Mary Ellen Miller
was educated at the universities of Princeton and
Yale receiving her Ph.D in History of Art in 1981 from Yale,
where she now holds the post of Professor of History of Art
and she also chairs the department. Professor Miller has
worked extensively in Central America, particularly
Mexico, Guatemala, Belize, and Honduras, where she has
carried out research in Maya art, architecture, and culture.
She has written many articles on Mesoamerican art for
learned journals, and her book with Linda Schele, *The Blood
of Kings* (1986), is considered a landmark in Maya
studies. She is also the author, with Karl Taube, of *The
Gods and Symbols of Ancient Mexico
and the Maya* (1993).

WORLD OF ART

This famous series
provides the widest available
range of illustrated books on art in all its aspects.
If you would like to receive a complete list
of titles in print please write to:
THAMES AND HUDSON
30 Bloomsbury Street, London WC1B 3QP
In the United States please write to:
THAMES AND HUDSON INC.
500 Fifth Avenue, New York, New York 10110

Printed in Singapore

MARY ELLEN MILLER

THE ART OF MESOAMERICA
from Olmec to Aztec

186 illustrations, 23 in color

Revised edition

THAMES AND HUDSON

Pronunciations and spellings of Mesoamerican names require some attention. In the sixteenth century, the letter *x* in the Spanish alphabet was pronounced like the phoneme *sh* in English today. In general, names in native Mesoamerican languages with this consonant require the *sh* sound – as in Yaxchilán, for example. Most *c*'s regardless of the following vowel are hard. When *u* precedes another vowel, the resulting sound is similar to a *w*, as in Náhuatl. Spanish words ordinarily have a stress on the final syllable unless they end in a vowel, *n*, or *s* (when preceded by an *n* or a vowel) – in which case the penultimate syllable is stressed. Hence, in this text, Uxmal has no accent, since the stress falls as it would in Spanish on the last syllable. To indicate stresses that differ from normal Spanish usage, accents have been added – for example, as in Dainzú or Ahuítzotl. In general, vowels are pronounced as they are in Spanish. Although spelling controversies are raging right now among Mayanists, the spellings here are the standard ones found on maps published by national governments.

Frontispiece: Once set near the Pyramid of the Moon at Teotihuacan, this great basalt water goddess seemingly wrings moisture from her very garments. Early Classic.

© 1986 and 1996 Thames and Hudson Ltd, London

First published in the United States of America in 1986 by
Thames and Hudson Inc., 500 Fifth Avenue, New York, New York 10110
Revised edition 1996

Library of Congress Catalog Card Number 95-70510

ISBN 0-500-20290-7

Printed and bound in Singapore

Contents

Chronological table

		CENTRAL MEXICO	OAXACA	GULF COAST	WEST MEXICO	MAYA HIGHLANDS / PACIFIC COAST	LOWLAND MAYA South	North
1519	LATE POSTCLASSIC	*Tenochtitlan* *Tlaxcala* (Aztecs)	Mixtec independent kingdom	Totonacs *Cempoala*	Tarascans	Maya independent city-states *Mixco Viejo, Iximché, Utatlán*	*Tayasal* (Itzá)	*Tulum* *Sta Rita*
1200		*Tula* (Toltecs)						*Mayapán*
900	EARLY POSTCLASSIC TERMINAL CLASSIC	*Xochicalco*	*Mitla* *Yagul*	Huastecs				Chichen Itzá (Toltec Maya)
600	LATE CLASSIC	*Cacaxtla*	Monte Albán IIIb	Classic Veracruz *Remojadas*		*Cotzumalhuapa*	Tepeu Late Classic Maya	Puuc and Central Yucatán
300	EARLY CLASSIC	(Teotihuacan Phases I–IV)	Monte Albán IIIa	*Cerro de las Mesas* (El Tajín)	*Ixtlán del Rio*	Kaminaljuyú *Escuintla*	Tzakol: Early Classic Maya	*Dzibilchaltún*
	PROTO-CLASSIC		Monte Albán II					
AD / BC	LATE FORMATIVE	*Cuicuilco*		*Tres Zapotes*	Chupícuaro *Colima*	Izapa, Kaminaljuyú, *Abaj Takalik*	Cerros	
300								
600	MIDDLE FORMATIVE	*Tlatilco*	*Dainzu* Monte Albán I	La Venta (Olmecs)				
900	EARLY FORMATIVE			San Lorenzo	*Teopantecuanitlan Xochipala Capacha*	Ocos		
1500								
	ARCHAIC							

When I wrote the first edition of this book a decade ago, I imagined my readers to be undergraduate students who had previously depended on archaeological texts for their classes in Precolumbian art history. What I've seen evolve over the years, however, is an audience of travelers, armchair archaeologists, and museum-goers interested more in works of ancient art and their meaning than in their archaeology.

The amplifications and changes in this book have been driven by these various sets of readers, who immediately let me know that the treatment of Olmec art, for example, was too cursory. New discoveries, as well as sustained campaigns of archaeology, and the assembling of major exhibitions of Mesoamerican art have all fuelled my thinking in this new edition. At the time of the first edition, major exhibitions of Aztec and Maya art had already focussed keen attention on the works of art from those cultures, and so the reader may find the chapters on Classic Maya art and the Aztecs less changed than others. The 1993 exhibition of Teotihuacan has added much to our understanding of that ancient city's art and architecture, as, to a lesser degree, have the 1996 exhibitions of Olmec art. Despite a steady supply of new readings of Maya glyphs, I have sought not to let the Maya and their writing dominate this book – and I recognize that their remarkable art merits a separate study.

My ideas about Mesoamerican art have been developed in the classrooms of Street Hall, often through the thoughtful give and take with both graduate and undergraduate students at Yale. The seminar system at Yale has given me the opportunity to explore subjects in depth, from Maya pots to Aztec sculpture, with smart undergraduates, who, although new to the subject, offer fresh insights on the material. I am grateful to those who first taught me the history of Mesoamerica: Gillett Griffin, George Kubler, and Michael Coe, and to the scholars who keep changing the nature of that history, particularly Karl Taube, Stephen Houston, and Linda Schele. My generous colleagues and friends in Mesoamerican archaeology and art history have shared ideas and speculations about their work over the years, and once again, they have been kind enough to share drawings and photographs for this book.

My children and husband have often visited ancient Mesoamerica with me in recent years, whether through quick trips to U.S. museums or through extended travel abroad. Their questions have led to some of the answers herein.

1 Gold repoussé disks were dredged from the Sacred Cenote, Chichen Itzá, at the turn of the century, and, like the paintings in ill. 154, they show Toltec warriors gaining domination over the Mayas. The graceful human proportions suggest lingering Classic traditions.

CHAPTER ONE

Introduction

At the time of the Spanish Conquest, the Aztec ruler Motecuhzoma II kept tax rolls that show tribute paid from regions far to the north and south, from the limits of the barbarian ('Chichimec') north to the rich, cacao-producing coast of modern Guatemala. If we extend these limits across their respective lines of latitude, 14 to 21 degrees north, we define Mesoamerica, a cultural region united by use of the ritual 260-day calendar and a locus of New World high civilizations for over 3,000 years, from 1500 BC until the arrival of the Spanish. Although the Caribbean, lower Central America, northern Mexico, and the United States Southwest all had contact with Mesoamerica, they remained separate from it, with independent traditions stronger than those they shared with Mesoamerica. Among the high civilizations that flourished in Mesoamerica are the Olmec, Maya, and Aztec.

Despite its narrow latitudinal range, Mesoamerica is a place of great climatic and topographic diversity, depending on both altitude and rainfall. The tribute paid to Motecuhzoma II ranged from jaguars to eagles, from exotic bird feathers to gold and jade treasure, materials and resources found in greatly varying ecological zones. The high, cool valleys provide a sharp contrast to the steamy lowland jungles, and then as now the valleys attracted dense populations. Certain critical resources, such as obsidian, the 'steel' of the New World, were found only in the highlands, while cacao and cotton grew in moist, tropical regions. Trade in these goods brought highland and lowland Mesoamerica into constant contact.

Most civilizations of ancient Mesoamerica were located either in the highlands or lowlands, although the Maya inhabited both. The earliest civilization, that of the Olmecs, rose along the rivers of the tropical Gulf Coast. Most Maya development also took place in the lowlands, under tropical conditions ranging from rainforest to scrub jungle in Yucatán, Chiapas, Guatemala, and Belize. The ancient cities of Tula and Teotihuacan, as well as Tenochtitlan, Motecuhzoma's city, were located at high altitudes, and the center of highland life was the Valley of Mexico. Modern Mexico City is built on top of the Aztec capital, and so the

Valley of Mexico still dominates Mesoamerica as it did in antiquity.

According to some archaeologists, man first entered the New World 20,000 or 30,000 years ago, when he began periodically to cross what was then a land passage at times of low sea level from Asia to Alaska. At least some peoples had probably arrived within the boundaries of Mesoamerica 10,000 years later. Waves of migration continued to bring newcomers from the north into Mesoamerica, however, and this process ceased only with the Spanish Conquest. These waves affected the political geography of Mesoamerica, for each succeeding movement of peoples required re-adjustment on the part of the others. For instance, some think that Nahua speakers were late arrivals, entering the Valley of Mexico at the fall of Teotihuacan in the seventh century AD and perhaps in part responsible for that city's decline. These Nahua speakers soon dominated the highlands, developing first as Toltecs and later as what we know as Aztecs. Now lost in the shuffle are the people of Teotihuacan, whose ethnic identity remains unknown.

Little that is of interest to the history of art remains of the earliest colonizers of the New World. Fine projectile points, such as the Folsom, were crafted almost 10,000 years ago, and village life thrived throughout Mesoamerica by the second millennium BC. Only with the rise of Olmec civilization around 1500 BC, however, did art and architecture appear which combined ideological complexity, craft, and permanence.

Compared with the Old World, the Mesoamerican high civilizations seem to have lagged behind technologically: the wheel was never used for anything other than miniatures, and obsidian tools and weapons served in place of wrought metal ones. Lack of a draft animal may explain the absence of the wheel; obsidian, though easily chipped, in fact makes such a sharp instrument that it has been returned to modern use by ophthalmic surgeons! New World technology did in any case develop slowly. Metallurgy, for example, was first used in the ancient Andes about 3000 BC, and metalworking techniques were gradually passed north, traveling up through Central America and arriving in Mesoamerica about AD 800. Even then, however, metals did not replace stone and obsidian functional objects, and precious metals were worked instead into luxury goods: jewelry, masks, and headdress elements – although gold never completely replaced jade as the most precious material. Hernando Cortés's men quickly learned that the people of Mesoamerica valued greenstones more than any other material, and gold was willingly traded for green glass beads. Throughout Mesoamerican history, the finest objects were worked from jade and other green materials, such as feathers. What has come to be called 'Motecuhzoma's headdress,' for *176* example, was made of long, green quetzal feathers, jade disks, and tiny hollow gold beads.

Long before the emergence of high civilization in Mesoamerica, humans had domesticated corn, beans, squash, tomatoes, and chili peppers. Later they created innovative methods of high-yield agriculture that allowed human energy to be devoted to the arts. Poetry was written and recited. The movements of the heavens were charted. By Classic Maya times a calendar of interlocking cycles was in use that is as accurate as any known today, and more accurate than the Julian calendar used by Cortés and his men. Powerful lords commissioned a monumental architecture characterized by both pyramidal constructions and ranging palaces, frequently with rich burials, caches, or offerings deep within, that testify both to the value of the arts and personal power.

Because of its realistic system of human proportions and complex hieroglyphic writing, Maya art long seemed a reflection of a pinnacle of civilization, and by 1950, most students of its art called its florescence between AD 300 and 900 the Classic. Preclassic and Postclassic were the terminology then assigned to the predecessors and successors of the Classic Maya. Despite the suggestion of value that these terms bear and repeated efforts to replace them with such conventions as those used in the Andes (e.g. 'Late Intermediate Period'), these terms survive, although the Preclassic is often referred to today as the Formative. Formative, Classic, and Postclassic should now be considered chronological markers, not descriptive terms. The Olmecs flourished during Formative times, approximately 1500 BC to 100 BC. Some Classic civilizations, such as that of Teotihuacan, rose before the Classic Maya, and others, such as the Classic Veracruz florescence at El Tajín, persisted after the eclipse of most Maya cities in AD 800. By the tenth and eleventh centuries, many Postclassic traits had developed, but the most important of Postclassic peoples, the Aztecs, did not found their capital city of Tenochtitlan until AD 1325. By 1531, ten years after the Conquest, the Precolumbian artist, architect, and patron had shifted artistic production to a new, colonial mode.

Not all the art and architecture of ancient Mesoamerica was lost from view as culture succeeded culture. Teotihuacan in the Valley of Mexico was visited regularly by Motecuhzoma II as a place of pilgrimage, and Western visitors have traveled there since the Conquest. Indeed the

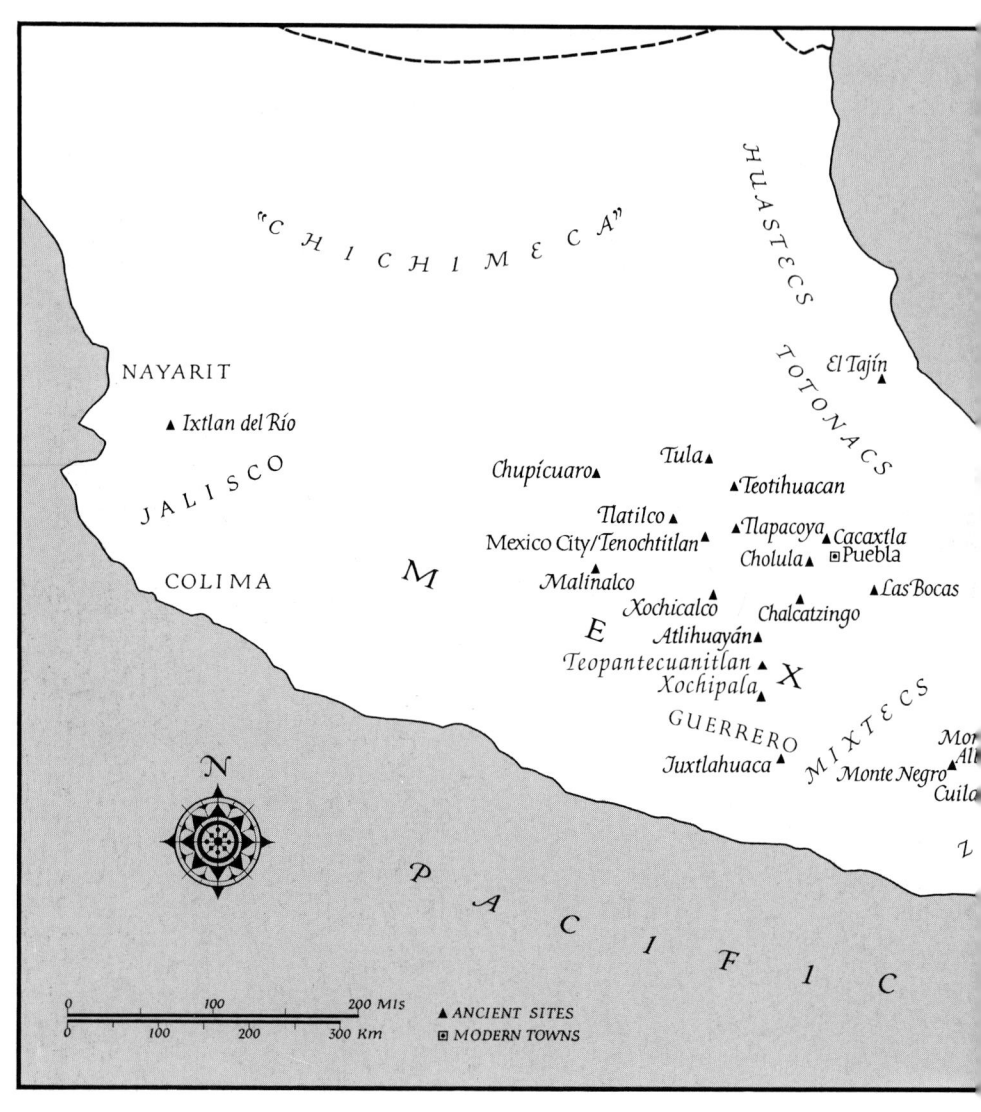

2 Mesoamerica, showing sites mentioned in the text.

GULF

OF

MEXICO

YUCATÁN

Dzibilchaltún
Chichen Itzá
Cobá
Tancah
PUUC AREA
Mayapán
Tulum
COZUMEL I.
Uxmal
Kabah
Jaina
Sayil
Labná
CHENES AREA
Etzná

MAYA LOWLANDS

Santa Rita
Cerros
Río Bec
Altun Ha
El Mirador
Lamanai
San José
Uaxactún
Naranjo
Tikal
Yaxha
San José de Motul
Tayasal
Palenque
Pomoná
Piedras Negras
Yax-chilán
Toniná
Xoc
Bonampak
Seibal
Altar de Sacrificios
PETÉN
BELIZE
Pasión R.
Usumacinta R.

veracruz
Remojadas
OLMEC HEARTLAND
de
Mesas
Zapotes
La Venta
Laguna de los Cerros
San Lorenzo
Las Limas
Coatzacoalcos R.
TABASCO
OC
CHIAPAS
Chiapa de Corzo
gul
Mitla
xaca
Dainzú
ECS

MAYA HIGHLANDS

GUATEMALA

Quiriguá
Motagua R.
Nebaj
Mixco Viejo
Cahyup
Copán
Utatlán
Iximché
Kaminaljuyú
Izapa
Abaj Takalik
El Baúl
Santa Lucía Cotzumalhuapa
Ocos
EL SALVADOR
HONDURAS

OCEAN

13

question of the recovery and understanding of the past preoccupied the Aztecs as much as it does archaeologists today (even if in a different way) – as recent excavations in the sacred precinct of Tenochtitlan have shown. Objects and treasures were uncovered by the Aztecs and brought to Tenochtitlan from throughout the realm, often with little appreciation of their original significance. These objects were then deposited in caches, leaving yet greater archaeological and chronological puzzles for the twentieth century.

Sources record that Motecuhzoma II's grandfather, Motecuhzoma I, sent out wise men to seek the origins of the Aztecs, but no answers were found. The Spanish wondered whether these new people were truly human at all. Did they, so it was asked, derive from the same creation in the Garden of Eden as they themselves did? Explanations were sought for the isolation of a New World race: were the Amerindians a Lost Tribe of Israel or refugees from Atlantis? Did they, as Father José de Acosta suggested in the late sixteenth century, enter the New World by a land bridge from Asia?

Even after it was accepted in the nineteenth century that Mesoamerica was populated by the means Father Acosta had suggested, Mesoamerica continued to be identified as the recipient of culture from the Old World. Egypt, Phoenicia, China, and Africa have all been cited at one time or another as probable sources, usually on the basis of nothing more than vague resemblances. For example, the distinctive scrollwork of El Tajín has often been associated with the scroll designs made in China in the late Chou dynasty. In Mesoamerica, the origin and use of the double scrolls is linked to the game played with a rubber ball. Rubber (as well as the game it gave rise to) is native to the New World. The Chou dynasty ended in 256 BC, long before the advent of the Classic era in Mesoamerica. Based on an interpretation of Olmec colossal heads, Afro-centrists have recently made broad and unfounded claims that Mesoamerican civilization depends on African contact. It is worth noting that useful technologies – just what one would imagine would be most likely to be exchanged – were generally not shared between Old and New Worlds. Powerful though such suggestions may be, one must also note that these claims are made by those unwilling to accept the modern Mesoamerican peasant as the descendant of creators of high culture. Although the question of contact remains unanswered in all its details, by and large it will be assumed here that ideas, inventions, and civilizations arose independently in the New World.

The systematic recovery of ancient Mesoamerica by modern man did not begin until almost 300 years after the Conquest. Starting at the end of the eighteenth century and continuing up to the present, explorers have searched for the ruins of ancient Mesoamerica. With the progress of time, archaeologists have unearthed civilizations increasingly remote in age. It is as if for each century logged in the modern era an earlier stratum of antiquity has been revealed. Nineteenth-century explorers, particularly John Lloyd Stephens and Frederick Catherwood, came upon Maya cities in the jungle, as well as evidence of other Classic cultures. Twentieth-century research has revealed a much earlier high civilization, the Olmec. It now scarcely seems possible that the frontiers of early Mesoamerican civilization can be pushed back any further in time, although new work – such as in Oaxaca – will continue to fill in details of the picture.

The process of discovery often shapes what we know about the history of Mesoamerican art. New finds are just as often made accidentally as intentionally. In 1971, for instance, workers installing Sound and Light equipment under the Pyramid of the Sun at Teotihuacan stumbled upon a remarkable cave within the structure; this chance discovery has done as much for our understanding of the pyramid as any systematic study. Archaeology has its own fashions too: the isolation of new sites may be the prime goal in one decade, the excavation of pyramids the focus in the next; in a third decade, outlying structures rather than principal buildings may absorb archaeologists' energies. Nor should one forget that excavators are vulnerable to local interests. At one point, reconstruction of pyramids to attract tourism may be desired; at another, archaeologists may be precluded from working at what has already become a tourist attraction. Modern construction often determines which ancient sites can be excavated. In Mexico City, for example, the building of the subway initiated the excavations there and renewed interest in the old Aztec capital.

The study of Mesoamerican art is not based exclusively on archaeology. Much useful information about the native populations was written down in the sixteenth century, particularly in Central Mexico, and it can help us unravel the Precolumbian past. Although there are many sources, the single most important one to the art historian is Bernardino de Sahagún's *General History of the Things of New Spain*. A Franciscan friar, Sahagún recorded for posterity many aspects of prehispanic life in his encyclopedia of twelve books, including history, ideology, and cosmogony, as well as detailed information on the materials and methods of the skilled native craftsmen. Furthermore, traditional ways of life survive among the native peoples of Mesoamerica, and scholars have increasingly found that modern practice and belief can decode the past. Remarkably, some scholars have even turned this process around, teaching ancient writing to modern peoples who may use it to articulate identity in the twenty-first century.

During the past thirty years, scholars have also made great progress in the decipherment and interpretation of ancient Mesoamerican writing systems, a breakthrough that has transformed our understanding of the Precolumbian mind. Classic Maya inscriptions, for example – long thought to record only calendrical information and astrological incantations – can now be read, and we find that most glorify family and ancestry by displaying the right of individual sovereigns to rule. The carvings can thus be seen as portraits, public records of dynastic power. Although scholars long believed that Mesoamerican artists did not sign their works, David Stuart's 1986 decipherment of the Maya glyphs for 'scribe' and 'to write' opened a window on Maya practice, where at least one painter of ceramic vessels was the son of a Naranjo king. Now the names of known Maya painters and sculptors – all male – exceed most other ancient traditions. Knowledge of the minor arts has also come in large part through an active art market. Thousands more small-scale objects are known now than thirty years ago, although at a terrible cost to the ancient ruins from which they have been plundered.

Linda Schele and David Freidel have demonstrated that the Maya believed that this era of humanity began when the gods set the three hearthstones of creation in place, back in the fourth millennium BC. The Spanish conquerors who first saw Mesoamerica in 1519 were awed by the pomp, but in its constructions of glorious palaces and pyramids three hearthstones lay within – the kernel of civilization symbolized by this humble act of setting up the center of human domesticity. In a very general sense, we can find the first steps from mere domesticity to monumentality in the enigmatic Olmec culture of the Gulf Coast.

CHAPTER TWO

The Olmecs

By 1500 BC, population growth, competition, and a successful agricultural base gave rise along the Gulf Coast to the complex culture now called Olmec. A misnomer, 'Olmec' derives from Olmeca-Xicalanca, the name of the successful Gulf Coast polyglot traders of the Conquest-era, rather than the Mixe or Zoque speakers that most linguists believe began to establish a formal order of artistic expression back at the hazy origins of Mesoamerican civilization. The ethnic identity of Olmec civilization itself remains unknown.

These early Olmecs established major centers along the rich riverine lowlands of the modern Mexican states of Veracruz and Tabasco, particularly at the sites of San Lorenzo, La Venta, Laguna de los Cerros, and Tres Zapotes, or what is called the 'heartland' of Olmec culture. At distant Teopantecuanitlan, Guerrero, Olmecs established a sacred precinct, the first such monumental evidence of the Olmecs in the highlands. But, as we shall see, the Olmecs had an advanced social and economic system, with networks for commerce extending far to the west and south. The fertile Gulf plain probably allowed for an agricultural surplus, controlled by only a handful of individuals. From the art and architecture of their ceremonial centers (we know too little about Olmec domestic life to call their sites 'cities'), it is clear that social stratification was sufficiently advanced for a major emphasis to fall upon the monumental record of specific individuals, particularly in the form of colossal heads.

Long before radiocarbon dating could testify in mid-century to the antiquity of this culture, archaeologists and art historians had become aware of the powerful physiognomy of Olmec art through individual objects. Some identified this Olmec culture as the oldest of Mesoamerican civilizations, perhaps a 'mother culture,' as Miguel Covarrubias called it, from which all others derived. Eventually, much to the chagrin of Mayanists, the antiquity of Olmec culture was confirmed, and today many important elements of Mesoamerican art and architecture can be seen to have had a probable Olmec origin: ballcourts, pyramid

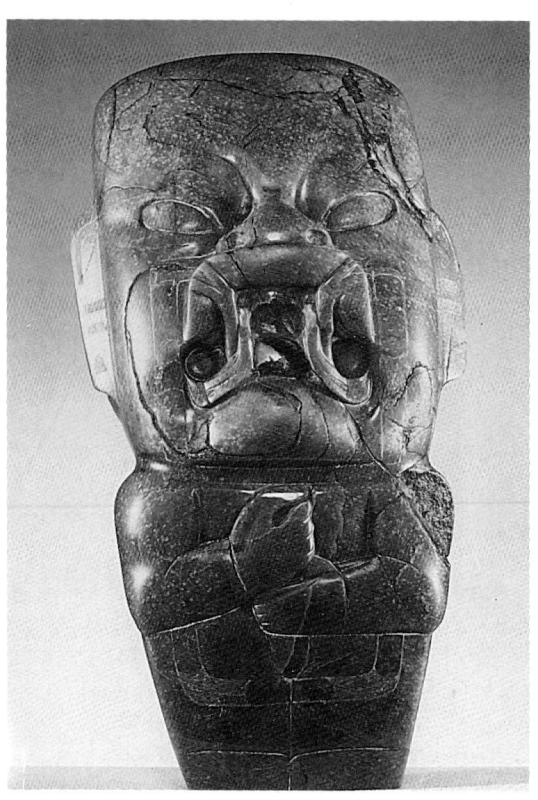

3 The Kunz Axe is a jadeite effigy 'were-jaguar' which grasps a miniature axe in its hands. Pieces of the precious greenstone have been cut away from the back of the figure. Middle Formative.

building, portraiture, the making of mirrors. Some later deities probably derive from Olmec gods, and even the 'Maya' calendrical system was in use by peoples in the Olmec area during the Late Formative.

3   One of the first important Olmec objects to come to modern attention was the Kunz Axe, acquired in the 1860s in Oaxaca and then brought to world attention by the semi-precious gem expert at Tiffany's, in New York, where the carving still remains at the American Museum of Natural History. It puzzled and intrigued investigators for years. It was clearly neither Aztec nor Maya: in fact, it had no features that could be linked with known Mesoamerican cultures, yet it had surely been made in Mesoamerica in antiquity. The axe exhibits many qualities of the style we now call Olmec: precious blue-green translucent jade, worked to reveal a figure in both two and three dimensions. The large-scale face was drilled to facilitate carving of the hard jade surface. More than half the celt is devoted to the creature's face – the open, toothless mouth, and

18

closely set, slanting eyes which have often been likened to the face of a howling human infant. The viewer's attention first focuses on the open mouth, and then the more subtle qualities of the rest of the creature's body become evident. His hands are worked in lower relief, and in them he grasps a miniature version of himself. Feet and toes are indicated only by incision, and incision also marks the face, ears, and upper body, perhaps to suggest tattooing, ear ornaments, and a tunic. For over two millennia the large, precious Kunz Axe was presumably kept as a treasure or heirloom. Sections were periodically cut from its rear, each slice perhaps carrying something of the power and magic of the whole. It was not until 1955, after several seasons of excavation at La Venta had produced many fine jade objects and a convincing series of radiocarbon dates in the first millennium BC, that objects such as the Kunz Axe were at last understood by scholars to embody the principles of the first great art style of Mesoamerica.

Early students of the Olmec style noticed a repeated pattern of imagery on the carved stone objects. Many 'howling baby' faces were found, and other faces seemed to combine human and jaguar features in a sort of 'were-jaguar.' Today, while the presence of jaguar imagery is still acknowledged, scholars have discovered that aspects of many other tropical rainforest fauna can be identified in the carvings. The caiman (a kind of alligator), harpy eagle, toad, jaguar, and snake all appear in the Olmec supernatural repertoire. The sharp cleft in the forehead of many Olmec supernatural beings may be associated with the naturally indented heads of jaguars or toads, or it may simply indicate the human fontanel. David Joralemon has suggested that most of the motifs and images can be allocated to a few Olmec deities. The 'paw-wing' motif, for example, can be shown to be an element of the winged dragon, itself perhaps derived from the harpy eagle and caiman. This whole intricate symbolic code appears to have been in use from the first appearance of the Olmecs, and to have been employed consistently for a thousand years.

SAN LORENZO

The earliest Olmec center was probably the great earthen platform at San Lorenzo Tenochtitlan, where careful testing by Michael Coe and Richard Diehl in the late 1960s revealed that the entire complex was manmade, honeycombed with drainage systems, and perhaps planned in a zoomorphic shape. The elaboration of the drains themselves was remarkable:

4 Colossal Head 5, San Lorenzo. Jaguar paws, perhaps emblematic of family lineage, drape across the head and brow of this early Olmec ruler. Early Formative.

Monument 52, for example, a sculpture of a crouching Olmec rain god, was hollowed on its back to guide copious waterflow that eventually poured out into a recarved duck at the base, forming a duck fountain. Freestanding architectural forms were limited to low-lying mounds, possibly including an early ballcourt of two parallel structures. At about 900 BC, 300 years or so after the founding of San Lorenzo, monumental sculptures at the site were systematically interred along the ridged outline of the earthworks, and many fine works were ritually 'killed.' Stone monuments were brutally defaced: great pits were bored into colossal heads, recognizable features were ground down on altars, and human sculptures such as Monument 34 were decapitated. In some cases the work of destruction must have been as laborious as that of the original creation. The ritual interment was equally thorough: Monument 34, for example, was placed on a red gravel floor and covered with a specially prepared limestone fill.

Among the early Olmec sculptures dealt with in this manner are *4* masterful works representing humans and deities. Colossal Head 5, a freestanding basalt boulder, probably depicts a ruler of the region. Like small-scale works such as the Kunz Axe, the features of the colossal head were drilled, giving emphasis to the deep-set eyes, nostrils, and strong, slightly asymmetrical mouth. Eight round dimpled pits were bored into the head, and the prominent ones on chin, lip, and cheekbone do not detract from the stern gaze. Jaguar paws are shown draped over the figure's forehead, and perhaps the individual wore the feline pelt as a lineage title or symbol of office. (Much later, in Mixtec manuscripts and Maya inscriptions, many lords are named with a jaguar title.)

Ten colossal heads have now been found at San Lorenzo, including two of substantially smaller scale and pop-eyed appearance. The most recent discovery features a single jaguar paw, perhaps linking this lord's identity to the man featured on Colossal Head 5. Both physiognomy and insignia vary from one head to another, reinforcing their individual identities. The raw basalt of Colossal Head 5 weighs about 18 tons, and was brought from the Tuxtla Mountains, some 60 miles away, probably floated in on rafts. The very process by which these sculptures were obtained and created informs us of the power held by these early kings.

For some monuments, defacement was a step on the route to recycling and recarving. James Porter has offered provocative evidence that some thrones were recarved into colossal heads, perhaps a means of converting active power and position into more static memorials. San Lorenzo Colossal Head 7 may retain signs of a deeply carved niche on the side of its head; Monument 14, a throne, has been smashed almost beyond recognition, but in its surviving form, seems to reveal the nascent shape of a colossal head.

Monument 34 from San Lorenzo also reveals the strong three-dimensional qualities of early Olmec art. Perishable and movable arms were once attached to the torso, and it is easy to imagine the torsion of the figure, from the tense, compact, lower body to the moving arms. The tucked right foot is like a coiled spring, about to be released. Special attention has been given to costume detail, and knots in particular are carefully drawn. The figure wears a concave disk as a pectoral decoration, which probably represents a concave mirror of the sort recovered from Olmec contexts. Magnetic materials appealed to the Olmecs, and they worked ilmenite and magnetite into dark, shiny disks. Indeed, such objects were highly prized throughout Mesoamerican history. The polished surface not only showed one's reflection, but it also cast light; the bearer is revealed to be not only a lord but also a priest and diviner.

The so-called Wrestler, discovered in the nineteenth century near   5 what is now the town of Antonio Plaza, Veracruz, has three-dimensional qualities similar to those of Monument 34, and other early Olmec art. The human figure is completely released from the solid block in contrast to much Mesoamerican sculpture. The artist must originally have intended it to be viewed from all sides. The long diagonal line of the figure's back and shoulders is as beautiful and commanding as the frontal view. The beard and mustache, as well as the look of deep concentration, reveal a masterly portrait, one whose individuality would be enhanced by long-lost perishable attire and ornament. These early Olmec monuments, of which this sculpture is typical, are among the most powerful three-dimensional portraits of the ancient New World. The Aztecs may have sought such antiquities when creating the vocabulary for their own art style, for it is only among their works that we find Mesoamerican stone freed to three dimensions in a comparable way.

In her work at San Lorenzo, Ann Cyphers Guillen has brought remarkable works to world attention, not only colossal heads but also a unique set of large paired figures found on the side of nearby Zapote Hill. Two similar crouching felines, apparently recarved from some other

5 In the Wrestler, as this sculpture is known, the artist has captured the torsion of the human form. Early Formative.

6, 7 The discovery of two nearly identical Early Formative sculptures near San Lorenzo has prompted some scholars to propose that they represent the Hero Twins, known in later times as Maya culture heroes. San Lorenzo, Early Formative.

sculptures, faced two identical kneeling males. No other comparable sculptures of this sort have ever been found. With their striking physiognomies, tight grips of scepters at their knees, these young men project serene and confident power. Were they part of a yet-larger assemblage, focussed on a colossal head, or are these ideal men prototypes of the Maya Hero Twins, as Cyphers suspects?

6, 7

Some features of Mesoamerican art and materials come into coherent focus for the first time at San Lorenzo. Remarkable trade routes brought precious materials from distant realms: mica, jade, and serpentine were all desired, but porters carried ilmenite, a magnetic iron ore favored for the making of mirrors, to San Lorenzo by the ton, probably for on-site manufacture. Local builders used local rock and clays, but elite status depended on imports, a lasting aspect of Mesoamerican elite economy. What is also clear is that a systematic destruction of San Lorenzo took place about 900 BC, and a new center of Olmec civilization was established at La Venta.

LA VENTA

La Venta occupied a small, swampy island in the Tonalá River, where oil derricks now mark the landscape. During the 400- or 500-year occupation of the site, both monumental architecture and earthworks of colored clays and imported stones were completed. The most important structure is a large pyramid toward the end of the northern axis, in the form of what has been called a 'fluted cupcake.' This impressive mound may have been intended to echo the shape of a Central Mexican volcano, or

8

8 Reconstruction of the major mound cluster at La Venta. The ceremonial center extends north from the 'fluted cupcake.' Ancient Olmecs placed structures in bilateral symmetry either side of the north-south axis.

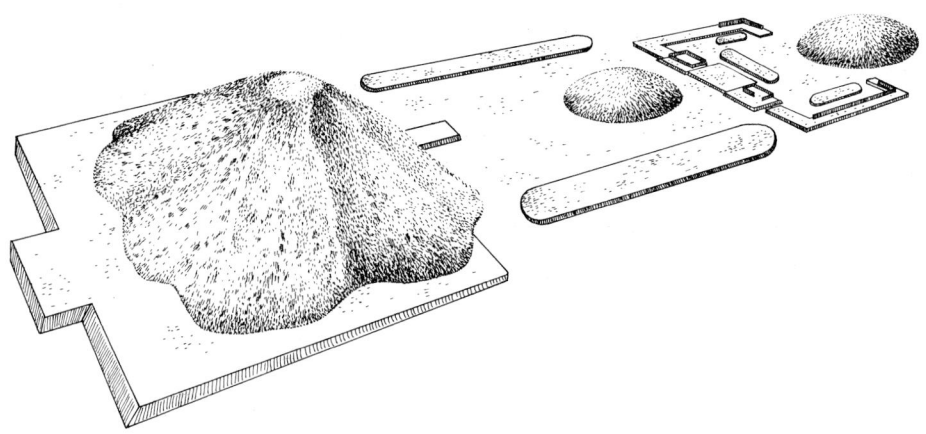

9 Made of large serpentine blocks, this abstract mosaic mask was systematically buried under colored clays and adobe bricks at La Venta. Tassels decorate the chin, and a cleft marks the top of the head. Middle Formative.

it may simply be the eroded remains of a pyramidal platform – the first of a long series in Mesoamerican history – designed to raise a perishable shrine above the plaza level. The excavators discovered fine burials in the 1950s under other structures at La Venta, but they failed to penetrate this main mound, which may yet hold the tomb of an individual whose portrait appears as one of the four colossal La Venta heads. Parallel mounds lead north from the pyramid to a sunken courtyard flanked by massive basalt columns. Great basalt sarcophagi were found buried in the court. A smaller stepped pyramid with a single staircase then ends the axis to the north.

Following a bilaterally symmetrical pattern, vast deposits of serpentine, granite, and jade celts were laid out and buried at the entrance to the sunken northern court. Some of the slabs formed mosaic masks, such as the one illustrated here, a cleft-headed monster. Few of these construc- 9 tions were meant to be seen, and most were buried immediately after they had been created. Such works show the relation of art to architecture for the Olmecs, and the interest in process over product. We can think of these works as a sort of 'hidden' architecture.

The whole of La Venta was laid out on a specific axis, eight degrees west of north, establishing some principles of architectural planning that

10 Once set facing out from the ceremonial precinct, La Venta colossal heads guarded sacred architecture. Middle Formative.

were repeated many times in the history of Mesoamerica: ceremonial cores laid out along astronomically determined axes; concern for natural topography – a sort of geomancy – which may have inspired the erection or overall orientation of individual structures (as for instance the 'fluted cupcake'). The plaza, a 'negative space' seen in the sunken court of La Venta, was as significant as the structure or 'mass' that defined it. The process of interring works of art may also have been as important as their execution. But above all the visual emphasis fell on the pyramid.

10 The four colossal heads at La Venta were set as if to guard or protect the ceremonial core of the site, three to the south and one to the north. If erected during the reign of a ruler, such heads would have been effective images of royal power; if erected posthumously, fearsome memorials. The La Venta heads are somewhat broader and squatter in general than those of San Lorenzo, but like the latter they suggest a series of powerful men who held absolute sway over the populace.

26

Other sculptural types are known from La Venta, including the so-called altars and stelae. Through time, the monuments of La Venta became increasingly two-dimensional and specific in terms of setting, costume, and ritual paraphernalia. These developments suggest a growing preoccupation with the trappings of the ruler. Altar 4 shows a ruler carved in rich three-dimensional form seated within a niche or cave, holding a *11* rope wrapped round the perimeter of the stone which binds two-dimensional captives in profile to the lord on the front. The lord's power is emphasized by his action, the holding of the rope, and by the technique, which subordinates the two-dimensional figures. Such altars may well in fact have served primarily as thrones; the painted figure at Oxtotitlan (see *22* below), for instance, is represented sitting on a throne similar to Altar 4, and Altar 4 may once have been decorated in the brilliant colors of the painting. The surface of the monument is carved with a jaguar pelt, a royal cushion on the seat of power.

Altar 5 may emphasize a different aspect of Olmec rulership. As on Altar 4, a highly three-dimensional figure, about life-size, emerges from a niche on the front of the monument, while two-dimensional figures are shown on the sides. The central figure in this instance, however, holds

11 Altar 4, La Venta. An Olmec ruler emerges from the mouth of a schematic cave at the front of the stone. Such 'altars' may also have been thrones from which the reigning lord would have presided. Middle Formative.

out an infant, who lies limp in his lap. The Las Limas figure (see below) is also of an adult and infant, although there the child is clearly supernatural. The representation on Altar 5 may reflect a concern with legitimate descent, and perhaps the ruler is displaying an heir, as in some Maya paintings and carvings. The subsidiary figures on the sides of Altar 5 are also adults and infants, humans who hold rambunctious Olmec supernatural children.

12 On Stela 3, two men face one another while small figures, perhaps deities or ancestors, hover above. The man at left carries a baton, and the one at right wears what appears to be a beard, winning for this monument the nickname 'Uncle Sam.' Indeterminate shapes, perhaps architecture or landscape, appear behind the two men, thus suggesting that the setting for a particular event is being recorded, not just historical figures. This is a new preoccupation at La Venta, one not emphasized at San Lorenzo, and it may be a precursor of historical records written in a script. Even the notion of carving an upright finished stone slab, or stela, is new, introduced here for the first time.

Offering 4, excavated at a corner of the basalt courtyard at La Venta, records history in a different fashion, as well as in a different medium:

12 Stela 3, La Venta. Against a schematic background, two Olmec lords meet. The beard and towering headdress of the figure at right has earned this monument the nickname of 'Uncle Sam.' Middle Formative.

13 (right) Offering 4, La Venta. Like the monumental deposits (ill. 9), Offering 4 was buried after being laid out in just this configuration. The single figure of granite (foreground) appears to be regarded in a hostile fashion by those made of precious greenstone. Middle Formative.

jade and serpentine, which, carved into sinewy figures, reveal Olmec mastery of the material. The hardest rock commonly found in the Mesoamerican world, jade found its keenest masters among the Olmecs. Six celts and fifteen jade and serpentine figurines were specifically set out in Offering 4 so that the one figure made from a base stone – granite – faced the group made from precious stones. The celts placed behind recall the columns of the La Venta sunken court where this offering was laid, and it is entirely possible that the scene recreates an action against the lone figure that once occurred within inches of its small-scale, tableau-like memorial. About a century after its interment, this offering was uncovered and then reburied, as if an important event needed to be reconfirmed. The later exhumation was made with precision, indicating that records were kept. Other individual, sinewy jades – warm, plastic, and

13

15, 16

14 Mexican peasants who found this large greenstone sculpture near Las Limas, Veracruz, believed it to be a madonna and child. In fact, it represents a youth holding an Olmec rain deity in his lap. Middle Formative.

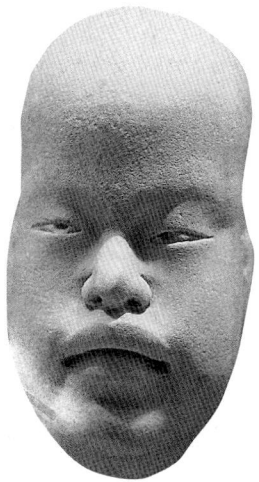

15 This jade Olmec head came to Guatemala perhaps as an heirloom or trade piece.

16 (*right*) From hard jade Olmec sculptors created small-scale and human forms that beg to be handled. Middle Formative.

almost feline in their posture – have been found, and were among the objects that attracted the attention of collectors early in this century. It is likely that they came from similar groupings elsewhere.

Of all Olmec greenstone sculptures, the largest and most beautiful is the Las Limas figure. When it was discovered in 1965, villagers considered it a miraculous madonna, and it was brought to the church of Las Limas. The sculpture, however, is no Christian mother and child. A youth, neither specifically male nor female, holds an infant in its lap, a reference, perhaps, to legitimate descent. The infant has the monstrous face of the Olmec rain deity, and the knees, shoulders, and face of the larger individual are incised with the faces of other supernatural images from the Olmec realm.

Although a single wooden Olmec mask had been found in a cave many years ago, time had effectively erased any evidence of Olmec perishable arts until *campesinos* took Mexican archaeologists Ponciano Ortíz and María del Carmen Rodríguez to El Manatí, where they had come upon an unusual series of deposits in what is now a mangrove swamp. Preserved for 3000 years in mud, powerful Olmec wooden busts, some nearly half life size, have survived, with associated offerings indicating that these individual portraits were parts of large bundles. Rubber balls also emerge from El Manatí's muck, testaments of games once played.

THE OLMEC FRONTIER

Scholars of the Olmec early in the twentieth century had pondered the relationship of the Gulf Coast sites to isolated objects that turned up in Guerrero, Chiapas, and in Central Mexico. The Olmec search for precious jade and other raw materials was clear enough, as was the widespread presence of Olmec materials in the highlands. Olmec ceramics, for example, have survived poorly, if at all, in the petroleum-rich soil of Veracruz, while they are found in abundance in the highlands, although often in association with more obviously local materials. Now, since the discovery in 1983 of the site of Teopantecuanitlan, it is clear that at least some Olmecs considered Guerrero home.

18   At Xochipala, Guerrero, solid, life-like figurines had emerged as an indigenous tradition by 1500 BC. Expressive gestures, naturalistic forms

17 Framing a sunken courtyard at Teopantecuanitlan, four nearly identical sculptures feature the Olmec Maize God. Although 400 miles from the Olmec heartland, these images nevertheless convey standard Olmec imagery. Early Formative.

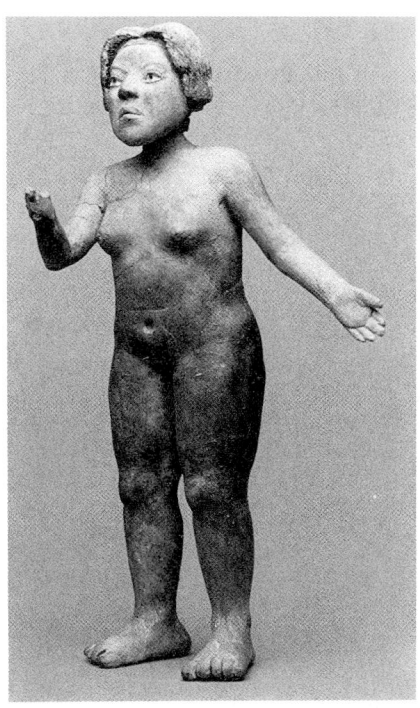

19 A vessel in the shape of a fish from Tlatilco. Ceramics recovered from this brickyard on the edge of Mexico City first revealed the spectrum of terracotta works of the highlands. Animal effigies, particularly of ducks and fish, are common. Other vessels show the schematic symbols of Olmec art. Middle Formative.

18 (*above*) A ceramic female figure from Xochipala. The surface of this extraordinary portrait is flecked with hematite. Perishable garments probably once adorned her. Early Formative.

20 (*right*) A hollow 'baby' ceramic figure from Las Bocas. A rocker-stamp motif associated with an Olmec deity runs down its spine. Early/Middle Formative.

of hair, breasts, and plastic arms and legs, make the early and rare Xochipala figures among the finest ceramic works of the ancient New World. Many of the figures, both male and female, are naked, and they may once have been dressed with jewelry and perishable garments.

Such local traditions may have made the region attractive to the Olmecs, for just across the Mezcala River from Xochipala lies Teopantecuanitlan, which thrived from 1400 BC to 600 BC, with the greatest construction from 1000 to 800 BC. During that brief period, Olmec lords constructed a monumental sunken court lined with green travertine rock, and marked by unusual T-shaped sculptures on west and east sides. These sculptures feature Olmec Maize Gods, who define the four corners of the universe. In later Maya ideology, the Maize God is reborn in a ballcourt: at Teopantecuanitlan, as if to indicate such belief, a ballcourt occupies much of the sunken patio.

At Tlatilco, on the outskirts of modern Mexico City, a rich cemetery revealed a figurine cult perhaps dedicated to fertility. Swelling breasts and thighs were emphasized, as well as narrow waists. The hair and face received great attention, and these figurines are often known as 'pretty ladies.' Others are grotesques, and their split 'Janus'-like faces appealed to artists of the early twentieth century.

The Tlatilco 'pretty ladies' were found in association with large Olmec-style ceramic figures, known also from Las Bocas, Atlihuayán, Tlapacoya, and other places in Central Mexico – incomplete ones have been discovered at coastal sites too. The fine-grained, plastic white kaolin of Las Bocas may have freed its artists to produce the finest of these figures. Although many of the sculptures seem to be babies, the loose, hanging flesh also suggests age, perhaps not unlike late medieval representations of the Christ child, where both age and infancy are portrayed. The hollow figure from the Metropolitan Museum sucks his thumb; his hair is groomed in the shape of a helmet. A red cross-bands-and-wing motif runs down this baby's back, perhaps made by a rocker stamp. Similar motifs carved on ceramic vessels, such as the hand-paw-wing, are repetitions of the constant Olmec symbolic system, coded references to particular deities, and are suggestive of writing. Other pots were worked as three-dimensional effigies, such as the fish illustrated here.

Another important class of Olmec works of art was identified in the 1930s at Chalcatzingo, Morelos. Here strange figures and fantastic creatures were carved in three distinct groups on the surface of a great natural rock formation, an igneous plug that marks a pass through the eastern

34

21 Petroglyph 1, Chalcatzingo. Set within a cave mouth in a schematic landscape where maize flourishes, an Olmec ruler, probably a woman, sits on a throne. Middle Formative.

22 A cave painting at Oxtotitlan. The ruler's face can be seen in X-ray fashion, within a great bird suit. Drawing by David Joralemon. Middle Formative.

end of the modern state of Morelos and access to the rich Valley of Puebla. The most striking of these carvings is known locally as 'El Rey,' a representation of an enthroned ruler (probably female, given the skirt the figure wears). This may be an Olmec overlord or governor, who could well reflect the extent to which power was imposed by the Olmecs in this frontier region, far from the Gulf Coast and the heartland of their civilization. She sits within a section of a cave or niche, like that depicted three-dimensionally on Altar 4, La Venta. In the petroglyph, the cave lies within a schematic landscape where phallic raindrops fall on young maize plants. Petroglyph 4, on the other hand, shows large felines attacking human figures with supernatural characteristics. The foreshortened human forms suggest that their outlines might first have been traced from cast human shadows. The petroglyphs at Chalcatzingo are remarkably varied: some portray warring Olmecs, others simple natural motifs, such as squash plants.

The earliest Mesoamerican paintings survive only in caves, their condition and presentation not unlike Paleolithic cave art in France, although not on the same magnificent scale, and not, lamentably, from such an early date. Fine examples have been found at Oxtotitlan and Juxtlahuaca caves in Guerrero. One from Juxtlahuaca shows what may be the mating of a human male with a female jaguar, perhaps the source of the race of 'were-jaguars' so common in Olmec imagery. A badly battered sculpture from the Olmec heartland also shows such mating, but in that instance a human female and a male jaguar are represented.

A large painting at Oxtotitlan, 3.8 × 2.5 m, set 10 m over the entrance to the cave, depicts an Olmec lord wearing a green bird suit, cut away in X-ray fashion so that we see his face and limbs. The bird's eye was probably inlaid with a precious material, and the lord sports a jade noseplug. His throne resembles Altar 4 at La Venta. The palette of these early Olmec paintings was broad, including bright greens and reds, although simpler black-on-white paintings have also been found. As Kent Reilly has argued, this lord is a shaman, transformed and flying out of the cave. 22

Far to the south, at Copán, Honduras, kings of this period, whether Maya or Olmec, were buried with Olmec pomp: their paraphernalia consisted of jade celts, jade necklaces, and vessels worked with Olmec symbols. Also distant from the heartland, at Xoc, Chiapas, an Olmec petroglyph was discovered depicting a male Olmec carrying a great burden. One wonders what this lord bore in his bundle: could it have held cult objects, perhaps even a sculpture like the Kunz Axe? A maize plant in full tassel is drawn over the bundle's exterior, revealing the significance of the plant to Olmec ideology. Whatever the content of the bundle, the very presence of Olmecs so far from their coastal origins raises the possibility of widespread dissemination of Olmec culture. In establishing contact from Honduras to Guerrero, the Olmecs came close to defining the geographic boundaries of Mesoamerica.

During the Late Formative, and certainly before 100 BC, the once successful Olmec culture weakened and collapsed for reasons that are still unknown. The first of the great Mesoamerican civilizations to rise, flourish, and fall, it influenced all the civilizations that were to follow.

CHAPTER THREE

The Late Formative

The Olmecs continued to hold sway in some areas into the Late Formative, but the great centers of La Venta and San Lorenzo were already in eclipse by the end of the Middle Formative. Olmec contacts with distant regions apparently broke down; the ceramics of Central Mexico, for example, were no longer infused with the symbolism of elite Olmec culture. Of the major Olmec sites known today, only Tres Zapotes enjoyed sustained occupation and development during Late Formative times (that is, 400 BC–100 BC and continuing on for perhaps 200 years more). Yet there was a minor florescence of Olmec culture in highland Guatemala at this time, and several smaller but still colossal heads were made. Even more surprisingly, perhaps, it was at just this point that early Mesoamericans made their most lasting contribution to New World high civilization: the creation of sophisticated writing and calendrical systems. The very disorder of the period may have fostered the development of a uniform symbolic system.

The disintegration of Olmec long-distance trade routes probably made it possible for strong regional and ethnic styles of art and architecture to develop under independent local elites. It was in this era that the Zapotecs first flourished at Monte Albán, Oaxaca, subsequently their capital for 1500 years. In West Mexico, the shaft tombs of local elites were filled with fine ceramics. Among the Maya, the first cities of the Petén were built. But the most interesting art and architecture of the Late Formative appeared along the Belize coast and in the highlands of Guatemala and Chiapas.

WRITING AND CALENDRICAL SYSTEMS

The roots of all Mesoamerican calendrical systems – highly varied though they subsequently became – lie in the Late Formative era. Two such means of recording time, the 260-day calendar and the 365-day calendar, evolved at the very beginning of the period and were generally used simultaneously. In terms of intellectual achievement, however, the most important system was a slightly later development, the continuous record called the Long Count, used in conjunction with the 260- and 365-day calendars. An appreciation of the intricacies of all three systems as they appear in ancient inscriptions is necessary, not only to help us date monuments, but also to understand the concepts of time and thought expressed in Mesoamerican art and architecture.

The 260-day cycle is the oldest and most important calendar in Mesoamerica. Stone monuments in Oaxaca indicate its use as early as the sixth century BC when Zapotecs began to chart achievements publicly, and it is still employed in Guatemala today for ritual divining. Indeed, use of the 260-day calendar effectively defined the limits of high civilization in ancient Mesoamerica and provided an aspect of cultural unity. Yet its origins remain obscure. Some have noted that 260 days is the period of time that elapses between solar zenith passages (when the sun lies directly overhead at noon) at a latitude of 15 degrees north – the latitude along which the important sites of Izapa and Copán lie. Zenith passage is a relatively easy phenomenon to observe in the tropics, but it seems an unlikely basis for a calendar first recorded to the north of the 15-degree latitude. A much more fundamental unit of 260 days in the human life cycle is the length of gestation, from first missed menstrual flow to birth. Mesoamerican peoples were named for the day of their birth in this calendar and were perceived as having completed a 260-day round at birth, so this seems a considerably more likely origin for the 260-day cycle.

The 260-day calendar was not subdivided into weeks or months as our year is, but into a round of 20 different day names. Counting systems around the world on the whole use a base of either 10 or 20 depending upon whether fingers or fingers and toes are used, and throughout Mesoamerica the base was vigesimal rather than decimal. But the 20 day names were also associated with a cycle of 13 day numbers, which ran at the same time. Each day, therefore, had one of 20 day names and one of 13 day numbers, so the cycle would take 260 days to complete.

This cycle always had its own name in various Mesoamerican languages: the Aztecs, for example, called it the *tonalpohualli*, and the written version of the cycle – the fundamental tool of the diviner – was called the *tonalamatl* (*amatl*, or *amate* in modern Spanish, refers to the fig paper on which such a manuscript was often written). The 260-day system is the 'almanac' of Mesoamerican calendrical cycles.

A child was named for the day on which he was born in this cycle – 13 Monkey, for example, in the *tonalpohualli* – and the diviner or calendar priest was consulted to study the augury both for that day and for the period of 13 days within which it fell. According to the Aztecs, some entire such periods were afflicted by either certain shortcomings or gifts. Those born under the period of 1 Death, for example, would suffer drunkenness. To try to alter the prediction, a naming ceremony was often held on a more auspicious day.

In conjunction with the almanac a 365-day calendar was used. This corresponded roughly with the true solar year, and was divided into 18 'months' of 20 days each, plus 5 'nameless' days at the end of the year. Each group of 20 days had its own month name, and was linked with a number from 1 to 20 or 0 to 19, depending on the region. Each year took a name, usually the day name and number of the day in the 260-day calendar that coincided with the 360th day of the solar calendar. Because of the nature of the calculation, only 4 days can be 'yearbearers.' For example, in Aztec times, Quetzalcóatl was awaited in each year named 2 Reed. There is no evidence that the approximate solar year was ever corrected in the calendar to allow for the extra days that accumulate in the true tropical year, but the Maya calendar priests at Piedras Negras noted true tropical anniversaries in their records. Without the addition of leap days, the 365-day calendar wandered, eventually passing from one season to the next, and requiring movable agricultural feasts.

23   When the 260-day calendar and 365-day calendar were set in motion, it took exactly 52 years of 365 days for a given day to recur. This period of 52 years is called a calendar round, and we may liken it to a century in our own system. The end of this 52-year cycle was widely celebrated, particularly by the Aztecs, who held a New Fire ceremony at its completion. The 5 nameless days which preceded the end of the cycle were especially dangerous: the gods might choose that moment to end life on earth. Certain behavior was required: all pots had to be smashed, pregnant women kept indoors, and fires doused. At midnight before the first day of the new year, a sacrificial victim had his heart ripped out, and there, in his open chest, a flame was started with a fire drill. The burst of light assured the light of the morning sun and the opening of a new 52-year cycle.

The calendrical systems described so far were based on relatively short periods of time that could be easily related to human experience. It is true that the completion of an entire round of 52 years by any individual would have meant a very long life in Mesoamerican terms, but it was possible to survive to this age, barring death in infancy, war, or pregnancy.

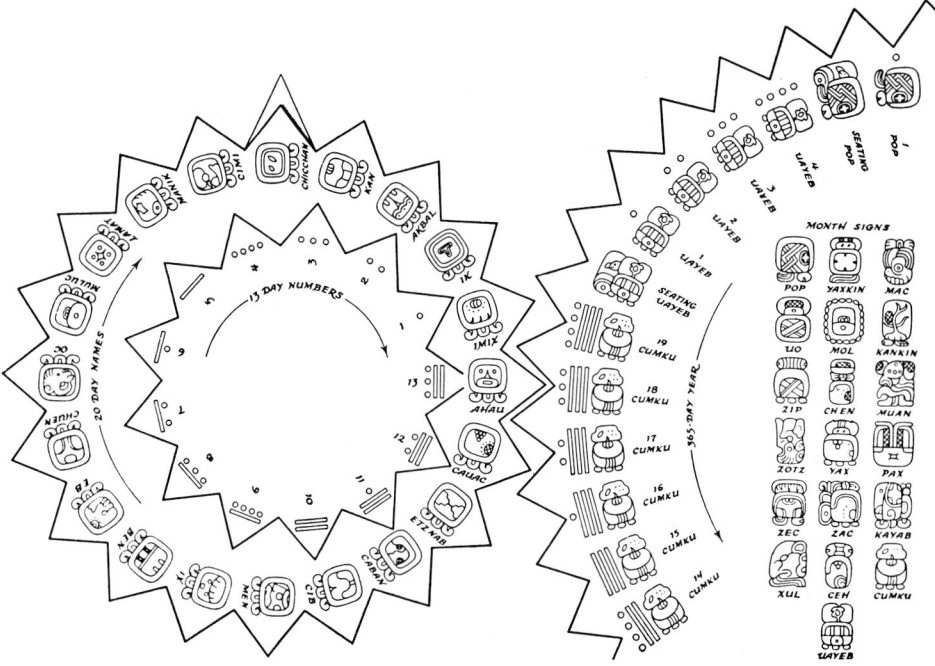

23 All Mesoamerica observed the 52-year cycle, created by the intermeshing of the 260-day calendar (left) and the 365-day calendar (right). It is drawn here as a system of interlocking cog wheels and follows standard Maya notation, although the days and months had different names and symbols in each culture.

The 260-day calendar was perhaps the most basic to Mesoamericans. It is the first one for which written records survive, and it is the one still in use today among some Highland Mayas. It is composed of 20 day names (outer wheel) and 13 day numbers (inner wheel), both of which rotate endlessly. It takes 260 days for all the combinations to occur.

The 365-day calendar is composed of 18 months, each of which has only 20 days, numbered 0–19 or 1–20, depending on the region, and the 5 unlucky days (known as Uayeb among the Maya). In this larger wheel, the end of the month of Cumku and the 5 unlucky days (the Aztec called them *nemontemi*, or 'nameless' days) are shown – other month glyphs are at right.

Here, 13 Ahau (left) and 18 Cumku interlock. It will take 52 × 365 days (in other words, 52 years) before the cycles will all reach this point again. This is the calendar round.

Over longer periods of time, dates in the calendar round may have been difficult to order chronologically, since any given year name recurred once every 52 years. The use of the last two digits of our year calendar produces a similar effect: is '49 a reference to the California Gold Rush or the beheading of Charles I? At some point during the Late Formative, perhaps to eliminate just such ambiguity in historical records, another calendrical system, the Long Count, was introduced, and it was perfected by the Maya in Classic times.

Long Count dates record the complete number of days elapsed since a starting point corresponding to a date in 3114 BC in our calendar – hence the alternative modern name, Initial Series dates. The Maya later held that the 'zero' date fell within an era of divine activity, as does the zero date of our calendrical system. But even this zero starting point was no blank slate but rather the end of a previous grand cycle. For the Maya, the initial day of the calendar, 4 Ahau 8 Cumku, was also the last day of the old cycle, or 13.0.0.0.0. On this day, the gods set three hearthstones of creation in place, giving rise to the era of civilization. In the Long Count, time was normally recorded in periods of 400 years, 20 years, years (in this count all years have 360 days), 20 days, and days – i.e. to five places running from largest to smallest. Most dates of the Late Classic period, for example, begin with 9 periods of 400 years, and the date 9.10.0.0.0 can be correlated with the year AD 633. The achievement of this calendar was the ability to pinpoint events in time without ambiguity. Particularly for the Maya, this very record was a focus of artistic achievement, and Maya artists transformed what could have been simple notations into beautiful works of calligraphy. Although other cultures must have known of the inscribing of these initial dates with their formulaic notations of time, only in the Olmec and Maya regions of Mesoamerica did the practice take root.

Long Count dates can be easily read. They were always placed at the beginning of inscriptions and recorded in a system of bar-and-dot numeration, in which the bar equals 5 dots. The development of the null cipher, a placeholder similar to our zero, was a crucial step forward intellectually. In the history of mankind, it was achieved only in the Indo-Arabic and Mesoamerican numerical systems. The Maya generally represented this symbol as a maltese cross, perhaps derived from the human body with all four limbs outstretched, indicating the 20 digits. In Postclassic manuscripts a shell is used for the null cipher, and in Classic Maya inscriptions a head or full-figure variant could also be substituted.

The earliest known Long Count date is 36 BC, recorded on Stela 2 at Chiapa de Corzo. The cessation of the system in the tenth century (AD 909 at Toniná is the last date known) generally marks the close of the Classic era. The *katun* (the period of 20 years) count persisted up to the sixteenth century, thus allowing a correlation to be established between the Mesoamerican and European systems.

24 The Maya used three basic symbols in their numbering system: a dot for one (a), a bar for five (b), and to represent the null cipher similar to our zero a maltese cross (d) during the Classic (which became a stylized shell (e) in the Postclassic). The number six, for example, was made up of a dot and a bar combined (c) – the space either side of the dot being filled by so-called 'spaceholders' which are not counted.

As well as this standard numeration, the Classic Maya sometimes introduced a head or full figure as variant: the number nine, for instance, in its common form (f) (four dots and a bar) also appeared as the head in (g) or the full figure in (h).

The importance of this accurate calendar to the art historian and archaeologist should not be underestimated: when inscriptions are present, the calendrics precisely document Classic Maya chronology in a way not known elsewhere in the New World. A subtle difference of style between monuments, for instance, can be shown to reflect a ten-year difference in their erection, and this knowledge can be used subsequently to date monuments and ceramics without such calendrical inscriptions, even those outside the Maya area.

The Maya recorded hundreds of dates, generally of the Classic period, but on occasion they reckoned mythological dates deep into the past and future. In some inscriptions, calendrical information can occupy a third to a half of the glyphs. For years, scholars made progress in deciphering only the calendrical content of Maya writing. This led some of them, particularly Sir Eric Thompson, to posit that the writings were purely calendrical, glorifications of the passage of time itself. The same thinking prompted the notion that the human figures carved on Maya monuments must have been anonymous calendar priests. But, as we shall see, Thompson's hypothesis and its corollary that the Maya were a pacific people, their lives overseen by astronomer priests, were abandoned as scholars determined the meaning of non-calendrical inscriptions.

During Late Formative times, non-calendrical writing also appeared, both in association with and independent of calendrical statements. Glyphs occur with human figures, perhaps as names or events, and in long passages. Little progress has so far been made in reading these non-calendrical Late Formative glyphs. Some of the earliest Maya inscriptions, however, are recarved Olmec objects, as if an Olmec heirloom were later

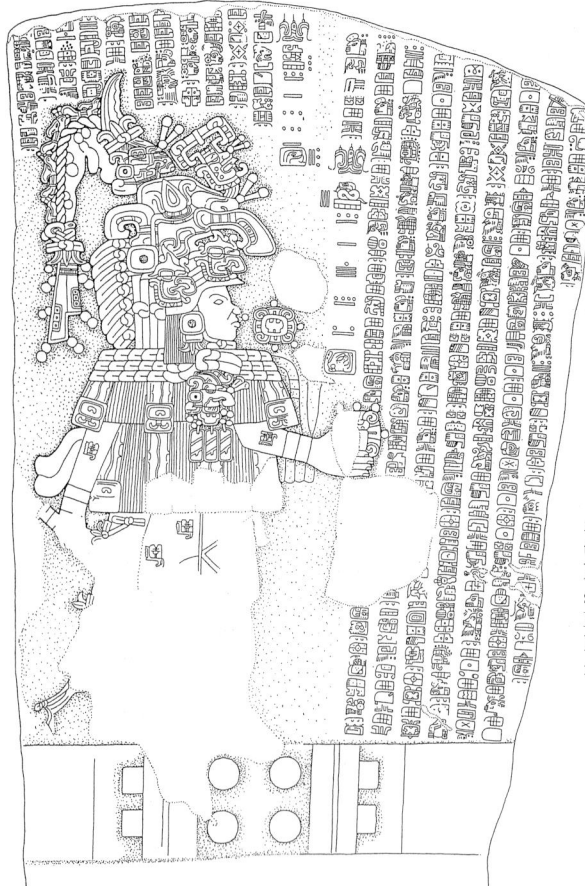

25 Worked of fine, dense limestone, this stela from La Mojarra features a lord in the elegant attire of the second century AD. The Principal Bird Deity imagery evident in the headdress also prevails on other monuments of the period.

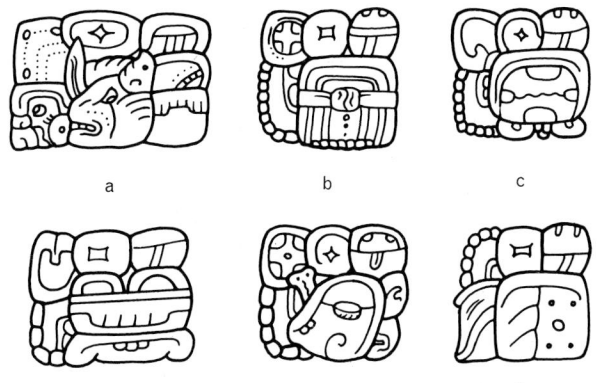

26 Maya emblem glyphs indicate lineage or place. Here is a sampling: (a) Copán (an Early Classic form); (b) Tikal; (c) Palenque; (d) Yaxchilán; (e) Bonampak; (f) Piedras Negras.

worked with a new owner's name. A fine Olmec greenstone pectoral now at Dumbarton Oaks, for example, was incised with a long Maya text, perhaps at the end of the Late Formative.

The mid-80s recovery of a huge carved stela from La Mojarra, 25 Veracruz, in the region thought of as the Olmec 'heartland,' has revealed previously unknown sophistication and skill in early writing. Two Long Count dates run in columns at the center of the monument, recording dates in AD 143 and 156. Other signs and their syntax can be recognized, but not 'read.' Adorned in the headdress of the Principal Bird Deity, the standing lord wears regalia that the Classic Maya would subsequently emulate, including the celt assemblage on his chest.

When John Lloyd Stephens visited the Maya area in 1839, he found inscriptions that he believed represented a single system used from Copán in the south to Chichen Itzá in the north. One day, he felt sure, a new Champollion would rise to the challenge of translating the names and places of the ancient kings of the New World. About 120 years later, and 80 years after Long Count dates were first cracked, two breakthroughs began to fulfill his prophecy. They also began to explain just why the Maya (and probably the Olmecs and Zapotecs before them) were so absorbed in chronological reckonings: they needed a means to fix historical information firmly in time. Heinrich Berlin first noticed in 1958 that a particular glyphic compound closed many Maya texts, yet the main element of this cluster varied from site to site. It quickly became evident that these glyphic compounds must refer either to place or family, if not

45

27 Lintel 8, Yaxchilán. Bird Jaguar, at right, captures 'Jeweled Skull,' whose name is emblazoned on his thigh and at the bottom of the column of glyphs at left. Bird Jaguar's name is the second in the column of glyphs at far right, and it is followed by the Yaxchilán emblem glyph. Late Classic.

both. (Similarly the name York, for example, refers to both a lineage and a place in England.) These glyphs have now been identified for most Maya sites with inscriptions. The text of Naranjo Stela 24, for example, includes two different 'emblems,' as Berlin called them. One might suspect trade, warfare, alliance, or marriage as the motivation for such an inscription, and in fact the hefty woman depicted on the monument was a foreigner who married into the Naranjo dynasty. Both the emblem of Naranjo and that of her place of origin appear in the text.

At about the same time that Berlin was working on emblems, Tatiana Proskouriakoff explained how the pattern of dates at Piedras Negras implied their historical nature. She hypothesized verbs – to do with birth, accession, capture, and death, among other things – and names – 'Bird Jaguar' and 'Shield Jaguar' at Yaxchilán, for example. She also showed the importance of royal women, and documented a 'female indicator' glyph.

A look at Yaxchilán Lintel 8 shows why she began to suspect that such 27 inscriptions had historical content. A skull within a beaded cartouche is inscribed on the thigh of the captive at right: this same glyph appears as the fourth glyph in the text above, left. The first two glyphs yield a date in AD 755; given modern Maya syntax and the frequency of the third glyph in passages associated with armed men and captives, Proskouriakoff then hypothesized that the third glyph was a verb, probably meaning 'to capture,' since that activity is depicted. To the right, the text continues. The last glyph could already be identified as a Yaxchilán emblem (cf. ill. 26d); the glyph preceding it is a jaguar head with a small bird superfixed. Based on its frequency in texts dating from about AD 750 to 770, Proskouriakoff proposed this glyph to be the ruler's name in that era, and she called him 'Bird Jaguar.' Thus, if we ignore the caption material that appears in the middle of the scene, the text might be paraphrased: 'On 7 Imix 14 Tzec [in AD 755] was captured Jeweled Skull by Lord Bird Jaguar, of the Yaxchilán lineage.'

By this time studies had also been completed by Yuri Knorosov in St. Petersburg, who was able to show the phonetic values of many glyphic elements. Unlike Proskouriakoff or Berlin, who worked with Classic inscriptions, Knorosov took the sixteenth-century manuscript of Diego de Landa, bishop of Mérida, and the three Postclassic Maya manuscripts surviving in Europe as his focus of study. Landa had asked an educated Maya source to write Maya characters beside the letters of the Spanish alphabet. In this way, some thirty-odd Maya glyphs had been written down. Knorosov used these to begin to determine the phonetic value of the texts.

The capture glyph in the passage decoded by Proskouriakoff was one to which Knorosov had already turned his attention. He read the three elements of the glyph at A3 as *chu-ca-ah*, or *chucah*, literally the third person of the verb 'to capture' in many Maya languages today. With the publication of Proskouriakoff's work, the phonetic interpretations of Knorosov began to gain acceptance.

These initial understandings of the nature of the Maya script changed the way scholars perceived the ancient Maya. The first group of glyphs deciphered showed them to have been territorial; the next stressed the role of individuals and their quest for power at various Maya cities. With a few strokes of the pen, the notion of a peaceful Maya had become obsolete and insupportable. As a result, scholars began to seek evidence for similar cultural patterns through Mesoamerica, and the impetus to decipher other scripts gained renewed energy.

The Zapotec writing system was also used to record names and places. Names were indicated by their position in the 260-day calendar, and the places recorded were those conquered by the successful lords of Monte Albán. Javier Urcid has recently identified several missing elements of the calendar, and the script may have been more complete than scholars previously assumed.

By means of logographic manuscripts, the Mixtec of the Postclassic (and probably earlier as well, but the manuscripts no longer exist) recorded their genealogical histories. Names are either the calendrical day names or logographs (that is, word pictures) which first appear attached physically to given individuals. Events are symbolized by widely understood signs: an umbilical cord denotes birth, a couple seated on a reed mat marks marriage. With this kind of record, the reader must provide the words to a story for which places, dates, events, and persons are specifically indicated.

Among the Aztecs, dates and logographic writing also prevailed. Writing was used by individuals for divining manuscripts and genealogies and by the state for keeping track of the prodigious tribute collected from the whole of Mesoamerica. At the time of the Conquest, Aztec writing had become sufficiently sophisticated for it to have both phonetic indicators and a type of rebus writing, in which homophones are substituted. Ritual manuscripts charted festivals and divinations; histories and genealogies tracked lineages from the supernatural past; tribute books enumerated the prodigious tribute collected from the whole of Mesoamerica. Nevertheless, the elegant poetry recited at the time of the Conquest was probably not written down until the introduction of the Roman alphabet, although a guide with cues could have existed.

Late Formative Art and Architecture

MONTE ALBÁN

The most spectacular early development in Oaxaca took place at Monte Albán. The city was founded at the beginning of the Late Formative, pre-

28 Danzante at Monte Albán. These limp, mutilated figures, long thought to be 'dancing,' may be sacrificed captives of war. Monte Albán I.

sumably as the Zapotec capital. A mountainous outcrop overlooking three important valleys of central Oaxaca was reworked into a great manmade acropolis. In the first era of occupation, a main axis running *62* roughly north-south was established and at least some structures were erected to define the main plaza as the ritual core.

Monte Albán has no natural source of water, and one might legitimately surmise that it took an advanced social organization to sustain a community high above the fertile valleys below. Various ideas have been put forward to explain the selection of this remote mountain for settled life, and all depend upon the most important early temple there, the Temple of the Danzantes, and the nature of its reliefs. While some scholars have imagined Monte Albán as a site of pacific unification, others have seen in its early writing and art patterns of conquest and domination more typical of Mesoamerica.

The Danzantes, or 'dancers,' were so named in the nineteenth century *28* because of their free, loose postures. In Late Formative times, over 300 individual slabs were carved with these figures, and about 140 were incorporated into the Temple of the Danzantes. About the same number were set into Mound J, a slightly later structure, and others were re-used in later contexts. In the Temple of the Danzantes, the slabs are set so that some face out, away from the main plaza, while others line a narrow

49

passageway and yet others flank the main façade. Some, particularly those considered 'swimmers,' form a flight of stairs. No single figure is arranged with regard to another, insofar as can be determined now.

Each slab is different in its imagery, but all were worked in a simple incised technique with little relief. One assumes that the carver simply followed a charcoal sketch made directly on the stone. Most bodies are shown frontally or in three-quarter view, while the heads are in profile. All are male. Hands and feet hang limp. The closed eyes of most figures indicate that they are dead. Although some retain a necklace or an earplug, they are all naked, normally an indication of humiliation in Mesoamerica. Scroll motifs streaming from the groin no doubt reveal an ancient pattern of genital mutilation in Oaxaca. A few are accompanied by glyphic cartouches, probably names.

In all likelihood, these slabs show the victims of war. To Richard Blanton, who has studied early settlement both in the valleys and on Monte Albán, the Temple of the Danzantes suggests a war memorial, erected at the beginning of Monte Albán's growth, to commemorate the end of divisive strife among the three valleys. Prisoner galleries, however, occur in later art, particularly among the Classic Maya, and in general they indicate a different sort of memorial. The north wall of Room 2 of the Bonampak paintings, for example, shows a group of tortured captives at the feet of victorious warriors on a flight of stairs. If we were to repop-

29 Mound J, Monte Albán. From the south, the dramatic, arrow-like positioning of the structure can be seen. Monte Albán II.

ulate the 'swimmer' staircase of the Temple of the Danzantes, we would have a similar scene. In the later Maya cases, it is clear that the captives were displayed to proclaim the prowess of the victors, not to discourage the horrors of war. In accordance with Mesoamerican patterns, the message conveyed at Monte Albán is likely to have emphasized the power held by those who dominated the valley.

Somewhat later, probably after 200 BC, the Zapotecs erected Mound J in the center of the plaza at Monte Albán. By this time the symmetrical guide lines of the plaza had been laid out; but Mound J was set prominently off axis and given unusual form. The structure looks like an arrow pointing to the southwest, yet its unusual configuration cannot be observed from the north or east. From the northeast, the building shows only a wall of steps, flanked by broad balustrades. The pointed head of the building is honeycombed with tunnels that are vaulted with stone slabs slanted to touch one another, creating a visual pointed archway but with no structural strength. Both these odd tunnels and the unusual shape of the structure itself have given rise to the idea that Mound J may have had an astronomical function. Recent studies have borne this out. Thirty-one miles to the east, at Cabellito Blanco, a structure nearly identical to Mound J has been found. At zenith passage both mounds point to particularly bright stars. Mound J, then, is one of the first buildings in Mesoamerica that we can consider a giant chronographic marker. Its purpose was to acknowledge the passage of time, and – interestingly enough – it appears about the same time as the proliferation of the written calendrical system.

The evolution of the writing system is also evident in Mound J. Carved slabs, technically similar to those of the Temple of the Danzantes, were set along the façade, the projectile wall, and within the tunnels. On these slabs, although the genital mutilation persists, the figures show more costume details. The writing too is far more elaborate; it seems to record

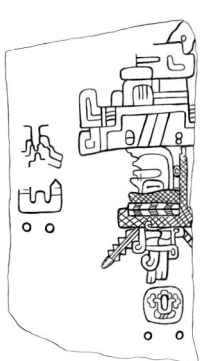

30 Incised on a slab from Mound J, this glyph for 'hill,' indicating a place name, includes the upside-down head of a lord, probably recording his defeat.

battles with dates and placenames, as distinct from the more general record of conquest shown previously on the Danzantes temple. A rough incision, probably following a charcoal sketch, characterizes the Mound J carvings. On one, a human head is shown upside-down under a placename, indicating conquest, and the accompanying glyphs suggest a date in the 52-year calendar.

Monte Albán was very much the main center in Oaxaca during the Late Formative, but it was not unique. To the southeast, at Dainzú, another great mountainous outcrop was the focus of occupation. In this instance, the main architecture arose on the valley floor, and a large temple structure there had inset carved slabs technically similar to the Danzantes. Individuals with masks or helmets, perhaps ballplayers, form the majority of the representations. Above, on the peak itself, steps and chambers were carved from the living rock, and the site may have functioned as a religious shrine.

The careful excavation of the tombs at Monte Albán produced a dependable chronological sequence long before radiocarbon testing could provide a second check. The two earliest periods are known as Monte Albán I and Monte Albán II. Ceramics show the most periodization; other architectural innovations of the Late Formative, such as the construction of masonry ballcourts or the use of columns, show a steady development into Classic forms.

Most of the tomb goods from Monte Albán I were simple offerings of gray-colored ceramics. Strong affinity with Olmec conventions of physiognomy can be seen in the earliest effigy pots, the best of which come from Monte Negro, also in the modern state of Oaxaca. Slightly slanted eyes and a strongly downturned mouth are typical of these early wares. By Monte Albán II, the technical qualities that characterize later Monte Albán tomb offerings are evident, although stylistically distinct. Many large full-figure hollow effigy sculptures were made in animal and human forms. Technically, large ceramic figures may have derived from Olmec precedents, but the imagery is particular to Oaxaca.

A carefully formed large standing figure of this period holds his hands out as if to warn away tomb robbers, and Alfonso Caso found these figures at tomb entrances. Life-size hollow pumas and jaguars wear scarves and adornments, indicating their supernatural qualities: surely such guardians acted to deter potential violators of these entries to the Underworld! But the figures represented encompass a wide range of human expression. The Scribe of Cuilapan, with his slight asymmetry,

31 An early Monte Albán king was buried with this jade bat assemblage. He probably once wore it on his chest, like the lord of La Mojarra (cf. ill. 25), or as a belt adornment, as demonstrated by later Maya lords (cf. ills. 85, 87). Monte Albán II.

32 (*right*) Hands outstretched, this large hollow tomb figure from Monte Albán II discourages anyone seeking to violate the space of the dead.

uneven shoulders, and partly opened mouth, seems simply to capture a portrait of a contemplative young man.

Fine pieces of Olmec jade have been collected in Oaxaca, perhaps treasures originally held by early Zapotecs. By Monte Albán II, the Zapotecs themselves were skilled lapidaries. One of the most splendid of their works of this time is the jade leaf-nose bat belt assemblage. This object would have been worn at the waist or chest, the three shiny jade plaques dangling. (The so-called Leiden Plate was once part of such an assemblage made by the Maya.)

31

87

WEST MEXICO

The history of ancient West Mexico is in many ways one of separate development from the rest of Mesoamerica. There is, for example, no evidence that the Mesoamerican calendrical systems were known or used. The relationship of the region to the high civilizations also remains obscure: neither the art nor the architecture indicate direct contact. Moreover there is no clear florescence of culture during one era, and it seems likely that the political developments of the Olmecs or the Aztecs barely touched the region. This does not mean, however, that the works of art produced there lacked subtlety or craftsmanship. Far from it. West Mexican ceramic figures and groups – almost all of which have no archaeological provenance – are among the most directly appealing of all Mesoamerican artworks. Charmed by their apparent lack of elite symbolism, the modern artist Diego Rivera made a large collection of them – now in the Anahuacalli Museum in Mexico City – and regularly incorporated images based on their styles in his murals. Needless to say, this demand for West Mexican ceramic sculptures has not only promoted the looting of ancient tombs but also nurtured an industry of modern forgeries and pastiches. Peter Furst linked the modern shamanistic practices of the Huichol to West Mexican ceramics, infusing them with specific ritual meanings, and bringing these sculptures into the greater Mesoamerican tradition.

For the sake of convenience, West Mexican artifacts are grouped here under geographic headings, principally the modern states of Colima, Jalisco, and Nayarit, plus one river, Mezcala. What links these finds together is the context in which they were deposited – the shaft tomb. At anywhere from one to six meters below ground level, such tombs consisted of a chamber opening out of a narrow shaft. In the chamber lay multiple burials, often deposited over a considerable period of time. Convincing dates for the tombs are rare, but most belong to the Late Formative, although the chronological span extends from the Early Formative to the Early Classic. Reports of the discovery in 1993 of a complete and untouched tomb revealed that families probably used their crypts for generations, adding new bodies and offerings through time. A single chamber held over 300 vessels, including many effigies!

The earliest documented works from West Mexico are from what is known as the Capacha complex, in central Colima. Shaft-tomb goods there have been dated to 1500 BC by radiocarbon techniques. Early vessels include stirrup-spout types remarkably similar to those found in contemporary contexts on the north coast of Peru. Does this imply links between the two areas? On the whole, contact between Mesoamerican and Andean civilizations is believed only to have been intermittent, if it occurred at all (the Aztecs, for example, knew nothing of the Incas at the time of the Conquest); but these early vessels may provide evidence for such contact. Crops, weaving and ceramic techniques, as well as elite lore, may have been shared at just this horizon, perhaps via Ecuador. On the other hand, the stirrup-spout jar, a convenient vessel for carrying water without spillage or evaporation, could well have been invented simultaneously in response to similar needs in both areas.

Two principal types of figures have been found in Colima, and they probably reflect a chronological sequence. Flat figures – often considered to be the earlier type – use a slab-and-appliqué technique, with animated postures, and are sometimes grouped together. Better known are the hollow figures of reddish clay, burnished to a high luster, and often spotted with black, white, and grey mineral accretions slowly deposited over the centuries in the tomb. The majority of such figures also double as vessels, whose pouring spouts are usually the tails of the animal effi-

33 A terracotta dog with human mask, Colima style. Great numbers of native hairless dogs were immortalized in Colima clay sculpture, but the mask of this one makes it an overtly supernatural creature.

gies. Indigenous hairless dogs were worked in particularly lively forms:
33 playing, sleeping, even nipping one another. Others, such as the dog with
a human mask, may have a meaning that goes beyond anecdotal charm.
Headrests were made in the form of half-dogs, and the resultant image
was of a human head on a dog's back, the dog thus bearing his master
into the afterlife. Colima potters formed clay into the shapes of squashes
and gourds, the perishable templates for all vessels. Most human figures
are males with clubs poised to strike. Like the large felines of Monte
Albán II tombs, they may have warded off unwanted visitors, but the
single horn protruding from the forehead of many of them has suggested
that they might be shamanistic figures for communication between the
living and the dead. But these horns may also be the tips of conch shells,
worn to signify rulership.

Shaft-tomb deposits from Jalisco are stylistically distinct from other
West Mexican ceramics, although not unrelated technically. The potters
of this region produced both small solid figures and larger hollow ones.
Some of the smaller ones, with pointed heads, and typically showing
musicians and performers, have been recovered in lively groupings.

Limited ceremonial architecture has been discovered in West Mexico,
although vast adobe mounds have been mapped in recent years by Phil
Weigand. The most important stone structure is at Ixtlan del Río,
Nayarit, where a tiered round platform like a wedding cake came to light.
Although the platform may be late in date, other round buildings like it
but of perishable materials have been found in West Mexico, and it is a
type that seems to have lasted for generations. We should not therefore
be surprised to discover that round architectural features often occur in
ceremonial groupings of Nayarit figures, and in general, Nayarit ceramics include more architecture than the other regional styles. One of the
most common themes is of figures in or near thatched houses, and the
groups that show tiny figures underneath houses have been interpreted
as funeral scenes related to the act of interment.

Ballcourts also have a prominent place in the group repertoire, and one
day actual stone courts may be located in the Nayarit region. The figural
scenes at any rate demonstrate the importance of the ballgame at an early
34 date in the area. The court grouping illustrated here shows three or four
men in a team, playing with a soccer-sized ball. Dozens of spectators look
on: they huddle together under a blanket or gently hug a child in an artistic expression that captures the warmth of everyday life.

The Nayarit potters also made large, hollow figures, often in male-

34 Players in two teams compete on this Nayarit-style clay model of a ballcourt while spectators watch in eager anticipation of the outcome.

35, 36 (*below*) A male and female couple, Nayarit style. Such male-female pairs were frequently placed in shaft tombs, perhaps to accompany interred married couples. The man at left wears a beaver skin on his head, a pelt still associated with shamanic transformers.

female pairs, which are perhaps marriage portraits interred with the dead. The bright patterning of the ancient textiles worn in Nayarit is recorded in the slip painting of the figures' costumes. The shifts donned by Nayarit men are uncommon in ancient Mesoamerica, and Patricia Anawalt has drawn attention to the presence of this sort of garment in the Andes during the same period, possibly showing contact. The couple in the *35, 36* example here may be of high status, to judge by the elaborate ornaments they wear in ears and nose, and they bear instruments, perhaps to provide musical accompaniment in death.

The drainage of the Mezcala River in West Mexico has yielded a great number of fine stone pieces of unknown date. The Aztecs coveted these serpentine, granite, and cave onyx (the Aztec *tecali*) carvings so much that they demanded them in tribute and interred them in the Templo Mayor in Tenochtitlan. Although the date of these objects has long been the subject of speculation, Louise Paradis has recently secured good radio-carbon dates for Mezcala stonework, confirming the early date (*c.* 300 BC) that artists like Miguel Covarrubias long suspected intuitively.

37 Using string-saw technology, Mezcala artists produced small temple models in abundance. The temple façades they represent are not matched by the architecture so far known from the region, and they suggest a familiarity with developments in Oaxaca. Some of these façades, for

37 Stone temple models, Mezcala style. Miniatures like this may record the perishable temple façades of long-lost architecture.

instance, resemble those of Mound X at Monte Albán, which dates to the Late Formative, and it is interesting to note that temple models have been recovered from Monte Albán II contexts.

Many functional stone pieces were also made by the Mezcala people: blades, axes, and bowls are known. What makes these materials so attractive to us is their lithic quality. The stone itself was admired by ancient Mezcala craftsmen, and its inherent 'stoniness' appeals to the modern eye.

THE MAYA REGION

Important developments occurred in the Maya area during the Late Formative. During the Middle Formative, the Olmecs had sustained contact with the Pacific coast, and their carvings have been found from Chiapas to El Salvador. During the Late Formative various population centers emerged where art and architecture of an apparently indigenous style was erected, particularly in the Chiapas/Guatemala highlands, at Izapa, Kaminaljuyú, Abaj Takalik, and El Baúl, and by persons who may not all have been ethnically 'Maya.' Excavations in the Central Petén – at Uaxactún and Tikal, the loci of Early Classic florescence – have shown that settlements had been established at both these places by the Late Formative. It was another Petén site, however – El Mirador – which apparently outstripped them in size and importance at this early date. Elsewhere, along the Caribbean coast, Cerros is the best-known site.

Late Formative building materials were often perishable, leaving only large collapsed adobe mounds in the highlands. Moreover, at Kaminaljuyú (with very probably the most substantial highland Late Formative architecture of all), only a handful of structures could be excavated before the modern real estate development of Guatemala City covered the greater part of the ancient ruins. In other locations, later structures still house earlier constructions. Probably the finest of known highland buildings is the great platform E-III-3 at Kaminaljuyú, which covered two rich tombs, in the pattern that Classic Maya architecture later followed.

However, at Cerros, in modern Belize at the mouth of the New River, we see dramatic new architectural expressions that were critical to the formation of Classic Maya patterns. About 100 BC there was an unprecedented spurt of building. All previous constructions were razed and new ones, some exceeding 20 m in height, were built with clean, new rubble cores. At Lamanai, farther up the New River, even taller structures rose

38 Structure 5, Cerros. Huge masks adorn the façades of Maya structures at Cerros and give evidence of the sudden rise of a solar cult. Late Formative.

38 to adorn the city. Giant stucco mask façades flanking the stairs are common in these new buildings at Cerros and Lamanai. The masks seem to display a new, codified imagery. *Kin*, or sun, symbols decorate the cheeks of great supernatural faces, in association with jaguar elements. The masks would thus seem to refer to the jaguar sun, an iconographic identification of the sun at night, and a prominent supernatural force among the Classic Maya. This combined imagery and architecture spread – almost as if it were some new orthodoxy – to other places, probably including the Central Petén, and perhaps instilling an ideological unity that gave force to the Early Classic within a few generations.

Some of the most exciting excavations of recent years have taken place at El Mirador and Nakbé, both in northern Petén, where a hitherto unobserved florescence of Maya civilization at the end of the Middle and beginning of the Late Formative has been discovered. The powerful ideology that united the Maya first took monumental form, perhaps already shared and transmitted by writing on perishable materials that no longer survive. Some of the largest pyramidal forms ever constructed in ancient America were erected in Late Formative Petén, broadcasting the power of the Principal Bird Deity and the Jaguar Sun, among other gods, whose power still compelled the faithful at the time of the Spanish Conquest. Few carved fragments of stone sculpture have been recovered to date, but at Nakbé, Richard Hansen has uncovered a nearly complete Middle or Late Formative carved stela with two standing figures rendered on it – what may well be the earliest representation of the Hero Twins. Rubble at El Mirador has yielded carved fragments that more clearly relate to subsequent Early Classic Maya works. At El Mirador's demise, when Tikal and Uaxactún were already growing into powerful polities, El Mirador's enemies may have stormed through the center of the declining city, smashing every sign of its former glory.

At the same time that such dramatic changes were taking place in the lowlands, the highlands too were seeing new developments. Perhaps following an earlier use of perishable materials or perhaps deriving directly from Olmec forms, highland societies began systematically to erect monumental stone carvings during the Late Formative. Boulder carvings – the ones most likely to have had Olmec precedents – were made at

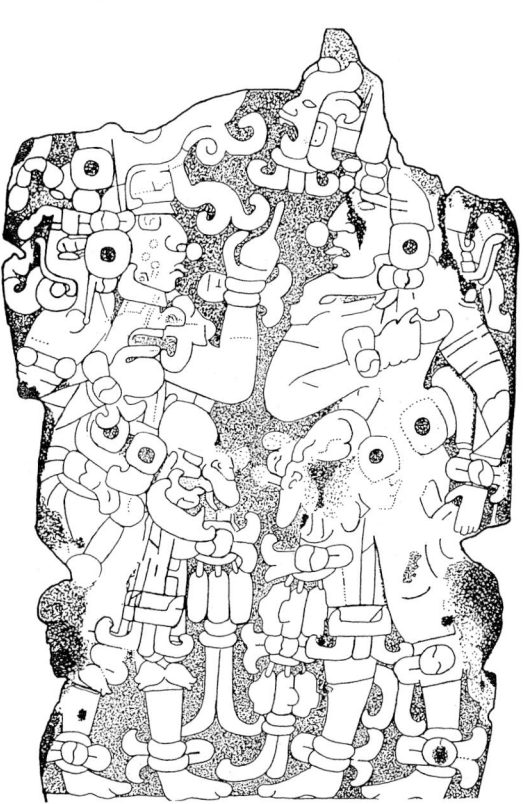

39 Stela 1, Nakbé. These two carved figures may be the earliest Maya depiction of the Hero Twins to survive. At left, the figure with jaguar pelage on his cheek may well be Xbalanque, facing his brother Hunahpu. Middle/Late Formative.

many sites, but other forms, the stela and altar, predominated. Despite the proliferation of the stela 'cult,' as it is often called, imagery and style remained distinct at the various highland centers: Izapa, Kaminaljuyú, and Abaj Takalik.

The Late Classic Maya reset the monuments of Izapa, but most of the stelae and altars there were carved during the Late Formative. Many of the altars (perhaps used as thrones by the lords) appear in the shape of large toads and frogs, perhaps symbols of the earth. A supernatural world is illustrated on the stelae, and many of the gods so key to Classic Maya religious narrative make their appearance on Izapa stelae. Furthermore, narrative art, with obvious sequence and story, makes its first appearance at Izapa. One stela, for example, depicts a standing figure, one arm rent from his body, who apparently appeals to the Principal Bird Deity perched in a caiman tree, an apparent rendering of the story of the Hero Twins and Vuqub Kaquix from the *Popol Vuh*, as written down in the mid-sixteenth century.

40 On Izapa Stela 1, Chac, god of rain and lightning, stands in water and fishes with a net, his already well-stocked creel on his back. A millennium later, on a pair of bones buried in Ruler A's tomb at Tikal, three

40 Fish basket on his back, Chac the rain god nets fish from the body of water he stands on. Chac is one of a handful of Maya gods clearly present in Late Formative iconography. Izapa Stela 1.

41 (*above left*) Stela 5, Izapa, may explain Izapan beliefs of world origins: beings both human and supernatural flow from the central tree while an old couple casts lots at lower left. Sky symbols mark the upper margin, and water defines the lower. Late Formative.

42 (*above right*) Stela 11, Kaminaljuyú. The standing warrior on this monument wears a bird suit and wields an axe. He is framed by a sky god above and terrestrial symbols below. Late Formative.

43 (*left*) A silhouette sculpture in Kaminaljuyú style, reportedly collected at Santa Cruz Quiché in the nineteenth century. The 'bowtie' at center is typical of weapons of sacrifice, and the beaded lines above may indicate blood. Late Formative.

squabbling Chacs catch fish in their bare hands and store their catch in similar creels. In this early representation of one of the most important Maya deities, Chac has his characteristically reptilian snout, a feature he would bear right up to the time of the Conquest. Not only the god of storms, Chac was probably the patron of fishermen.

41   Stela 5 depicts a mythic origin from a central tree. Representations of natural flora are rare in Olmec and Maya art – the two traditions most clearly related to Izapa – and the tree of Stela 5 is a supernatural one, from which human forms flow, as if released by the large figure to the right, who uses his nose to drill an opening into the trunk. The scene may be designed for oral reading, with components recorded as if in simultaneous narrative. The old couple at lower left who divine with kernels may be the ancestral couple (referred to in later sources) from whom all subsequent human beings descend. World trees, perhaps related to this earliest one at Izapa, appear also at Palenque and in Mixtec and Central Mexican manuscripts.

Borders above and below the Izapa scenes would seem to mark heaven and earth, quite possibly the first use of such conventions. Like the rest of Izapa monuments, these stelae emphasize mythological or supernatural scenes. As far as can be determined, the preoccupation with history evident on later Maya monuments is missing at Izapa.

The greatest florescence of the Late Formative in the highlands took place at Kaminaljuyú, where the richest burials of the era have been recovered, and many monuments have been found in its style over a 50-mile radius. Fine carved stelae show both supernatural figures and *42*   humans. Stela 11 depicts a standing lord adorned as the Principal Bird Deity, like the roughly contemporary ruler at La Mojarra (ill. 25). His eye peers out from the mask, and his cape flares out behind him like a pair of *cf. 84*   wings. An ancestor floats in the sky, and two smoking braziers rest at his feet. His deeply-carved feet press into the toponym he stands on, and the knapped surface of the hafted blade at right reveals a skill at carving that the lowland Maya did not achieve until centuries later. Other human *43*   figures are worked in silhouette, as is the unusual one illustrated here. This odd monument would seem to be a personified eccentric flint. Beaded elements appear here on the 'blade' of the monument. Such 'dots' or 'beads' often represent blood in Classic art, and this monument may commemorate ritual sacrifice in a bloodied blade.

At Abaj Takalik, stone monuments were also erected in stela/altar combinations, as they were at Izapa, but the imagery is different. Stela 2

64

shows two figures flanking a central column of text with a Cycle 7 (that is, before AD 41) date. Like La Venta Stela 3, Kaminaljuyú Stela 11, and the Early Classic portraits of Tikal, the upper margin has a supernatural character. The two humans below were probably historical figures. On Stela 5, two persons also flank a column of text, in this case a legible Long Count date of 8.4.5.17.11, or AD 126. The impossible posture of frontal torso with profile legs and face was a widespread convention later to prove typical of Early Classic Maya representations as well.

The second century AD brought an end to these achievements in the Guatemalan highlands, and the focus of progress shifted to the Central Petén, where the Early Classic began to take shape. From the forms established at Izapa, and already known in the lowlands, the Early Classic Maya derived mythic imagery; from Abaj Takalik, the conventions of historical portraiture. When the Early Classic emerged in full flower at Tikal and Uaxactún, it clearly drew upon precedents in the highlands for sculpture and from the Caribbean coast and El Mirador for architecture. Indeed, in most of Mesoamerica, Classic achievements in art and architecture were founded upon those of the Late Formative.

CENTRAL MEXICO

During Early and Middle Formative times an Olmec presence had made a profound impact on sites – and their grave goods, in particular – in the valleys of Central Mexico, but this presence ended in the Late Formative period. These established centers were not cities, and they did not have major ceremonial centers. We might consider them elaborate villages. At Tlatilco, for example, during the Late Formative period, figurines continued to be made; to the west, at Chupícuaro (now under an artificial lake in Guanajuato), charming figurines and vessels with distinctive red geometric slip patterning were produced.

By 100 BC at the latest, two new centers had emerged in the Valley of Mexico, Teotihuacan to the north, and Cuicuilco to the south. Positioned like rivals at extreme ends of the Valley, each grew dramatically in size and population. At Cuicuilco, a huge (135 m in diameter at the base) round platform was the focus of construction, rising in four concentric tiers like a giant wedding cake. About 50 BC, the volcano Xitli erupted, burying much of Cuicuilco. Another eruption occurred about 150 years later. Like Pompeii's population, the people of Cuicuilco fled. Teotihuacan no longer had a rival, and it grew rapidly in power and size.

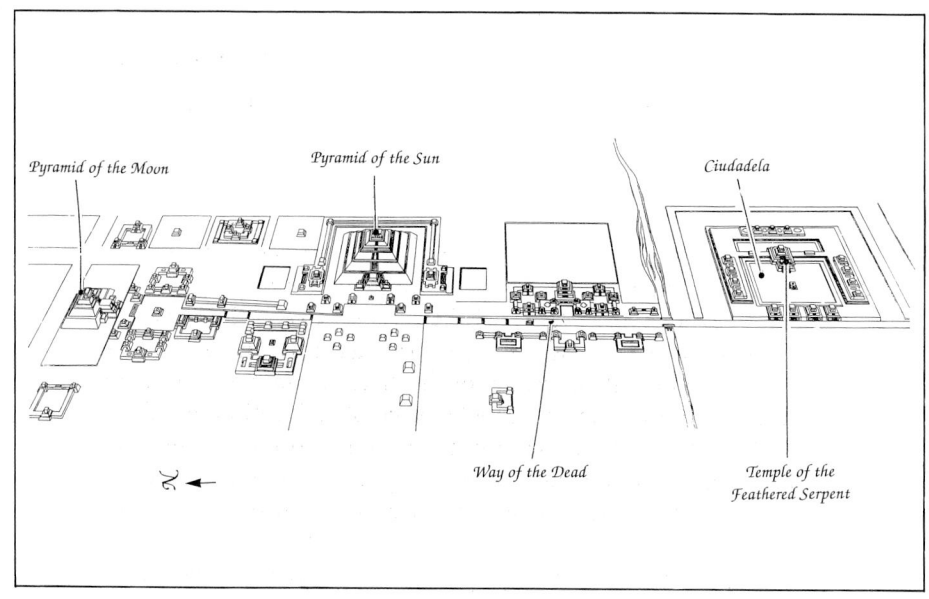

Pyramid of the Moon

Pyramid of the Sun

Ciudadela

Way of the Dead

Temple of the
Feathered Serpent

44, 45 Teotihuacan: an isometric view (*above*) of the main north–south axis, the Way of the Dead; and an oblique airview (*below*) from the north. The interstices of the grid were completely filled with buildings near the center of the city.

CHAPTER FOUR

Teotihuacan

The great city of Teotihuacan – a metropolis in the Valley of Mexico of perhaps 125,000 people at its height – had an impact on both commerce and art in the ancient New World comparable with that of Constantinople in the Old. It was a city of prestige and influence rivaled only by the later Tenochtitlan, capital of the Aztecs, and may have been the first great Tollan, or 'place of reeds,' a place of civilization, emulated by cultures all across Mesoamerica. Even as a ruin, Teotihuacan retained great importance, and it was never 'lost.' For the later Aztecs it was a setting for cosmic myth, and their last ruler, Motecuhzoma II, made regular pilgrimages to the site.

Decades of archaeological research have produced the single most detailed map in existence of a Mesoamerican city, but profound questions remain about Teotihuacan, including the very ethnicity of its powerful, urban population. Names of the city and buildings all come down from the Aztecs, and some of them may well be the names once spoken at the city, including 'Teotihuacan' itself, which means 'the place of those who have the road to the gods,' according to Thelma Sullivan. Recent investigations have begun to penetrate the complexity of its religion. A female deity, the 'Great Goddess,' dominated cave and mountain ritual, divination, and may have also had solar associations, while a male god, the 'Storm God,' presided over water and violent weather, like his later Aztec counterpart Tlaloc.

The notion of a 'Classic' era was first conceived to define the span of time during which the Maya used Long Count inscriptions, or about AD 250 to 900 – a period originally thought of as peaceful and theocratic throughout Mesoamerica. Though the idea of peaceful theocracy has since been abandoned, the term Classic remains in use, if only to characterize the richness, variety, and growth of the art and society of the time. Recent archaeological studies have shown that the Classic era in fact began by at least AD 150 in Central Mexico with the rise of Teotihuacan. The Classic era survived the burning of Teotihuacan in AD 650, and Classic traditions were sustained for at least two more centuries, particularly at Cholula, in the Valley of Puebla.

Random settlement during the Late Formative to the northwest of the city included elaborate cave precincts, particularly at the site of what would become the Pyramid of the Sun in future years. By the time of Christ, Teotihuacanos had begun to modify every aspect of the cave, from widening its entryway to lining the chambers with a mud mortar. From the cave entry, a siting line to the west was drawn that linked the cave, the rising of the Pleiades during the two annual passages of zenith, and the arc of solar passage at that same occurrence, forming a powerful east-west axis. Perpendicular to this was drawn another great axis, terminating at the mountain today known as Cerro Gordo, and by the end of the first century AD, these two axes had determined the grid that informed all positioning at Teotihuacan, with ritual focussed at the Pyramid of the Moon (by AD 150), Temple of the Feathered Serpent (by AD 200), and the Pyramid of the Sun (by AD 225). Low-lying apartment complexes filled the interstices in the ensuing centuries, and the great cosmopolitan center flourished, reaching its apogee *c.* AD 400–600. Archaeology has produced evidence of ethnic neighborhoods and barrios of craft specialists, but all lived along the immutable grid. Miles away, isolated structures still conformed to the city's right-angle geometry and the orientations determined by its grid. (With a population that archaeologist René Millon estimates at 125,000 or so, Teotihuacan would have been the sixth largest city in the world in AD 600, in an era when the half-million souls of Constantinople formed the world's largest urban center.)

44, 45   At Teotihuacan, the architecture is of both mass and space – mass in the great temples, open space in plazas, temple enclosures, ritual walkways, and interior space within the palace compounds. Although it is often difficult to distinguish palatial or bureaucratic structures from reli-

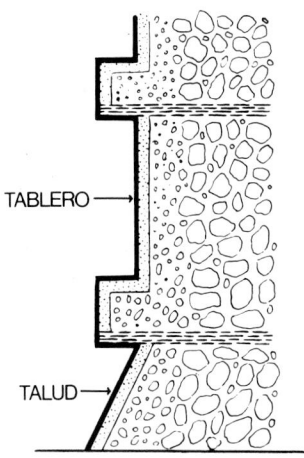

46 The vertical *tablero* sits on the sloping *talud*. This schematic drawing shows the sort of workmanship typical of many Teotihuacan structures. The exterior is finished with fine plaster and polished.

TABLERO →

TALUD →

47 The Pyramid of the Moon at Teotihuacan, framed by Cerro Gordo, a dead volcano, in the distance.

gious edifices or domestic dwellings in ancient Mesoamerica, the distinctive profile known as 'talud-tablero' delineates much sacred architecture at Teotihuacan, particularly among the smaller structures and within palace compounds. The sloping *talud* (talus) supports the vertical *tablero*   46 (entablature), which is often the surface for architectural ornament or stucco paintings. Perhaps more than any other aspect of its culture, talud-tablero architecture marks the presence of Teotihuacan abroad, and the execution of such profiles in adobe at Kaminaljuyú, for example, nearly   59 700 miles to the south, is a provincial manifestation of the great city.

The axes themselves took on architectural qualities, not only in orienting the city, but in ordering particular views of the city for participants in ritual. The north-south axis, called 'Miccaotli,' or Way of the Dead, by the Aztecs, may refer to the ancestral shrines that line it, and some may yet hold undiscovered tombs and offerings to the dead. Often thought of as a 'street,' the Way of the Dead changes elevation several times, forcing pedestrians up and down stairs and commanding attention as a two-dimensional architectural feature. This processional requirement recalls the passage in the cave under the Pyramid of the Sun, where supplicants shifted from kneeling and crawling to walking upright.

The Way of the Dead leads to the Pyramid of the Moon, and then   47 beyond to Cerro Gordo, a vast clefted mountain, a dead volcano with a sunken cone. Slightly smaller than the Pyramid of the Sun, the Pyramid of the Moon also features a huge open courtyard in the rough configura-

69

tion of the Mesoamerican completion sign that flows from the smaller talud-tablero structure that abuts the pyramid. Dedicated to the Great Goddess and her cult, the pyramid appears to possess the mountain and channel her forces to the city, acknowledging and calling upon the greater rainfall and abundance at the still-gurgling volcano. The setting of mountain and pyramid is visually compelling at Teotihuacan, as if humans sought to place their works in perfect harmony with the landscape. Intersections of such striking topography formed portals to the sacred in ancient Mesoamerica, points of liminal transformation, and the Teotihuacanos made the most of them, focussing cults on mountains and caves and celebrating them with architecture.

53   Although later partly covered by a plain pyramid, the original Temple of the Feathered Serpent always remained in view, with its elegant display of severe, frontal War Serpent headdresses floating atop the undulations of a Feathered Serpent. At the center of the large compound called the Ciudadela, once perhaps the palace of an early charismatic ruler, the Temple of the Feathered Serpent celebrates and commemorates warfare. Recently, archaeologists have explored the structure and found over 100 skeletons, almost all victims of what must have been massive human sacrifice rituals, apparently dedications to the cult of war.

48   The Pyramid of the Sun is one of the largest structures of Precolumbian Mesoamerica – in fact, at some 61 m (even without the perishable superstructure that undoubtedly crowned it!) one of the tallest

48 The Pyramid of the Sun at Teotihuacan.

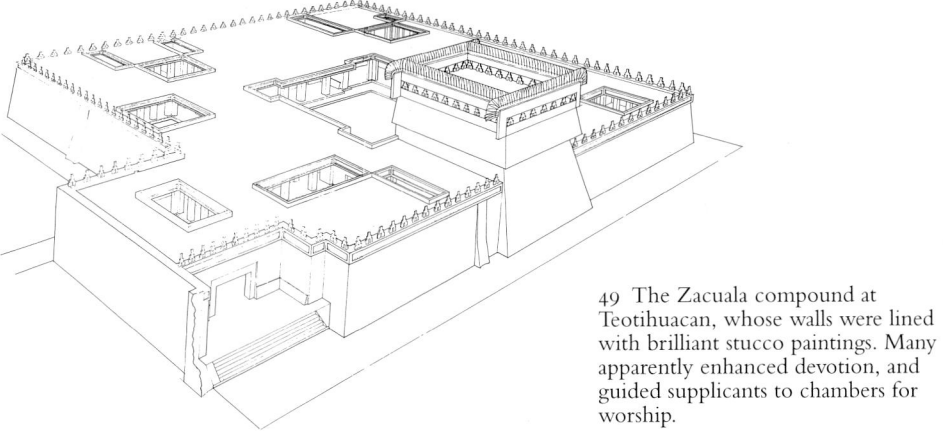

49 The Zacuala compound at Teotihuacan, whose walls were lined with brilliant stucco paintings. Many apparently enhanced devotion, and guided supplicants to chambers for worship.

and largest structures in North America until the twentieth century. Built over the multi-chambered cave that may have first galvanized the religious practice and civic order of Teotihuacan, the Pyramid of the Sun perhaps commemorated human creation and emergence from caves. The later Aztecs claimed to have come to Tenochtitlan from a mythic place called 'Chicomoztoc,' or Seven Caves: might not the underground chambers of Teotihuacan have entered into memory as a sacred place of origin?

Built at least twice, the Pyramid of the Sun rises in five distinct and giant levels. The broad staircase is the focus of the building. A single flight of steps divides into two and then merges together again: as attendants progressed up the stairs, they would have vanished and reappeared several times to the viewer on the ground. Like all Mesoamerican architecture, Teotihuacan structures formed specific backgrounds for rituals and public events. Scholars have not agreed on just what cult is celebrated at the Pyramid of the Sun, but it may have been the center for the Storm God, or perhaps another locus for the Great Goddess, who may have been honored in the caves below.

Residential compounds of various size fill out the Teotihuacan quadrants. Access to these compounds was extremely restricted, often through a single door, providing security and privacy within. Given the inevitable noise and confusion in this city of busy merchants and craftsmen, the inhabitants must have felt relief at escaping from the hubbub of the street to the seclusion of their quiet residences. Such urban life can be com- 49 pared to that of Old World, pre-modern cities, but it had no counterpart in the New World. Each residential grouping included three shrines and a platform for semi-public rituals, as well as many dwellings. Built to conventional standards and using stock materials, the compounds at Teotihuacan appear to have been the result of state construction. Only recently have archaeologists found evidence for slum-like dwellings pressed up against the apartments.

Such compounds sometimes housed foreigners, as discovery of a 'Oaxaca' barrio shows, where Zapotecs lived in typical Teotihuacan housing but whose mortuary rite included traditional Zapotec extended burials with Oaxaca urns. The Zapotecs at Teotihuacan imported utilitarian ceramics from Oaxaca as well. These foreign enclaves may have been embassies or merchants' quarters. Luxury goods in foreign style for the local inhabitants may also have been prepared there. Teotihuacan was truly a cosmopolitan city.

SCULPTURE

The stone sculpture of Teotihuacan is massive and prismatic, retaining the 'stoniness' that attracted the modern sculptor Henry Moore to Mesoamerican styles. In the sense of material and geometry, it is similar to the architecture. Static and serene, Teotihuacan sculpture and painting have long resisted interpretation, the absence of individuality and personality so keen that artistic expression has generally been considered a reflection of a corporate mentality that idealized the self-consciousness of

frontispiece uniformity. The most important Teotihuacan sculpture is the great female figure of the Great Goddess once set in the courtyard of the Pyramid of the Moon. The cleft in her head recalls Olmec works, but the 'blockiness' bears little resemblance to the plastic three-dimensional quality of Olmec sculpture. If set on axis with the Pyramid of the Moon, the cleft in the sculpture's head would have been aligned with the depression in

47 Cerro Gordo, and, as the figure brings her hands to her body, she seems to wring water from her *huipil*, or upper body garment, as if releasing the power of the mountain upon her people.

An unusual sculpture was found at La Ventilla, an outlying residential compound of Teotihuacan. It seems to have been a marker, or perhaps a banner stone, for a ballgame played without a masonry court of the sort generally associated with the game in Mesoamerica. The sculpture has four individual components, each worked with an elaborate interlocking

72

50 Teotihuacan masks feature no holes to breathe, but they gave life to mortuary or god bundles. The butterfly mouthpiece indicates a person of high rank.

scroll design. This type of scroll characterizes Classic Veracruz stone sculpture, particularly at the site of El Tajín, where the ballgame is celebrated with no fewer than eleven courts. One of the sloping talud paintings of the Tlalocan (see below) shows small, animated figures who play a game around a monument similar to the La Ventilla piece.

Perhaps best known of all Teotihuacan sculpture are the fine masks, *50* which Esther Pasztory believes may have been attached to perishable supports to form large assemblages that could have been dressed and worshipped. Made of serpentine, cave onyx (the Aztec *tecali*), or granite, these masks present clear, anonymous faces, neither male nor female, young nor old. Compare, for example, ill. 50 with the Frontispiece: these sculptures too wear the uniform face of Teotihuacan, isolated in the stone masks. Traces of deposits left in the sunken holes of some masks indicate that inlay of shell or pyrites once formed eyes. A few masks have been recovered with shell and turquoise mosaic intact; although beautiful, the inlay does not alter the quality of anonymity.

73

51 Small clay figurines, Teotihuacan, modeled in animated postures. Early Classic.

51 Ceramic figurines were made throughout the history of Teotihuacan, and the early ones, tiny, agile, and perhaps once dressed in perishable materials, are the most appealing. Like the stone carvings, these miniature figures wear the anonymous mask of Teotihuacan. They are found in great abundance, and by AD 450 or so were mold-made and mass-produced, richer in iconography but limited by their technology to static poses. A general move to mass production characterizes all Teotihuacan production, from ceramics to figurines.

54 Large-scale ceramic sculptures also survive. Brightly polychromed urns show human and animal faces peering out from almost architectural constructions of mass-produced, stamped elements. The flatness of the surface planes directs attention to the recessed, three-dimensional face. The Teotihuacanos themselves may have taken these assemblages apart and reconfigured different deities from the constituent parts.

Obsidian and precious shells were worked into fine objects that fre-
52 quently accompanied burials. Recent excavations at the Temple of the Feathered Serpent have yielded forty similar necklaces, each of which features shell worked into the shape of human teeth, sometimes accom-

52 During the second century AD, Teotihuacanos interred an unprecedented human sacrifice of at least 100 victims. Forty-odd necklaces featuring human jaws or their representation reveal the depth of commitment to the practice.

53 The Temple of the Feathered Serpent, Teotihuacan. Early in this century, archaeologists removed the exterior mantle of the structure and revealed more of the painted, sculptured façade of an earlier construction.

panied by whole jawbones, forming what must have been potent and eerie symbols of prowess in warfare and sacrifice.

PAINTING

The histories of painting and architectural sculpture at Teotihuacan cannot easily be separated, for painted ornament on early buildings would appear to give rise later to pure painting. Of all architectural ornament at Teotihuacan, the finest is that of the Temple of the Feathered Serpent, set *53*

54 Mass-produced of standardized parts large and small, this large urn with its owl imagery served the Teotihuacan war cult. Across Mesoamerica, the Teotihuacan owl entered the inventory of war iconography.

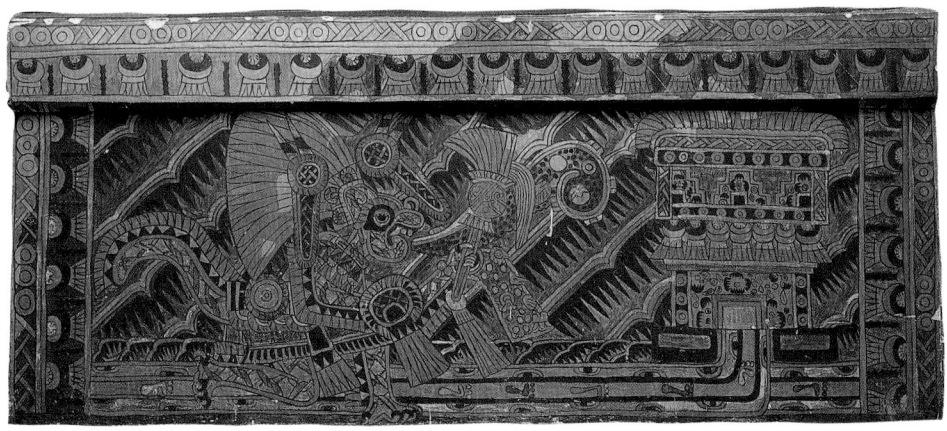

55 Representations of a clawed goddess from late Teotihuacan present her head upside-down and flung backwards, perhaps even severed like those of later Aztec earth goddesses. Flowers issue from her that symbolize fertility renewed by sacrifice.

56 A stucco wall painting from Tetitla, Teotihuacan. A human in a netted jaguar suit kneels on a path marked by footprints that lead to a temple.

at the western margin of a large enclosure, perhaps the palace of the ruler. On the talud-tablero façade uncovered and restored between 1917 and 1920, the huge feathered serpent heads of the balustrade weigh over four tons apiece, and elaborate tenons hold the complete assemblage in place. Because these sculptures were painted, we may consider this the earliest programmatic painting to survive at Teotihuacan, and daubs of blue, red, white, and yellow can still be seen. But by the third century AD, a true fresco painting replaced most sculptural ornament, and the palette brightened, with an emphasis on shades of clear reds, most of which depend on hematite as the essential pigment, and resulting in images that bring to mind medieval tapestries or Persian carpets. With little emphasis on line, the works can be hard to decipher, particularly when partly eroded. But many paintings are also highly repetitious, and reconstruction of the whole can often be determined from fragments.

Murals covered the tableros throughout Teotihuacan, and the apartment complexes in particular were brightly painted. Despite efforts to develop a sequence for paintings, both the range of subjects and nature of paintings from AD 400 to 750 seems to have been fairly consistent, with images of warfare, deities, and sacrifice prevailing. At the Atetelco complex and elsewhere, standard templates must have been used to achieve a repetitious patterning that looks like wallpaper to the casual visitor. Yet such templates were restricted to individual complexes and never repeated beyond a single precinct.

Many paintings are didactic and would seem to instruct observers to conduct themselves appropriately, and particularly to carry out sacrifice, exemplified in the many images of figures in profile, carrying incense bags and standing beside maguey spines and grass balls. Rows of profile figures, including the Netted Jaguar god, flank doorways, guiding processional movement. Elaborate backgrounds reveal temples, clouds, and abundant foliage. Processional warriors from Techinantitla follow a footprint-dotted path and speak 'flowery' scrolls; rare name glyphs appear in front of each one. The three-droplet tassel in each headdress represents an extruded heart.

Frontality was restricted to deities, and representations of the Great Goddess were painted all over the city. Remarkable images of her dominate the so-called Tlalocan patio paintings, so named by Alfonso Caso as an image of the Aztec paradise of water long before female deities were identified at Teotihuacan. On the upper tableros of each wall, the Great Goddess gives forth blue-green droplets while a pair of acolytes in profile

56

57 Teotihuacan potters crafted ceramics that were prized everywhere in Mesoamerica for their extraordinary thinness. This hunchback may have borne maize or gruel on his back.

attend and make offerings. From her head sprout plants along which butterflies flutter and spiders crawl. On the talud below, a myriad tiny individuals frolic in water flowing from a mountain; exuberant speech scrolls suggesting happy sounds. We might read this repeated mountain imagery as an invocation of the concept the Aztec would later call *altepetl*, or water-mountain, indicating a hearth of civilization.

Many paintings have eluded identification. One strange clawed goddess features an upside-down head and bosom, perhaps a prototype for the image of a decapitated woman deity, prevalent in Aztec art, who similarly throws her head backward, but with blood usually spewing from the neck. Like many Teotihuacan paintings, areas of feather were painted in blue-green malachite fresco, then outlined crisply in thin red lines. *55*

Many ceramics were stuccoed, generally showing a chronology and imagery similar to the monumental paintings, while others were worked in a thin orange clay (such as the one illustrated here), although often *57*

58 Stuccoed tripod vessel in Teotihuacan style. Symbols of Tlaloc, or the Storm God, adorn both the vessel and its lid. Tripod feet characterize Teotihuacan ceramics. Early Classic.

58 stuccoed too. Stuccoed vessels feature heavy, lipped lids with paintings to match the body; tiny slab cut-outs function as tripod feet. One *olla*, or open-mouthed jar, shows a bright blue goggle-eyed Tlaloc bearing an *olla* himself. At the time of the Conquest, the Tlalocs were said to pour water onto the earth from such vessels.

THE END OF TEOTIHUACAN

Constant rain and water crises at Teotihuacan exacerbated the difficulty of building and maintaining the city. The preparation of lime for mortar and stucco requires vast amounts of firewood to burn limestone or seashells, and the more Teotihuacan grew, the more the surrounding forests were depleted. With deforestation came soil erosion, drought, and crop failure. In response, Teotihuacan may have erected ever more temples and finished more paintings, thus perpetuating the cycle. The Great Goddess must have wrung her hands without profit, however, for the city was doomed. According to radiocarbon dating, Teotihuacan was ravaged about AD 650, with the core area of temples badly burned and savagely sacked. The perpetrators may have been semi-nomadic peoples just to the north, those most disrupted by the expansion of Teotihuacan, and perhaps occasionally in Teotihuacan employ as miners or laborers. The Teotihuacan map itself reveals greater density of construction along the northern perimeter, forming a wall to what was an open city. Although some occupation of Teotihuacan continued, the city never regained its importance, and the production of fine art and architecture ceased.

During the rise of Teotihuacan, the magnet of the great city drew people from valleys in surrounding areas, causing their depopulation. Conversely, when Teotihuacan declined, other Central Mexican cities began to expand.

Far to the south, in highland Guatemala, Kaminaljuyú was apparently the locus through which Teotihuacan had made contact with the Classic Maya, particularly during the Early Classic, when the Maya had become familiar with the foreign ideology and sought goods in Teotihuacan style. Although Kaminaljuyú had flourished in Late Formative times, during the Early Classic, a number of structures were built there in Teotihuacan style. Principal among these is a small-scale reproduction of the Pyramid of the Moon, carried out in adobe. Tombs at Kaminaljuyú were filled **59** with luxury goods, indicating the wealth accumulated by those who mediated between Teotihuacan and the Maya.

During the era of Teotihuacan's rise and development, Cholula, in the Valley of Puebla, also thrived. Curiously, about the same time as the burning of Teotihuacan, Cholula likewise underwent depopulation. During the Postclassic, however, the city was rebuilt and expanded. Most ethnohistoric sources link Cholula to Quetzalcóatl, at least during the era of Spanish Conquest, but the relationship may well be ancient.

The main pyramid at Cholula was used and rebuilt for nearly 2,000 **60** years, ending with a Colonial church on its summit. Archaeological

59 Reconstruction of B-4, Kaminaljuyú. At this site, in modern Guatemala, buildings in pure Teotihuacan style were executed on a diminutive scale in simple adobe during the great city's apogee. Early Classic.

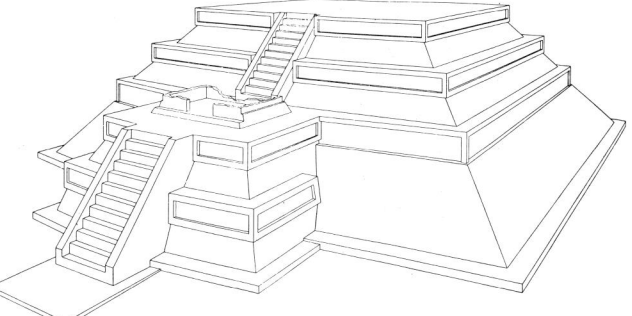

60 The main pyramid at Cholula flourished in many periods, and it probably benefitted from Teotihuacan's decline. A Colonial church caps at least 1500 years of prehispanic construction. This rather fanciful drawing from 1834 presents the great pyramid as if it were Mount Calvary.

explorations by the Mexican National Institute of Anthropology and History have revealed many aspects of the pyramid's construction. During the Early Classic, for example, paintings covered the talud–tablero temple exterior. These stucco works show great drinking rites and have suggested to George Kubler the drunken process of their very execution, for the painters would appear to have become increasingly intoxicated by the time they reached the later frames!

A longer sloping talud than that known at Teotihuacan characterizes the early pyramids at Cholula, and we may surmise that its population steered clear of Teotihuacan domination, despite the proximity, like the later city of Tlaxcala. At the time of the Conquest, Nahua speakers occupied the site. Despite years of archaeological study at Teotihuacan, however, the ethnic identity of the inhabitants there remains unknown. Were they Nahua speakers, like the later Toltecs and Aztecs, or were they Totonacs or Otomís, no longer dominant in the Valley of Mexico at the time of the Conquest? No one can say.

82

CHAPTER FIVE

Classic Monte Albán, Veracruz and Cotzumalhuapa

The Classic period produced the most widespread flowering of culture in Mesoamerican history. As we have seen, in Central Mexico Teotihuacan was the largest, most powerful and prestigious city to rise in the history of the ancient New World. To the south, in Yucatán, Guatemala, Honduras, and Chiapas, the Maya were equally important, although known for their diversity and variety rather than the monolithic power that characterized Teotihuacan. However, other regions fostered important Classic developments as well. Independent Classic styles of art and architecture flourished in Oaxaca at Monte Albán, in Veracruz at various sites, among them El Tajín, and on the Pacific coast of Guatemala at Cotzumalhuapa. At no other time in Mesoamerican history were so many fine and different kinds of works of art and architecture created. It was also an era of great international contact: just as there was interchange between Teotihuacan and the Maya, so too was there contact between Oaxaca and Teotihuacan and between El Tajín and Cotzumalhuapa. Nor were these cities insulated from the disruptions that closed the Classic era: Monte Albán and El Tajín both suffered depopulation and subsequent abandonment, and both regions witnessed separate developments during the Postclassic.

THE CLASSIC CIVILIZATION OF MONTE ALBÁN

At Monte Albán, the step from the advanced Zapotec architectural and artistic styles of the Late Formative to a Classic stage was easily taken. Some sophisticated works of art and architecture survived from Late Formative times, and the acropolis had already been artificially flattened. Most of the structures that flank the main plaza, however, date to the Classic era, either Monte Albán IIIa (Early Classic, to AD 400) or Monte Albán IIIb (the Late Classic phase, AD 400–900, according to archaeologists). The major architectural works of the era reflect an attention to the natural topography of the surrounding valleys. It is hard to capture the relationship of acropolis to mountains in photographs, but the cadence

61 Looking across the plaza on the mountaintop city of Monte Albán towards the North Barrier Mound.

of elevation to depression in the manmade structures on the west side of the plaza – to take one instance – so precisely repeats the rhythm established by the western range of mountains that the Monte Albán acropolis becomes a microcosmic replica of the surrounding valley of central *61* Oaxaca. If such a view is still apparent today, we can only imagine how much more vivid it must have been for the people of the time.

A plan designed to reproduce the rhythm of natural land forms may *62* also help to explain the approximate bilateral symmetry of the acropolis. Structures are not laid out on an axis or grid. Unlike the plan of *cf. 44* Teotihuacan, they do not radiate from a central point but rather frame

84

the negative space of the plaza. In its general north-south orientation, however, the plan of Monte Albán suggests an axial orientation far more than the organic site plans of Maya cities do.

The general organization of the Monte Albán acropolis also recalls the Teotihuacan Way of the Dead. That great processional way is lined by low-lying temples and modulated by changes in elevation. The North and South Barrier Mounds of Monte Albán not only frame the ceremonial core but also require movement up and down the processional way. Nevertheless, the ceremonial core of Monte Albán is small by comparison with Teotihuacan: the Monte Albán plaza with its surrounding temples could all be placed under the Temple of the Sun.

The constructions of the Classic era made the site as a whole, the plaza, and its component buildings more private. A wall enclosed over one square mile of the acropolis. Access to the plaza, both actual and visual, from the east, for example, was blocked by the replacement of numerous individual structures almost contiguous with one another. The proportion of balustrade to stair of these buildings is ponderous, and emphasis falls on the alternation between the two forms.

The corners of the plaza were no longer open: at the northeast, for example, the Zapotecs built an I-shaped ballcourt. (Such ballcourts were peculiar to this region in the Classic, but by the Postclassic the closed I-form court with sloping walls was known widely in Central Mexico as well.) On the west side of the plaza, similar compounds were erected to flank the earlier Temple of the Danzantes. Known as Systems IV and M, these buildings have been considered amphitheatres, where supplicants would gather in the closed court while attending rites performed on the principal façade. As with all Monte Albán structures, the perishable superstructures are gone. Tomb façades and small stone temple models found in tombs show that the distinctive Monte Albán profile molding was also repeated at the cornice level. Wrapped around exterior corners, this molding consolidated the structure, as did the apron moldings of Maya structures of the same period. In its two separate layers, the molding bears a similarity to the symbol for sky, perhaps indicating the generally sacred quality of architecture so delineated.

During Classic times the North Palace compound grew in size, and – particularly during Monte Albán IIIb – it became increasingly inaccessible. By the end of the period of construction, one climbed the North Barrier Mound, passed a colonnade, and descended into a courtyard similar to those of Teotihuacan, but on a smaller scale, and sunken in relation to surrounding structures. One then proceeded along a narrow passageway and up and down stairs before gaining access to palace chambers. Such restricted access has a parallel at Teotihuacan, particularly in the Quetzalpapálotl compound, and in the Maya region, where for instance the core of compound A-V at Uaxactún became virtually inaccessible in Late Classic times.

To the south, as Javier Urcid has recently shown, an early palace was dismantled, and carved lintels were set upright, like stelae, one side of their imagery now disoriented. Like the South Palace stones, many other monuments were reset through time, and most of them were grouped at the south end, honoring Zapotec lords. Some individuals appear as warriors; others engage in dialogue with what appear to be visiting Teotihuacanos. The Zapotecs wear tall headdresses with motifs similar to those of the ceramic urns (see below), as distinct from the tasseled head-

62 Plan of Monte Albán.

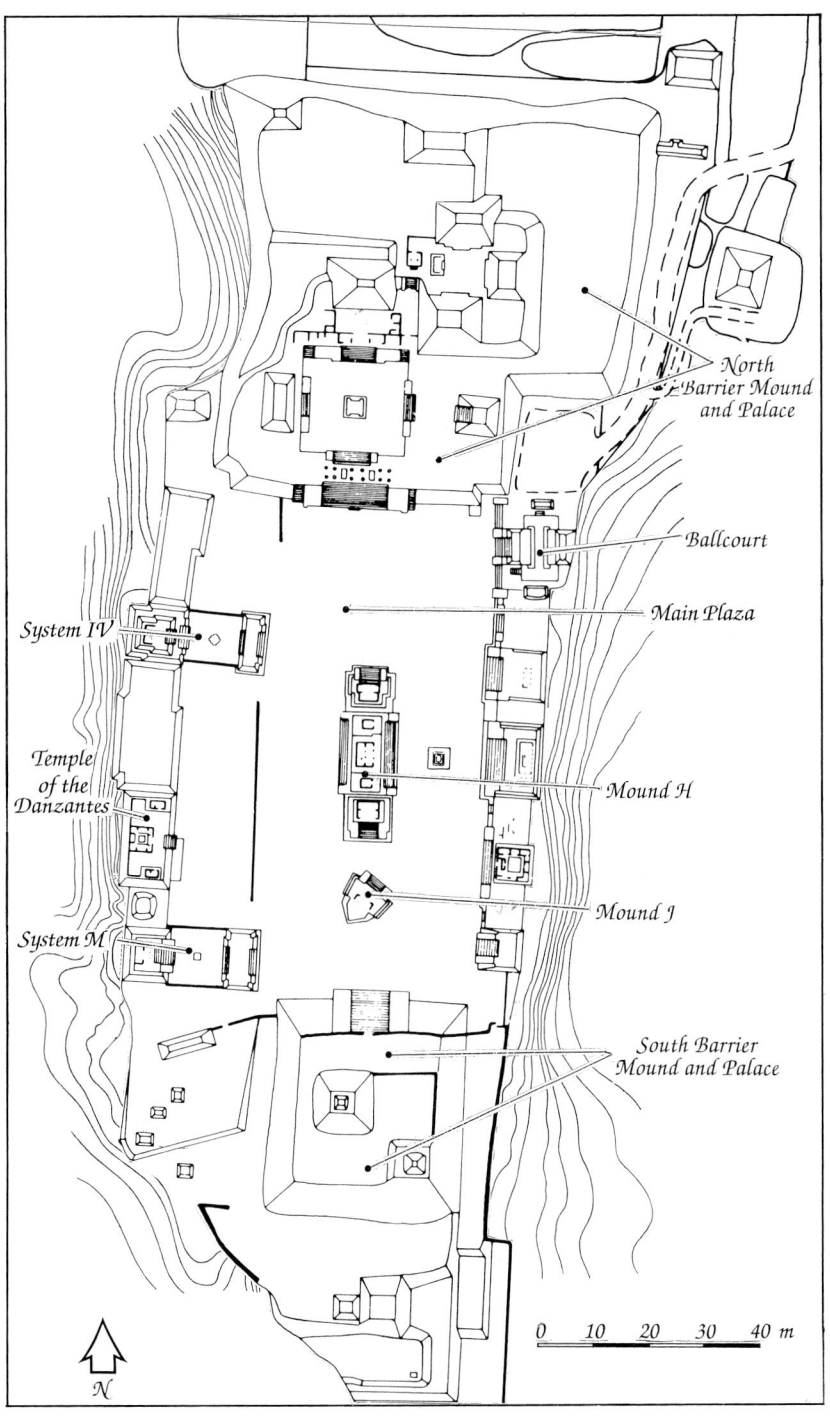

North Barrier Mound and Palace

Ballcourt

Main Plaza

System IV

Temple of the Danzantes

Mound H

Mound J

System M

South Barrier Mound and Palace

0 10 20 30 40 m

N

63 (*opposite*) Stela 4, showing a standing ruler, Monte Albán IIIa. Like the Early Classic Maya kings, Monte Albán lords adopted the fashions of Teotihuacan. The glyph 8 Deer appears at left, indicating either a name or date.

64 The façade of Tomb 104, Monte Albán. A fine ceramic urn remains in place over the entry to the tomb. Monte Albán IIIa.

dresses of the Teotihuacanos. Glyphs record dates in the 260-day calendar or calendrical names. Scrolls indicate speech or song, as they do in Teotihuacan art. Individuals are carved in profile in a flat, linear style.

Alfonso Caso directed excavations on behalf of the Mexican government at Monte Albán throughout the 1930s. He looked for burials in addition to cleaning and restoring structures. Many underground tombs thus came to light, both under structures and as separate chambers, some within the main precinct and others in residential areas. It remains to be established whether the structures that flank the compound were primarily dedicated to ancestor worship, as were many Maya buildings. Caso discovered fine burial chambers containing treasures from the earliest era right up to the Conquest. Many tombs of the Classic period were found to be painted, and, of these, Tombs 104 and 105 are the best preserved. 64–66 Tomb 104 is thought to precede 105, a chronological separation that probably reflects the difference between Monte Albán IIIa and IIIb. The palette of 104 emphasizes blue and yellow, while 105 has many more red

65 Interior painting, Tomb 104, Monte Albán. Hasty workmanship – indicated by spills and drips of paint – would suggest that the final decoration of this elaborate tomb was executed at the last moment. Reconstruction painting. Monte Albán IIIa.

tones, like later Teotihuacan paintings. Both had been quickly prepared and show signs of hasty work, such as drips and spills.

Tomb 104 displays an interesting unified use of architecture, sculpture, and painting. The chamber entry is framed by a doorway with the usual Monte Albán overhanging profile molding, and the door is surmounted by a very fine ceramic figure wearing a Cocijo, or rain god, headdress. A single skeleton was found extended in the tomb, feet at the chamber door. Sets of small, identical urns had been placed along the body, and other vessels positioned in the three cut-out niches of the wall. Two painted figures flank the side walls, in profile, attending the frontal cult image at the head of the tomb. One of them is an old god with a netted headdress, and Michael Coe has pointed out his similarity to the Maya God N. Iconographically, Cocijo and various maize gods dominate Monte Albán religious art, but Zapotec gods and ritual practice have remained among the most poorly understood in ancient Mesoamerica.

66 Interior painting, Tomb 105, Monte Albán. The painters here chose a darker, redder palette, more like that of many Teotihuacan works. Monte Albán IIIb.

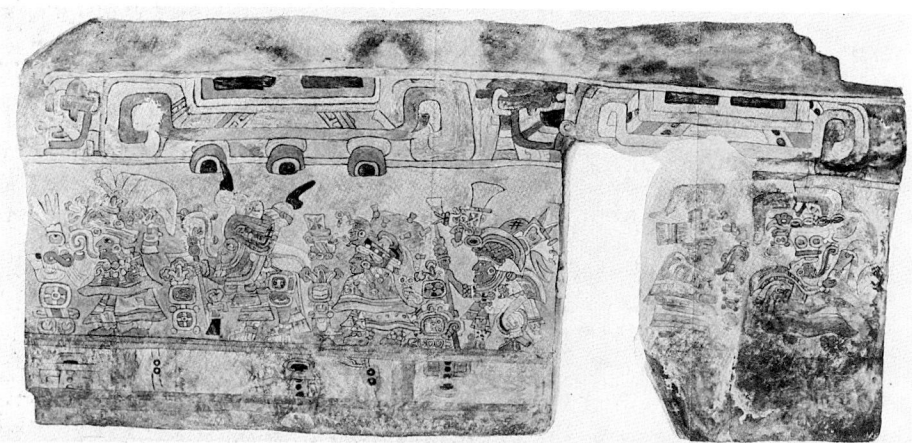

Compositionally, the painting resembles the central scene of the Tepantitla mural of Teotihuacan, the unwrapped composition of Tikal Stela 31, or even the more iconic Río Azul paintings. Given the emphasis on symmetry and frontality, the source for such compositions was probably Teotihuacan. The use of such similar conventions at Monte Albán and Tikal shows both the profound effect of Teotihuacan and the ability of regional artists to interpret its art for their own traditions. Curiously, tomb paintings as fine as this one or the Early Classic Maya ones are not known from Teotihuacan, where we find paintings set in a context for the living rather than the dead. The discovery of a major Teotihuacan tomb, however, could alter this perception. *85* *88*

In Tomb 104, each side figure gestures to the niche in front of him, directing the process of offering, and the central cult image seems to rise out of the central niche, as if sustained by the offerings placed within. Such paintings may have guided the attendants at the funeral rites of the interred and perpetuated those rites. *65*

The side and rear walls of Tomb 105 show nine male-female couples in procession, accompanied by glyphs that no doubt name them. A single calendrical day sign and coefficient occupies the front wall, probably naming the occupant or the date of his death. Symbols that resemble Monte Albán moldings form the upper register, and what presumably are *66*

67 One of several fertility gods in ancient Oaxaca, this maize god bears distinctive facial markings. He sits on what is probably a 'hill' glyph, indicating a toponym, perhaps 'hill of maize.'

earth signs lie underfoot. The nine couples represent ancestors who welcome the interred into the afterlife. Some headdresses include what would have been old-fashioned Teotihuacan elements, perhaps a sort of 'period' dress to indicate their antiquity.

31
64, 67 The tradition of making large, hollow effigy vases reached its apogee in Late Formative times at Monte Albán. By the Classic era, the urn had supplanted the hollow vase as the dominant form of tomb sculpture. These urns consisted of cylindrical vessels largely hidden by the attached sculptures of human figures. Evidence of burning in the vessels is rare, and it is more likely that they held foodstuffs or beverages for the interred rather than burnt offerings. They have been recovered both from tomb doorways and from the graves themselves, though many are without provenance. Most have headdresses of deities. Cocijo, the Oaxaca rain god, is worn by the Tomb 104 figure. Lines around the eyes of ill. 67 mark it as the 'God of Glyph L.' The maize of the headdress also indicates a fertility aspect for that figure. As more and more of the imagery of ancient America has been determined to be of historical persons, so the strong individual physiognomies of many Oaxacan urns have begun to suggest portraiture.

cf. 54 The ornamentation of the urns was built up in layers of pliable clay slabs until a rich three-dimensional texture was achieved over the hollow human form. Eventually, just as at Teotihuacan, individual elements came to be mass-produced. Some human faces are also mask-like and resemble contemporary Teotihuacan stone masks. Many urns have strong rectilinear qualities, despite their three-dimensionality, and can be described geometrically within a rectangle. In this way, they conform to a geometry like that seen in many Teotihuacan paintings.

At the end of Classic times, Monte Albán suffered slow and steady depopulation, as the focus of culture in Oaxaca moved to other centers, some of them Mixtec. Finally, Monte Albán became simply a necropolis and a place of pilgrimage, and it remains a place of pilgrimage today.

CLASSIC VERACRUZ

Distinctive art styles also flowered along the Veracruz coast during the Classic era. Today, Totonacs live in the region, but it is not certain that they were the makers of high culture in Classic times. Fifteen hundred years ago Huastecs and Otomís undoubtedly occupied some of the same territory, while at the time of the Conquest the Olmeca-Xicalanca dom-

68 The Pyramid of the Niches, El Tajín, as published by the explorer Carl Nebel in his 1829 account of his travels to the New World. Early Classic.

inated trade along the coast. We will simply consider the various elements to be 'Classic Veracruz,' without ethnic assignation. Connections with Teotihuacan and the Maya area were evident during the Classic, but the art and architecture of Classic Veracruz also depended upon its Olmec heritage from the Formative era.

Architecturally, the most important Classic city of the region is El Tajín, named after the Totonac rain god. Heavy rainfall yields dense rainforest where mountain meets plain. The Veracruz coast was known for its verdant croplands even in prehispanic times, and the Aztecs coveted the maize, cacao, and cotton grown in the area. El Tajín was discovered toward the end of the eighteenth century, just about the time that Maya sites began to catch Western attention. In 1829, the German explorer Carl Nebel visited the site, and the fine color lithographs he later published evoked the same kind of mystery as Maya ruins. Early travelers believed the Pyramid of the Niches to be the most important structure   *68* at El Tajín, which indeed it is in the sense that it dominates the main ceremonial core, at the center of hundreds of acres of ruins, despite its relatively small size (approximately 26 m on a side and less than 20 m high). It is generally considered to have been completed before AD 600. On a natural rise above the ceremonial core stands a group of structures known at Tajín Chico, which postdates the constructions below it.

The Pyramid of the Niches rises in six distinct tiers of an unusually busy talud-tablero and houses within it a smaller, and therefore earlier, similar pyramid. Each entablature supports a row of niches, making 365 niches in all, which implies that the pyramid refers to the solar year. The niches are each about 60 cm deep, and although it is tempting to think that they held offerings, no evidence is available that they did. Perhaps the niches were for purely visual effect: on a bright day they reflect and shimmer in the sun, giving the illusion of constant motion.

The Pyramid of the Niches has some unusual features that link it to Maya architecture at Copán; El Tajín may well indeed have had some direct contact with that site. Both the Hieroglyphic Stairs at Copán and the Pyramid of the Niches have balustrades with similar running fret designs. In fact, the abutments of the Pyramid of the Niches may have featured seated lords during public festivals, creating a diminutive assemblage closely akin to the Hieroglyphic Stairs at Copán. Moreover, the only true stela from El Tajín was found at the base of the Pyramid of the Niches. In some ways it looks like a crude Maya effort, and in its three-dimensionality, costume, and posture, it bears closest comparison to the stelae of Copán.

The low-lying galleried structures of Tajín Chico seem to have been largely for noble residential use. Geometric patterning worked on the building façades may correspond to the contemporary designs at Uxmal, in Yucatán, or they may have toponymic value. Dominating the group is the Building of the Columns, now collapsed, but once a very large structure with colossal carved columns. Narrations wrap around the columns on a small scale, many featuring the exploits of a late ruler, 13 Rabbit.

At least eleven ballcourts have been located in the central core of El Tajín. No other site in Mesoamerica has such a preponderance of masonry playing surfaces: indeed El Tajín was very probably a center for great ceremonial games, in the same way that Olympia served as the recognized meeting point for sportsmen from all over ancient Greece. El Tajín seems also to have been a major center for the collection of natural rubber, and perhaps the solid black rubber balls with which the game was played were made there. Various lineages could have sponsored their own court, or each successive ruler could have been obliged to commission a

69 The South Ballcourt at El Tajín frames the mountain behind, channeling its power to the plaza.

new one. For whatever purpose, the courts were made in profusion here, and their walls present the most extensive architectural sculpture of Classic Veracruz. As at other Mesoamerican sites, El Tajín lords sited buildings to powerful features of the landscape, and this can be seen most clearly with ballcourts, where rises are typically framed at the ends of 69 playing alleys.

Six narrative panels relate a ballgame myth or story along the vertical 70 surfaces of the South Ballcourt. In the first panel, the participants dress for the event; in another, one player conceals a knife behind his back. In the illustration shown here, set within a ballcourt (but oddly enough, one with an architectural profile different from that of the South Ballcourt itself), two players hold down a third and prepare to cut out his heart. A descending skeletal monster twists down from the upper margin, presumably to take the sacrifice about to be proferred, while another skeletal monster at left rises from a jar. As the narrative unfolds at El Tajín, the rain god perforates his penis, perhaps yielding pulque, the intoxicating beverage of ritual.

At the time of the Conquest, the ballgame was known to be played for various motives. As an athletic event, it was frequently the subject of much gambling. It could also be a gladiatorial contest, where a captive's or slave's strength and desire to avoid death were tried out. The sacrifice of players also informs us that the game was played in order to offer human blood to the gods. In Classic times, the game may have been played for all these purposes, not only at El Tajín, but also in the Maya area and at Cotzumalhuapa, and understood as a cosmic metaphor as well, necessary to the sustenance of the sun. Furthermore, the ballgame often plays a specific role vis á vis warfare. Set in the ceremonial precinct, the ballgame provided the means for controlled re-enactment of warfare. The use of the ballgame as a metaphor for other struggles was known at the time of the Conquest and is perhaps most clear in a Quiché Maya text, the *Popol Vuh*, where the confrontation of life and death is couched in terms of a ballgame.

152 The reliefs of the South Ballcourt were probably worked *in situ*, since several flat stones form a single carving surface, like those of Chichen Itzá. A distinctive double outline is used to work all the designs, but particularly the scrolls. The reliefs would now appear to have their origins in Middle and Late Formative Olmec styles, as well as in the curvilinear Late Formative style of Izapa. This double-outline workmanship is so characteristic of Classic Veracruz that it indicates the origins and relative
59 date of materials found as far away as Teotihuacan or Kaminaljuyú.

Three kinds of objects – frequently decorated with scroll motifs – have been recovered in great abundance in Mesoamerica: yokes, *palmas*, and *hachas*. Most of them come from Veracruz, but at both Palenque and

70 Carved panel, South Ballcourt, El Tajín. An unfortunate loser at the ballgame is being sacrificed by two victors while a third looks on. A death god descends from the skyband above to take the offering. Late Classic.

72 Three faces (two visible) of the defeated ballplayer, each with gouged eye, adorn this stone yoke, probably worn by a victorious ballplayer on ceremonial occasions. South Ballcourt panels (ill. 70) show ballplayers wearing similar yokes.

73 *Hachas* in Classic Veracruz style such as this one may have functioned as portable markers on the ballcourt. Late Classic.

71 A stone *palma*, in Classic Veracruz style. The heart has been removed from this unfortunate fellow. In ill. 70 the *palma* springs from the waist, as if directly inserted into the yoke. Despite such illustrations, it is still not clear just how these objects functioned in the ballgame. Late Classic.

74 (*opposite*) A large, hollow ceramic female sculpture, Late Classic Veracruz style. Black asphalt, a petroleum product known locally as *chapapote*, has been used to highlight the sculpture. Works of this sort continued to be made into Postclassic times.

75 (*right*) Stela 8, Cerro de las Mesas. Monuments from this site show affinity to Maya works. This one bears an Initial Series date in Maya style equivalent to a day in the year AD 514.

76 (*below*) A hollow clay figure with a 'smiling face,' perhaps from Las Remojadas, where many such ceramic sculptures were found. Late Classic.

77 (*below*) A wheeled Veracruz figure of the Classic period. Small ceramic figures with wheels such as this have been found among Classic Veracruz remains, but the wheel was apparently never used for practical purposes in ancient Mesoamerica.

Copán, Veracruz ballgame paraphernalia were found in a context contemporary with the abandonment of these sites. In at least one burial, a ballgame yoke framed a dead lord's head. The players on the South Ballcourt relief seem to show how at least two of these objects were worn. Yokes were fitted around the waist, attached sideways. Despite the doubt cast on whether these cumbersome stone objects could ever have been worn (the weight must certainly have altered a player's center of gravity), they were probably manageable for a skilled athlete. *Palmas* were inserted into the yokes at waist-level and extended to mid-chest height. *Hachas* may have served as markers for play. The scrollwork of the yokes is sometimes exceptionally fine and complex, and often the design cannot be understood until completely drawn out. Some motifs emphasize themes of the ballgame itself.

Full-scale stone carvings of Classic date have been found elsewhere in Veracruz as well, particularly at the site of Cerro de las Mesas, which may be best known for the huge cache of Olmec jades discovered in a Classic context. Stone stelae at the site bear Initial Series inscriptions that correspond to Early Classic Maya dates. Stela 8 records a date in AD 514 and shows an individual who was presumably a ruler of that era. Curiously, he wears a shield emblem in his headdress of the type prominent in the name glyph of Pacal of Palenque, the Maya king who came to power by the end of that century.

Fine hollow clay sculpture was produced at various centers throughout Veracruz during this era, perhaps continuing a tradition established by earlier Olmec artisans. It was a tradition sustained until the time of the Conquest, with the result that the exact date of some of these pieces is in doubt. Uncertain too is the specific provenance of the majority of the sculptures. Some have been traced to particular sites, but most are isolated finds. Those of Remojadas are particularly lively and are often characterized by 'smiling' faces, which may in fact be the result of ecstatic rituals. Charming couples are found in pairs or on swings, and little animals turn on wheeled feet. Such toys are the only known use of the wheel in ancient Mesoamerica. The potters painted many of these sculptures with shiny black asphalt, locally called *chapapote*, a naturally occurring petroleum product (no other use was known in Precolumbian times for the plentiful oil of Veracruz).

Probably of later date are the large-scale hollow figures, many of which represent Postclassic deities, although the chronology is far from certain. The one shown here is of a large seated woman. Others stand with arms extended, perhaps in greeting but perhaps to warn away a violator of a tomb or cache. Snakes form their belts, and some may represent a *cihuacóatl*, or woman snake, known in Postclassic times as an evil deity who lurked at crossroads.

COTZUMALHUAPA AND THE 'MIDDLE CLASSIC'

Connections among Classic Veracruz, Monte Albán, and Teotihuacan were close during the middle of the Classic era, particularly in the sixth and seventh centuries, at the end of Teotihuacan's splendor. Fresh research has brought to light the importance of the regional style of art and architecture known from Santa Lucía Cotzumalhuapa and its environs. Despite its location on the Guatemalan coast and its proximity to the Maya area, Cotzumalhuapa participated in the pan-Mesoamerican flowering, and it shared characteristics with other Classic cultures. The Isthmus of Tehuantepec may have made communication easier between Veracruz and the Pacific coast.

78 Stela 3, Santa Lucía Cotzumalhuapa. A ballplayer and a death god, both in ballgame yokes, stand in front of a temple. They reach toward a scorpion sun to offer a human heart.

The makers of Cotzumalhuapa art were probably not Maya, and, although they have often been identified with the Pipil (Náhuat speakers in Guatemala at the time of the Conquest), we will probably never know their ethnicity. We do know, however, that they carved stelae and panels rife with images of the ballgame, human sacrifice, and the sun. Glyphs were inscribed in round cartouches – some appear to be part of a Central Mexican calendrical system, although none of the glyphs have been securely read. The figures on the monuments are generally long and attenuated, of proportions similar to those drawn on Late Classic Maya vases from such highland Guatemalan sites as Nebaj. Right and left hands and feet are often confused in the Cotzumalhuapa depictions.

78 Ballgame rituals played between humans and supernatural beings appear on several stelae. Whether or not divine, the individuals wear ballgame equipment similar to that of Veracruz, and abundant *hachas*, yokes, and *palmas* have been collected at Cotzumalhuapa sites. Descending solar deities on the upper parts of the monuments may prefigure the Postclassic 'diving gods' of the Caribbean coast. These deity faces are worked frontally in three-dimensional relief, in striking contrast to the low relief
79 of the profile figures below. Some fully three-dimensional monuments were also created, and they may relate to the tradition of sculpture in the round at Copán.

79 Sylvanus G. Morley kneels beside this fragmentary stela from Pantaleon in Cotzumalhuapa style. Comparable three-dimensional portraits of the Classic period are known from El Tajín and Copán.

CHAPTER SIX

The Early Classic Maya

Classic Teotihuacan had already become an important center and cultural force by AD 150, but it was not until a hundred years later – about AD 250 – that the Maya entered upon their period of greatest prosperity and influence. By this time, Maya temples with corbeled vaults were being constructed, and stone stelae with Long Count dates and ruler portraits erected. All these elements appeared independently long before AD 250, but it was the beginning of their combined, continuous, and widespread use that roughly establishes the Classic era among the lowland Maya.

During the first 300 years of the Maya Early Classic (AD 250–550), major growth of cities was limited to the Central Petén, particularly at the sites of Tikal and Uaxactún. Contacts with Teotihuacan were strong, and local elites adopted Teotihuacan modes of dress and burial. Toward the end of the Early Classic, however – in the sixth century – many other Maya sites started to expand, Calakmul, Yaxchilán, Caracol, and Piedras Negras among them. The resulting competition led to warfare, and the largest and most powerful among them, Tikal, suffered terrible devastation at the hands of lesser polities. Simultaneously, the profound influence of Teotihuacan waned, and Teotihuacan motifs and costume elements, although they did not vanish, became so thoroughly incorporated into the Maya repertoire that they ceased to be foreign. By Late Classic times (AD 600–900), Tikal was only one of many well-established Maya cities, from Palenque in the west to Uxmal in the north, Altun Ha in the east, and Copán and Quiriguá in the south. At its height, Tikal may in fact have had a population of only 50,000, so these Maya cities were much smaller than Teotihuacan. They were united by the common use of the hieroglyphic writing system, but their monumental carvings and architecture reflect both regionality and innovation.

ARCHITECTURE

Archaeological work at Tikal and Uaxactún (literally 'eight stones,' a name given by Sylvanus G. Morley to refer to the early Cycle 8 dates there (and also a near homonym for 'Washington,' in honor of the sponsor), has revealed much of what we know today about the Early Classic.

Preliminary architectural and ceramic studies at Uaxactún, initiated in the late 1920s, indicated to the archaeologists that Group E, an isolated cluster of buildings, was the oldest part of the site. In a search for the origins of Maya high civilization, Structure E-VII was dismantled layer by layer, revealing a series of building phases. The earliest one, now known as E-VII-sub, is a small, radial pyramid just over 8 m high, with staircases on all four sides flanked by giant mask façades. The principal orientation of E-VII-sub is to the east, indicated by a stela at the base of the stairs on that side. Postholes on the upper level mark the remains of a perishable superstructure, which suggested to the archaeologists that the pyramid might antedate the general use of permanent superstructures. Indeed, E-VII-sub does seem to be a Protoclassic pyramid, probably preceding the widespread erection of dated stone monuments. What we now know is that most Petén sites hold such Protoclassic structures, and that E-VII-sub is no longer the prototype Morley imagined.

Functionally, E-VII-sub works as a simple observatory. From a point on the eastern stairs, the lines of sight that can be drawn to the three small facing pyramids mark the lines of sunrise on the days of the solstices and equinoxes. The maltese-cross plan of E-VII-sub resembles the Maya completion sign, as do plans of some other radial structures, and most such structures record the completion of some period of time. At E-VII-sub it is the solar year that holds significance, as it is at the Castillo,

80 E-VII-sub, Uaxactún, a radial pyramid, was probably completed before the first Early Classic stone monuments were raised at that site. A perishable thatched structure once stood on top of the pyramid.

81 Based on the archaeological exploration of Uaxactún, Tatiana Proskouriakoff drew reconstruction drawings (after which these are adapted) of the eight major phases of architectural development at the site. Single shrines of the Early Classic eventually gave way to multi-chambered galleries in the Late Classic.

Chichen Itzá, built much later. Twin radial pyramids at Tikal were erected on platforms to commemorate the completion of *katuns*, the twenty-year periods, during the Late Classic, while the maltese-cross emblem that functions as a frontispiece to the Late Postclassic Mexican manuscript Féjerváry-Mayer is a 260-day calendar. Thus radial configura- *181* tions, from their earliest appearance at Uaxactún until the Conquest, indicate the passage of time, and structures in such form are generally giant chronographic markers.

Excavations in Group A at Uaxactún revealed a different pattern of construction. A three-temple complex, A-V, was transformed over a *81* period of at least 500 years, its growth inspired by ritual interments of both important lords and stone monuments. The term 'temple' generally refers to an elevated platform with a relatively small superstructure where offerings were made. Because new temples were erected over rich tombs of important individuals, or in some cases the inscribed records of those individuals, one can only suppose that the structures were shrines to memorialized ancestors. As we shall see, a focus of Classic Maya religion and architecture was ancestor worship.

At complex A-V, by the end of the Early Classic, small temples obscured the courtyard of the three original temples, which had also been expanded through time. During the Late Classic, these single-chambered shrines of A-V gave way to multi-chambered galleried structures, the type of building normally considered a palace (and often called 'range-type' structures by archaeologists). These palace buildings drastically altered access to the old interior platform and shrines, and presumably function changed along with form. Although burials were deposited in the new structures, they were not elaborate and were limited to women and children. At the end of its life, when galleries had replaced all but one of the shrines, A-V had become a great administrative or bureaucratic complex, where most events took place away from public view, and where secular activities dominated sacred ones. A separate temple raised beside A-V can be interpreted in this light as a new focus for religious activity, and it probably housed a rich tomb.

Many elements of Maya city planning can also be observed at Uaxactún. The gently rolling karst limestone topography of the Petén provides islands of solid foundation separated by swampy *bajos*. Typically, the Maya built their sites so that clusters of monumental architecture on firm ground were connected by *sacbes*, elevated, stuccoed white roads which spanned the swamps. The result is a skyline of towering structures broken by open stretches. We might compare the result with modern Manhattan, where less firm rock has precluded the building of skyscrapers between Midtown and Wall Street. The skyline thus appears as islands of construction, connected by the great north-south avenues. At Uaxactún, Groups A and B are connected by a single causeway, and address one another across the north-south axis of the *sacbe*.

At Tikal, many years of large-scale archaeological exploration in the grandest of all ancient Maya cities has revealed an intricate pattern of architecture and urban planning. Like Uaxactún, Early Classic Tikal featured a massive radial pyramid with badly damaged stucco masks at the center of what is today called the Mundo Perdido ('Lost World') complex. A row of small temples flanks one side, while addressing the

83 (*right*) Late Classic Copán kings interred their Early Classic buildings with care, preserving color, stucco, and detail. Known as Rosalila, the building revealed here contained tombs of early kings – and yet another building smaller but equally elaborate lies hidden within.

82 Early Classic kings of Tikal were buried in North Acropolis structures (center). In the Late Classic, Temple II (at left, out of the picture) and Temple I (from where this picture was taken) framed the ancestors.

radial construction from the northwest is a large building constructed in something like Teotihuacan-style talud-tablero but in proportions that are unknown at Teotihuacan itself. Was this the focus for worship of foreign gods or a shrine constructed for resident foreigners?

Before AD 250, the North Acropolis and the Great Plaza were laid out to define the strong opposition of mass and space, north-to-south, that prevailed for the rest of the city's history. (The equally strong east-west axis created by Temples I and II was not established until Late Classic times.) Massive temples clustered on the North Acropolis functioned primarily as funerary monuments of Early Classic rulers of Tikal. Structure 34, for example, housed the richly furnished tomb of the king archaeologists have nicknamed Curl Nose. After his death, Stela 4 (his accession monument) was placed in front of the tomb. Once completed, the North Acropolis must have embodied the spirit of ancient kingship.

Typical features of these Early Classic funerary pyramids are their squat proportions and the massive apron moldings that wrap around corners. As archaeologists tunnel into the most ancient constructions at Copán, within the Great Acropolis, massive early buildings have been uncovered that retain almost perfectly preserved stucco ornament. On the exterior of what may be the most ancient structure to be discovered yet is the glyph for the founder of the Copán dynasty, Yax Kuk Mo', and his tomb may lie within.

In these Early Classic Tikal and Uaxactún structures, we see the most prevalent types of architecture to survive from the Classic Maya era: great chronographic markers, memorials to ancestors (probably religious structures), and bureaucratic structures. Were we to examine buildings of such different function from another part of the world, we would probably find that they were executed using different forms, perhaps separate architectural orders. Among the Classic Maya, there was no architectural style linked exclusively to religious structures that differentiated them from civil buildings. All Maya architecture was composed of elevated platforms and corbel-vaulted chambers, organized in a variety of configurations. This makes the precise identification of function not always an easy task.

The corbel vault has sometimes been disparaged as a false arch, but the true keystone arch was not a goal of Maya architecture. To form a corbel, masonry walls were built to the desired height. At the spring of the vault, flat stones were placed closer and closer together until they could be spanned by a single capstone. The weight and mass of the walls helped prevent collapse, as did cross-ties, many of which remain in place today. They were probably useful in raising the vaults. Exterior mansard roof profiles often followed the lines of the corbel, resulting in a stone architecture almost perfectly reproduced by the forms of Maya thatched houses today. The stone capstones conform to the hip roof of the thatched house, as if both to sanctify and exploit the domestic space. At Palenque, the conceit of the thatched house was emphasized in the buildings of the Palace, where sheets of shale were sheared off to look like thatch at the overhang of the mansard. On Late Classic buildings throughout the Puuc region, where sleek vertical lines supplanted the mansard profile, the architectural ornament at vault level featured thatched Maya houses, as if to inform the viewer of the relationship of permanent stone constructions to the humble, perishable dwelling. Almost all Maya interior spaces, then, repeat the forms of the Maya house. It is not a 'false' anything, but a 'true' Maya transformation of simple forms into elevated permanent ones.

SCULPTURE

At about the time that the Maya began to use the corbel vault, they also started to erect stone monuments carved with portraits of rulers and writings of their deeds. Royal individuals now commanded the power to have themselves honored in a permanent medium during their lives, and probably to be commemorated posthumously as divine. The earliest of these new monuments with secure date and provenance is Stela 29 at Tikal, *84* recovered from an ancient garbage dump in 1959 by archaeologists. (Other stelae were found tossed into piles of refuse or cut into building stone, but some had been reverentially buried and still others had evidently never been removed from public view in Maya times.) The roughly hewn shaft of Stela 29 was carved on one surface with a portrait of a seated Tikal ruler; the other face records a Long Count date, 8.12.14.8.15, or AD 292. Such dates denote important events and the names of their protagonists; unfortunately in this case the butt of the stela was broken off and lost in antiquity, thus depriving us of the complete record.

Typical of the representation of these early Maya lords are the very round and irregular forms. The right hand is drawn curled, as if in a mitten, and it presses a ceremonial bar to the body – many Maya kings throughout the Classic period are shown carrying this object. An ances-

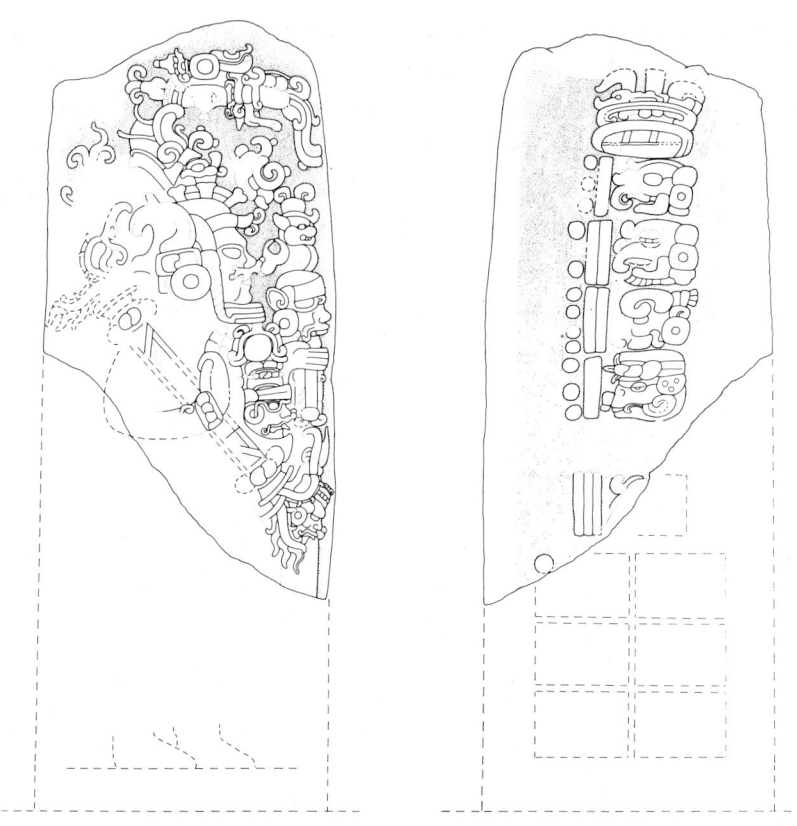

84 Stela 29, Tikal, records the earliest contemporary Maya Long Count date, 8.12.14.8.15, corresponding to a day in the year AD 292. This early king wears a deity mask and holds out another god, while his father's portrait faces downward in the upper margin. Drawing by William R. Coe.

cf. 4

tor figure looks down from the upper portion of the stela, in a manner similar to the deities in the upper margin of late La Venta stelae. With his left hand, the ruler supports an image of a supernatural figure generally known as the Jaguar God of the Underworld, identified by his tau-shaped tooth, jaguar ear, and 'cruller' over the nose. All early Tikal rulers carry this deity, and he is probably a patron of the city. The king himself wears a mask as well, and his hair is shaved into a 'mohawk' and studded with bones.

Stela 4, perhaps reset on the Great Plaza in Late Classic times, records the accession to power in AD 380 of the ruler known as Curl Nose. Technically, the monument is very similar to Stela 29, with its uneven

85 Stela 31, Tikal. Stormy Sky, as this ruler is known, is shown on the front of the monument. He is flanked on the sides (not shown) by warriors in Teotihuacan-style dress, or perhaps just two sides of the same warrior, and the long text at the back recalls the Early Classic Tikal dynasty, up until 9.0.10.0.0, or AD 445.

surfaces and low relief, but the image is distinct. Curl Nose is seated, like his predecessor, and he bears the Jaguar God of the Underworld on his right hand, but he is shown with a fully frontal face. He wears a headdress comprising a frontal head of a plumed jaguar and a collar of pecten shells. This attire mimics Teotihuacan fashions, as does the frontal representation, and along with a few eccentricities of the inscription this has led to the suggestion that Curl Nose may have been a usurper, a foreigner married to a Tikal woman, or perhaps a Mexicanized Maya from Kaminaljuyú in highland Guatemala. During the era of Teotihuacan's greatest prestige, Curl Nose expressed his own power by adopting its conventions.

85   About 9.0.10.0.0, or AD 445, Tikal Stela 31 was erected by a ruler today called Stormy Sky. Like Stela 29, Stela 31 too was removed from public view in antiquity; during Late Classic times, its broken shaft was hauled to the top of Structure 33 and interred with burnt offerings under a shrine. Stormy Sky had himself carved in a manner similar to the ruler on Stela 29, in what one takes to be an intentionally conservative style, perhaps invoking the legitimacy of the past. Stormy Sky bears abundant ritual paraphernalia, testimony of his high office. He holds the Jaguar God of the Underworld in the crook of his left arm, and with his right, he holds forth the headdress of rulership, crowning himself. Although we can consider this sort of sculpture a portrait, it is more a portrait of the trappings of office than the representation of a particular man.

Unlike Stela 29, 31's surface is smooth and uniform, a finer-grained limestone having been selected for the carving. Also, unlike Stela 29, Stela 31 was worked on all four surfaces of the stone prism. If we unwrap the design, Stormy Sky is flanked by a pair of individuals attired in more simple Teotihuacan garments, who also bear *atlatls*, or spearthrowers, in one hand and a shield in the other. We might also see this as two side views of the same individual, standing behind Stormy Sky, for shield and weapons are reversed. The more visible shield bears an image of Tlaloc, generally thought to have been a Teotihuacan rain deity, but now known also to have been associated with war and sacrifice in all Classic cultures. Although it is tempting to interpret these two figures as evidence of a Teotihuacan military presence in Tikal, it is just as likely, given the text above, that these figures represent Stormy Sky's father, Curl Nose, who is shown in what may be considered 'period' costume.

Most Uaxactún monuments have suffered such serious erosion over time that few remain legible except for their Long Count dates. At the

86 The so-called Po panel. Named for the glyph that appears on the thrones on which the two figures sit, this wall panel shows two Bonampak rulers of the Early Classic.

end of the Early Classic, monuments were erected at many other sites. In a number of cases, even these first hesitant works indicate the regional styles that later flourished at these places. Monument 26 from Quiriguá shows a ruler in frontal pose, like all later monuments at that site. In style, it probably drew on both the wraparound conventions of Central Petén stone monuments and early cache vessels: portable goods might have *93* influenced provincial developments. At Yaxchilán, the earliest figural monument shows a standing lord in profile who makes a 'sprinkling' or 'scattering' gesture. Multifigural designs appeared first far from the Petén, and the so-called Po panel may be the earliest work in stone where two *86* lords face one another across a panel of glyphs. Nevertheless, despite these developments, Early Classic stone sculptures were restricted in composition and theme, especially when compared with the exuberant Late Classic works.

In 1864, workers digging a canal near Puerto Barrios, Guatemala, came across one of the most remarkable of Early Classic sculptures, together with a Postclassic cache of copper bells. Now known as the *87* Leiden Plate, this beautiful piece of translucent jade was once a fancy costume element, one of three jade plaques hanging from a jade bar or head worn at the waist. The imagery suggests that the object may have been a kind of portable stela, for the ruler portrait on the front and the

113

87 The Leiden Plate. On this handsome jadeite ornament – perhaps it was a 'portable stela' – a Maya lord proudly stands on the captive underfoot. The date recorded, 8.14.3.1.12, corresponds to a day in the year AD 320.

inscription on the back conform to monumental Tikal works of the time. The Maya lord stands over a prone, bound captive, and bears a pliable serpent bar in his arms. Mitten-like hands and the parted profile legs also indicate the early date.

PAINTING

Several Early Classic wall paintings have survived the ravages of time. Perhaps the most beautiful of these is the tomb painting first encountered by looters at Río Azul, in northeast Petén. An early fifth-century Maya date and text are framed by deities, including the Maya sun god, at right, with a glyph for *kin*, or sun, in his cheek. The side walls are marked with wavy, beaded symbols that indicate liquid, probably the watery surface of

88

88 Archaeologist Ian Graham first recorded this beautifully painted monochromatic tomb at Río Azul, after grave robbers had uncovered it. A Long Count date of 8.19.1.9.13, or AD 417, is inscribed. The glyph at the bottom of the left-hand column indicates birth – perhaps to mean rebirth in the underworld.

the underworld. The deceased would have been laid with his head at the text, and his body just within the liminal, watery world that the Maya perceived as the entrance to the afterlife. The niches for offerings are similar to those of contemporary Tomb 104, Monte Albán (ill. 64).

The Río Azul painting is monochrome, a reddish brown hematite pigment on creamy stucco, and the line is sure, strong, and highly calligraphic, each stroke ending in a whiplash. Contemporary paintings at Tikal (Burial 48) are by comparison less well executed, although the configuration is similar: a Long Count date is surrounded there by symbols of preciousness, asymmetrically painted across the walls of the chamber. A bright polychrome scene found and almost immediately destroyed at Uaxactún showed musicians, families, bloodletting, and a meeting of important lords.

The great tombs uncovered at Tikal brought to light the finery and pomp of Early Classic funerary practices, and in many cases also gave meaning and context to the many objects known without such clear provenance. When Maya kings were prepared for interment, they were splendidly equipped for their journey and transformation in the underworld, and funerary furniture often reflected these concerns in its iconography.

Curl Nose died about AD 425. He was borne on a litter into his tomb – at first a perishable structure at the base of what would become after his death the building we call Structure 34. He was probably accompanied by a great procession of musicians who laid down their instruments, turtleshells and deer antlers in the tomb. Others in the procession, like those depicted in the later Bonampak murals, may have worn exotic costume: a set of crocodile scutes was also recovered from the tomb. Nine individuals, perhaps those very procession members, were then sacrificed and placed alongside the dead king. Many fine ceramics were placed in the tomb, some filled with cool frothy chocolate beverages or maize gruel. Many of these pots show strong Teotihuacan influence in terms of imagery, shape, and technique, but most were made locally. Many resemble those also produced at Kaminaljuyú, in the Guatemalan highlands. In fact, burial complexes there contained a similar configuration of exotic materials, and both may reflect a Teotihuacan tradition, although there are no known royal Teotihuacan burials with which to make comparisons.

Lidded, stuccoed tripod vessels predominated in Maya royal funerary offerings during the late fourth and fifth centuries. Shape and technique are similar to and perhaps derived from contemporary Teotihuacan pots, but the Maya products taper at the 'waist,' and the less weighty Maya lids often have anthropomorphic or zoomorphic knobs. The human head of the lid in the illustration here in fact suggests that the vessel itself is human. In certain instances the stucco technique is combined with incision of clay at its leather-hard stage, and the two techniques are occasionally worked together with dazzling finesse. Some of the pots, among them the recently excavated ones from Río Azul, have 'screw-top' lids; and others have rattles in the base of the bowl. Many ceramics of this era depict purely Maya imagery in the stucco painting, but Teotihuacan influence is also strong: a ring-stand bowl from Curl Nose's tomb shows Central Mexican deities.

89 Basal-flange bowls dominated Maya elite wares before the introduction of the tripod cylinder from Teotihuacan. Using both sculpture and slip, the vessel here conveys a slice of Maya cosmology, the cormorant riding atop a turtle, both features of the night sky. Early Classic.

90 An early Classic Maya tripod vessel, Burial 10, Tikal. This vessel in Curl Nose's tomb was made with the tripod feet typical of Teotihuacan pots of the time, but the anthropomorphic lid was a purely Maya device.

91 Four downward-facing peccary snouts support a fishing cormorant atop a lidded vessel, all layers of the Maya cosmos.

92 Two-part ceramic effigies have also been recovered from Early Classic tombs. An especially fine one from Curl Nose's tomb depicts a squat old deity on a stool of crossed human femurs holding a human skull in his hands. About twenty-five years later, a Tikal lord was interred without head, femurs, or feet. Although he might have been brought back from the battlefield in this state, his mutilated skeleton could also bear witness to the practice of collecting relics from royal persons. Years later, Ruler A of Tikal was buried with a collection of carved bones, some of them cut from human femurs. This old deity, then, may be the patron of a particular form of sacrifice, associated with ancestor worship and dismemberment.

89 Other types of fine ceramics were made in Early Classic times. Basal-flange bowls pre-dated the advent of tripod vessels in the Maya area, and many had dome-shaped lids. Painted with colored slips before firing, some pots reveal a remarkably wide range of colors, despite the low temperatures at which they were fired. Quadrupod vessels occur with the basal-flange bowls, and many are jaguar or bird zoomorphs. The finest are of dark clay, incised at the leather-hard stage and then burnished after firing. The artists enjoyed the interplay between two and three dimensions on these vessels, in a fashion similar to contemporaneous Moche *91* ceramics in the Andes. In the accompanying illustration, a three-dimensional cormorant eagerly eats a fish that shifts from a two-dimensional

92 This two-part effigy was found in the tomb of Curl Nose at Tikal. Smoke from burning incense placed within would have billowed from the mouth and forehead tube of the old deity, who holds out a severed head in his hands. He sits on a stool of crossed femurs.

drawn figure to a three-dimensional sculptural one. Like many Asian peoples, the Maya may have used cormorants to help them fish.

Carved and appliquéd cache vessels are also found, many of them formed of two parts – the lower part often with a human face, the upper, one or two supernatural headdresses. Others simply show deities, and one imagines that offerings were placed in these pots. Chac, god of rain, dominates these representations. He is marked by the curl in his eye, shark tooth, fish fins on cheek, and shell over the ear, and it is in this guise that a Tikal ruler appeared on Stela 2. 93

Early Classic jade was generally worked in soft, curving lines, rather than with the sharper drill-and-saw technique of the Late Classic. In some cases, the jade was incised; in others, the hard stone was cut into human and animal shapes. A large, fine Early Classic jade head depicts an early sixth-century Copán ruler. A few mosaic masks protected the faces of dead kings, and a particularly fine one was recently excavated at Calakmul. 87

EXTERNAL RELATIONSHIPS

One of the most important questions still to be answered about the Early Classic Maya is the nature of their relationship with Teotihuacan. Military domination by the latter has been suggested, as has an economic stranglehold. Both ideas stem in part from our knowledge of the later Aztec domination of Mesoamerica. There is certainly evidence for profound and sustained contact between Central Mexico and the Maya region, and in the highlands provincial architecture in Teotihuacan style at Kaminaljuyú may well support the notion of direct Central Mexican occupation there. But what of the lowlands? Although rulers at Tikal and Uaxactún adopted Central Mexican styles of dress, they bore Maya insignia of office, and the very records of their reigns were inscribed on a Maya invention – the stela – in the Maya script. It is true that Central Mexican religious imagery was so common that we may suspect the presence of a foreign cult. Well established by the second century AD Teotihuacan may have been seen as a hearth of culture by the Maya, and so the Maya emulated their ceramics, their weaponry, even their sacrificial practices. Nevertheless, all these clues tell us only that the Maya imitated their Central Mexican contemporaries and acquired similar material goods, not that Teotihuacan people invaded and occupied the Petén. We do not, after all, suppose that the late nineteenth-century 59 denizens of Boston, who wore China silk, ate from Chinese porcelain, and sat on Chinese furniture, were actually under the sway of the Chinese.

The salient physical characteristic of the city of Teotihuacan is its city plan, with its grid of right angles and its architecture of right-angle geometry. It bears no resemblance to the more random, asymmetrical and clustered plan of Tikal, with its architecture of rounded moldings and variable proportions. Only a single structure has been excavated at Tikal in what appears to be true Teotihuacan talud-tablero. Nearby Yaxha, where Teotihuacan influence was strong, developed an urban layout that in part followed 'streets,' perhaps an accommodation of Teotihuacan city planning to Petén geography; but it too is truly a Maya city, with causeways and clusters. Contact with Teotihuacan resulted in an increasingly cosmopolitan and luxurious life for the royalty of Tikal, but it did not necessarily deny the essential Maya character of Early Classic Maya civilization, particularly as expressed in writing, architecture, and much of the iconography.

Because no inscriptions were known from Tikal or Uaxactún for the period from AD 530 to AD 580, Sylvanus G. Morley recognized a cessation of cultural production, calling it the 'hiatus,' and used it to divide the Early Classic period from the Late Classic. At Tikal, where Teotihuacan influence had most potently affected religion, ritual, and artistic style, such influence ended abruptly. Although various explanations had been put forward to explain the lapse (Morley had thought Tikal established colonies at Copán and elsewhere in the period) and the absence of any true 'hiatus' outside the Central Petén had become clear in recent years, a recent discovery at Caracol, Belize, seems to provide the clearest explanation of all: according to Caracol Altar 21, in the mid-sixth century Tikal was besieged and defeated by its enemies, led by the lords of Caracol. Whatever the absolute goals of such warfare, Caracol enjoyed an economic boom while a reduced population at Tikal suffered grinding poverty and watched the destruction of monuments and buildings. The Tikal dynasty itself fractured, with a branch of the lineage establishing itself in the Petexbatun region, leading to further seventh-century wars. Cities and lineages far from this interminable conflict seem to have benefitted by their distance. When cultural production at Piedras Negras, Palenque, and Copán gained renewed vigor at the beginning of the seventh century, styles in art, architecture, and ceramics all showed dramatic changes.

93 Among the most prominent of Maya gods, Chac commonly occurs on Early Classic cache vessels, usually with characteristic shark-tooth tongue and scroll eyes. Beads and thin slabs of clay appliqué have been built up in layers to yield this image.

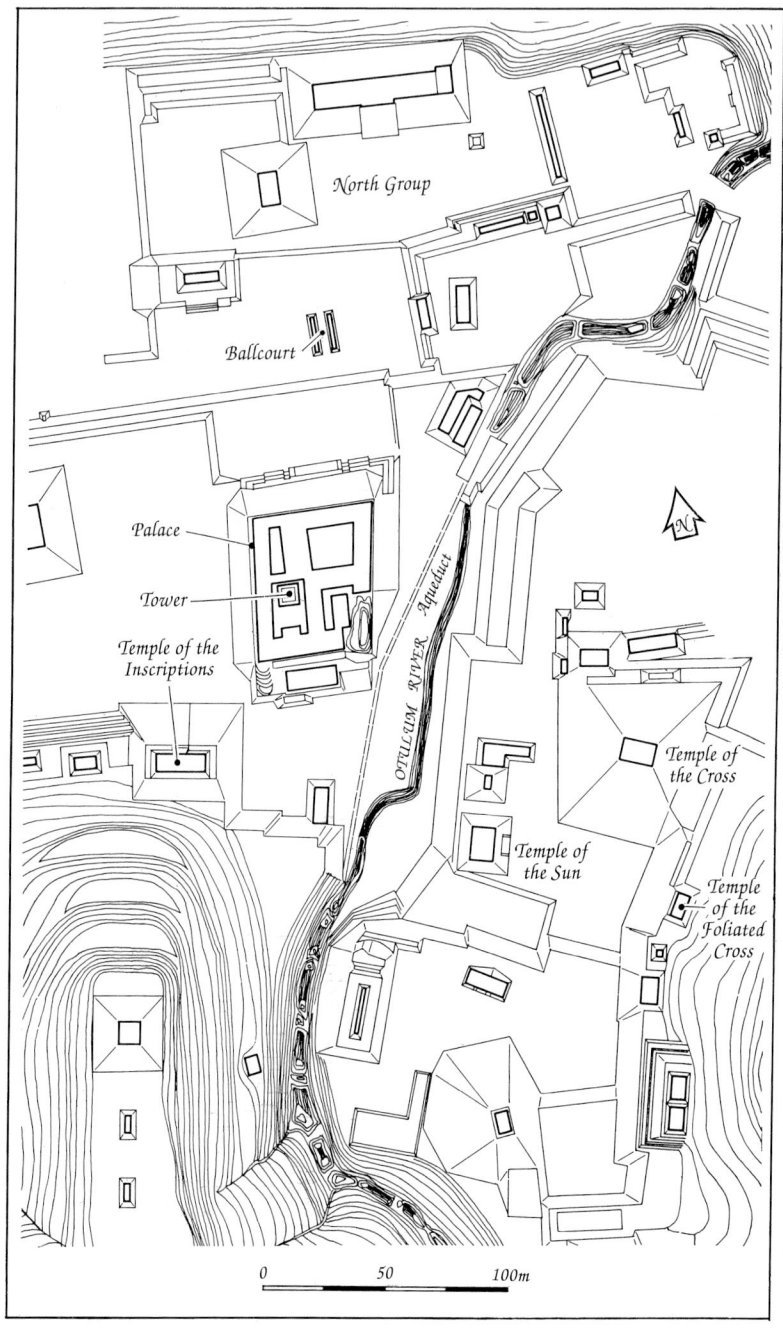

94 Plan of the Late Classic Maya city of Palenque.

CHAPTER SEVEN

The Late Classic Maya

Of all Mesoamerican art and architecture, that of the Late Classic Maya has long been the most esteemed. Even before the travels of John Lloyd Stephens and Frederick Catherwood brought the great temple pyramids and stone carvings to public attention in the 1840s, Alexander von Humboldt had remarked upon the naturalism of much of Maya imagery, and students of ancient art had praised the ability of the ancient Maya to draw the human figure. Late Classic Maya art is undoubtedly very human, and the attention to the individual, whether in the courtly Bonampak paintings or the solemn, three-dimensional stelae of Copán, has always attracted the modern, western viewer, as has the remarkable preservation of Late Classic buildings. Moreover, what has always been apparent is the simultaneous flowering of different styles during the Late Classic, in a profusion of artistic production.

Having already been abandoned to the tropical rainforest for centuries by the time of the Spanish Conquest, most Maya cities were too remote and ruinous to be pillaged in the sixteenth century. Only since World War II have roads opened the realm of the ancient Maya to the modern visitor, and only since 1980 has widespread exploitation of the rainforest run riot, with far-reaching implications for ancient cities, rainforest flora and fauna, and the modern Maya.

During the sixth century, the cities of the Petén went into decline, sapped by warfare. Simultaneously, peripheral regions – Chiapas, the Usumacinta drainage, Belize, and the southern lowlands – began to flourish, siphoning economic power and cultural energy away from the center.

ARCHITECTURE

Just about the year AD 600, in the foothills of the Chiapas *altiplano*, Palenque, the most westerly of major Maya cities, embarked upon a period of expansion. Over about 150 years and under the aegis of just a handful of rulers – in large part, the great king Pacal (whose name can be read phonetically in Maya and which means 'shield') and his two sons

95 The Palenque Palace as seen from the southwest. Behind the tower lies the East Court, famous for its carvings of captives (ill. 96). Subterranean passages honeycomb the section of the Palace in the foreground. Late Classic.

94 – the city grew in size, splendor, and importance. Its layout follows the rolling topography of the site, and temple structures crown and emphasize natural rises. The Otulum River passes through the city, and part of it was canalized to bring running water to the Palace. No *sacbes* characterize the architectural plan, but three distinct levels of construction can be discerned down the hillside.

Early Classic Petén masonry was clumsy and heavy, weighty roofcombs leaving little interior space. At Palenque a different aesthetic prevailed, 97 and its architects set corbeled vaults parallel to one another, with a light, 98 cut-out roofcomb over the central wall. Not only did this allow for greater interior space, but it also stabilized the whole construction, and it is partly because of this innovative technique that Palenque architecture is so well preserved today. Solid mass gave way to a web-like shell for the first time in Mesoamerican architectural history.

124

What one sees today of the Palenque Palace was probably built over a period of 100 years, the interior north-south buildings pre-dating the exterior colonnades and the tower. House E, unlike all other Palace buildings, was painted white and adorned with flowers. An inscription names it as the 'white flower house.' Panels celebrating the accession of several rulers were set inside Palace structures, and scenes on such panels undoubtedly reflect the luxury of courtly life at the time. The fine throne of House E was set under the Oval Palace Tablet and the doorway to the East Court was framed by a stucco bicephalic dragon of the sort that provides the border on accession stelae at Piedras Negras. The East Court was ornamented with large slabs of coarse limestone carved with subservient figures of gross and distorted features, including one with a huge scarred penis. Sacrificial rituals joined those of accession in the Palace, revealing the rights and responsibilities of kings. ₉₅ ₉₆

The final phase of construction in the Palace gave rise to the graceful three-story tower, a unique survival in Mesoamerican architecture. Narrow stairways wend around a solid core. Although the very idea of a tower has led several scholars to think in terms of an astronomical observatory, the building may also have had a defensive function, for from its upper story one can survey the whole plain to the north.

96 Individual carved slabs were placed together to create the great sloping talud of carved captives in the East Court of the Palenque Palace. Lords of the region would have entered the court by the staircase that these humbled figures flank. Late Classic.

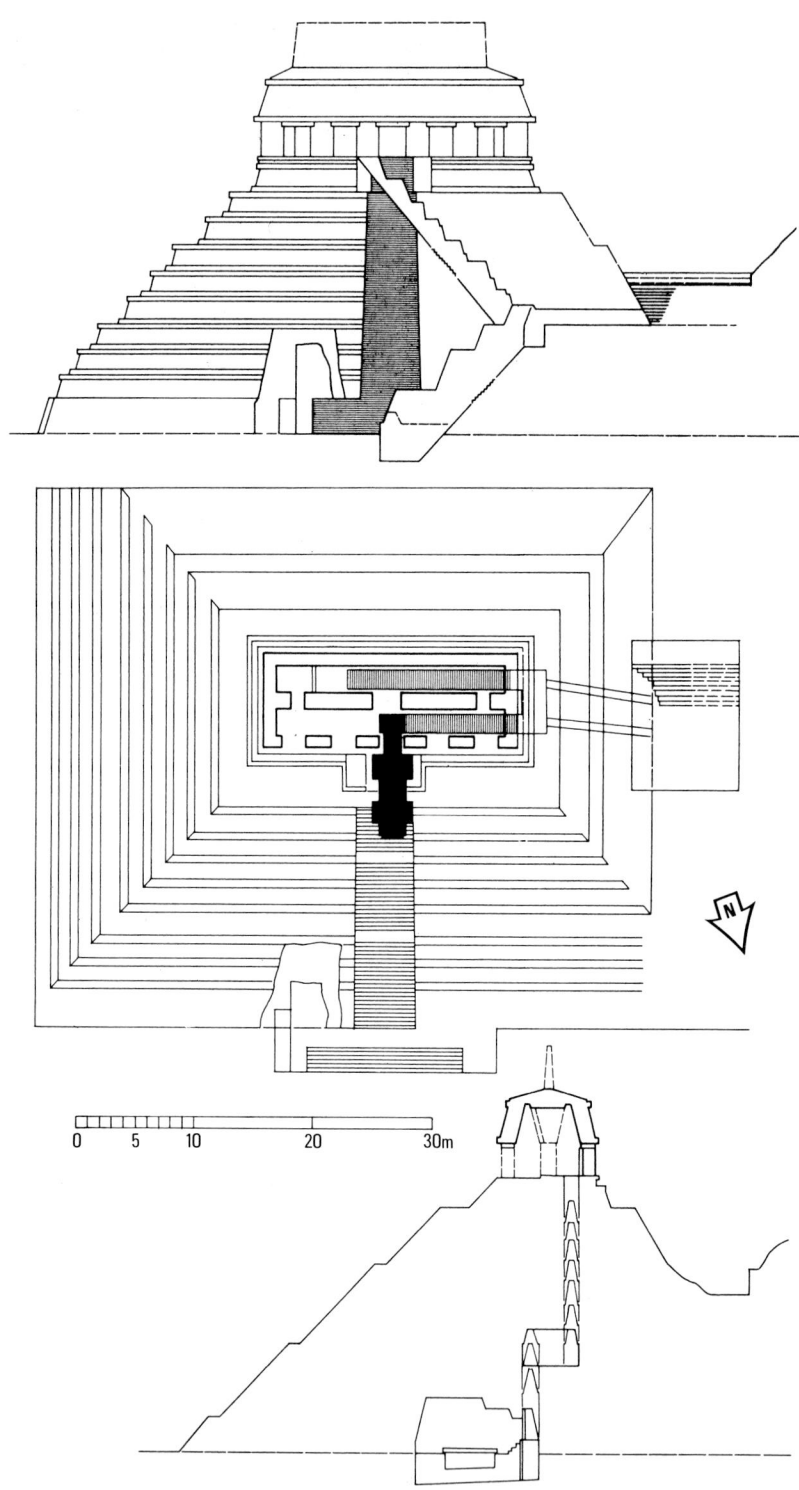

97, 98 Section, elevation, and plan of buildings at Palenque. (*Opposite*) Elevation, plan and section of the Temple of the Inscriptions. (*Right*) Cutaway model of the Temple of the Cross showing the light roofcomb resting on the central wall dividing the two parallel corbeled vaults.

Fitted with plumbing that draws on the ancient aqueduct, the Palace was a comfortable building. It seems to have served as the focus for the various royal ceremonies, rather than as a residence for the king's family. For dwellings, we look east of the aqueduct, where recent excavations by Mexican archaeologists have restored the graceful palaces alongside spectacular waterfalls and pools, and here we might well have heard the sounds of children and dogs and smelled the wafting scent of spicy sauces stewing.

The nine-level Temple of the Inscriptions stands just south of the Palace. Set directly into the hill behind, it is highlighted and framed by the landscape. After discovering that floor slabs of a rear chamber could be lifted to reveal interior constructions, the Mexican archaeologist Alberto Ruz cleared the staircase and in 1952 found the extraordinary tomb at the base of the pyramid, set on an axis, north–south, with the stairs. Within, a large corbeled chamber held the uterus-shaped sarcophagus of the great king Pacal, whose remains lay covered with jade and cinnabar. The sarcophagus lid shows the king at the moment of death, falling in rapture into the maws of the underworld. The sides of the sarcophagus display Pacal's ancestors, emerging from the ground, while nine stucco attendants flank the walls. The construction was designed for eternity: even the cross-ties were made of stone (the only examples known) and a small stone tube, or 'psychoduct,' as it is called, connects the tomb

99

100

127

99 The Temple of the Inscriptions, Palenque. The tomb of Pacal lay at the base of this pyramid, accessible for some time after the entombment by an interior staircase that ran from the tomb to the chamber at the top of the structure. Seventh century AD.

to the upper level and thence to fresh air. The Temple of the Inscriptions is unique among all Mesoamerican pyramids in having been built before the ruler's death, probably to his specifications.

Three panels of lengthy inscriptions in the upper chamber relate Pacal's life, and the exterior stuccos show his son as an infant deity, perhaps to demonstrate divinity even during the king's lifetime. Immortalized within funerary pyramids, Maya kings were worshipped after death, great ancestors united with deities and visible in the constellations of the night sky.

The Temple of the Inscriptions rises in nine distinct levels. At the time of the Conquest the underworld was perceived by both Aztecs and Mayas to have nine layers, and Pacal's funerary monument evidently conforms to the same idea of the afterlife, with the lord's tomb placed at the nadir of the pyramid. Likewise, at the Conquest, Mesoamericans believed the heavens to have thirteen levels, a vision of the universe reflected in the stratified Maya world of Pacal, for thirteen distinct corbels connect the tomb to the upper galleries. Later lords anchored themselves to Pacal's apotheosis, with burials in smaller funerary pyramids to the west, where Mexican archaeologists uncovered a significant tomb in 1994.

East of the aqueduct, the three temples of the Group of the Cross (the Temples of the Sun, the Cross and the Foliated Cross) show yet another architectural innovation. In this design – common to each of the temples – the two parallel galleries are intersected at right angles by another corbeled passage, creating a great chamber. Each temple also has an inner shrine at the rear of the building. The post and lintel doorway, as well as the usual mansard roof, conceal the interior space. At Palenque the achievement of private, interior space is as significant as the negative, public space defined by the volumes of the buildings.

Inscribed panels within the Group of the Cross shrines celebrate the birth of three patron deities of Palenque, back at the dawn of the current era in the fourth millennium BC, but under the sponsorship of the late seventh-century king Kan Balam, Pacal's oldest son. Stephen Houston

100 As if in the moment of death, the seventh-century king Pacal is depicted being swallowed by skeletal jaws on his sarcophagus lid at the base of the Temple of the Inscriptions, Palenque.

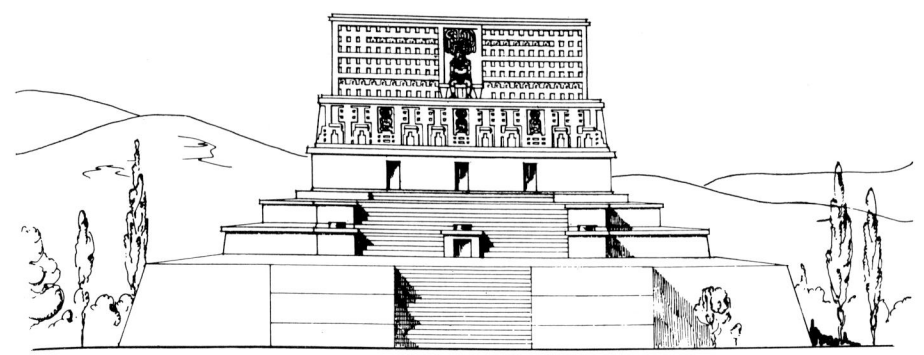

101 Elevation of Structure 33 at Yaxchilán.

has shown that these shrines symbolize sweathouses, places for birth and then the home for the resting image of the deity. Kan Balam probably stored cult figures here.

The Late Classic witnessed a burst of development along the Usumacinta and Pasión Rivers too, beginning at the end of the sixth century and continuing until about AD 800. River commerce along the Usumacinta was certainly one of the driving forces behind the growth of both Yaxchilán and Piedras Negras. At Yaxchilán, the river rounds an omega-shaped spit of land. Remnants of stone pilings in the silt perhaps indicate that there was once a bridge or toll gate here. Ranging single galleries are set both at plaza level near the river and on the surrounding hills. Structure 40 and Structure 33 celebrate the inaugurations of the two most important Late Classic rulers at Yaxchilán, nicknamed Shield Jaguar and Bird Jaguar. Rising up from great terraces built into the rugged natural relief, both buildings have commanding views of the river.

101 The architects of Yaxchilán created a few buildings of the double-galleried sort common at Palenque, but in general they were more conventional in their use of interior space. Moreover, they positioned roofcombs directly over vault capstones, which exacerbated the natural tendency of corbeled constructions to collapse and made it necessary to erect ponderous interior buttresses for added support. Most Yaxchilán structures have multiple doorways, and many have finely carved lintels.

At nearby Piedras Negras, only a day or two down-river, different influences are evident. Buildings relate to one another, rather than to the river, and they cluster in groups similar to those of Palenque. The inscriptions suggest a general development of the site from south to north that took almost 200 years. The early structures to the south are heavy and massive, with great rounded insets similar to those of the Early Classic Tikal North Acropolis. The West Acropolis at Piedras Negras consists of a central palace compound flanked by two great funerary pyramids, probably the shrines to Rulers 3 and 4 in the dynastic sequence. The palace structures feature double-corbeled galleries like those of Palenque. *102*

At Tikal, the 'hiatus' at the end of the Early Classic drifted on into the seventh century, as Tikal sustained further military and political losses. In the eighth century, however, a program of major new building work began that was sustained for about a hundred years. Instrumental in this revitalization of Tikal was Ruler A, who was buried about AD 727 in Temple I, a pyramid located directly across the Great Plaza from Temple II, which had itself been completed just a few years before. Temples I and

102 During the Late Classic, Piedras Negras kings developed a new complex on the West Acropolis. Within galleried palaces, kings reviewed their retinues from elegant thrones, framed by funerary pyramids that rose in great setbacks. Ruler 3's eight stelae stand in a line at right.

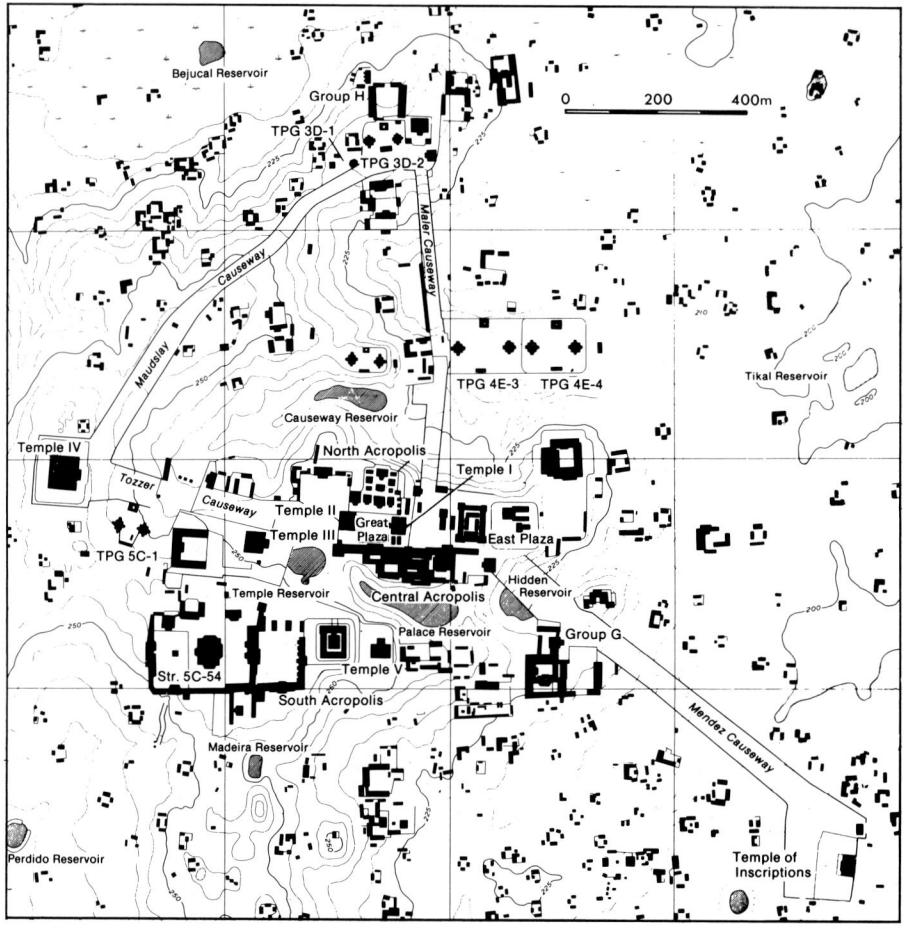

103 Plan of the central part of Tikal. The abbreviation TPG refers to the Twin Pyramid Groups or Complexes erected in the Late Classic. The early so-called Lost World pyramid is marked here as Str. 5C-54.

II dramatically altered the core of Tikal, changing the old north-south axis (conveyed by accretions of buildings with rounded corners and fussy *103* moldings) to an east-west one, defined by just two towering structures with clean lines.

104 Temple I, like the Temple of the Inscriptions at Palenque, is a nine-level pyramid, and – again like the Palenque building – it was conceived from the first as a complete memorial, from the carved wooden lintels

132

104 Temple I, Tikal and the Temple of the Inscriptions at Palenque (ill. 99) are the two most splendid funerary pyramids of the Late Classic Maya that archaeologists have yet explored. Both structures rise in nine distinct levels, as if a reference to the notion of nine levels of the underworld were incorporated into architectural iconography.

spanning the doorways to the funerary chamber below. Such an elaborate building must surely have been planned before Ruler A's death. Unlike the Palenque temple, however, none of the construction work can have started until the body of the ruler was sealed in the tomb at the base of the temple. Temple II was presumably dedicated to Ruler A's wife (though no tomb has been found), in which case husband and wife would have faced each other through eternity, framing their ancestors to the north.

Like great beacons rising above the jungle, other temples surround the original pair of the Late Classic dynasty. These unexcavated pyramids appear to be funerary monuments of later rulers who respectfully address their forebears. Temple IV is the greatest in both mass and height, rising to 65 m – or roughly the height of the Temple of the Sun at Teotihuacan. The Tikal pyramids remain visible 12 miles to the north, from the last great rise before Uaxactún.

Although freestanding and devoid of many of the ornamental moldings typical of Early Classic Tikal, these pyramids of the Late Classic retained characteristics of the North Acropolis that are not limited to their funerary nature. In Temple I, for example, a heavy roofcomb was set over the narrow, dark chambers that are accessible through a single doorway, and its weight runs down the spine of the structure. Inset moldings, more streamlined than those of the North Acropolis, both cover the corners of the structure and create a play of light and shadow across the surface.

The strong east–west orientation dominated not only the Great Plaza in Late Classic times but also the rest of the site, in outlying groups known as Twin Pyramid Complexes. At least six of these architectural clusters were erected in sequence, presumably to celebrate the twenty-year *katun* cycle which is recorded in each group. The elevated platform of each cluster has the shape of the Maya symbol for completion, and the two radial pyramids on the east–west axis recall the chronographic marker at Uaxactún, E-VII-sub. With a range structure to the south and a shrine to a ruler in the open structure on the north, this repeated and well-defined Tikal configuration would seem to reproduce the Great Plaza at its every appearance along the causeways.

No sculpture and little architectural ornament remain *in situ* to help us understand the function and meaning of the Central Acropolis. Its galleried chambers do, however, resemble a palace like that of Palenque, even if organized with less concern for overall plan. Furthermore, the

105 Reconstruction of a Twin Pyramid Complex, Tikal. Limited to Yaxha and Tikal only, these complexes were erected in the eighth century to celebrate *katun* endings. Although they might have been painted in antiquity, all the altars and stelae are plain today.

presence of a victor and his captive in eroded stucco – recorded on one of the structures flanking a trapezoidal court at the core of the Acropolis – hints that it may have been a place of sacrifice, like the East Court at Palenque, where humbled captives are depicted. A bank of four large hearths sustained a sort of institutional kitchen for the scribes, traders, priests, scholars, and nobles at work in the Central Acropolis. *96*

Using the same fundamental elements of Maya architecture – platform, stairs, and corbel vault – the architects of Copán, Honduras, developed a distinctive aesthetic. The local stone is an easily worked volcanic tuff, ranging from pink to brown to green, so that building stones could be cut and fitted together with a precision rare in the limestone structures of Palenque or Tikal. (The stone, of course, was cut with stone tools.) At Copán, however, as elsewhere, stucco coatings would have hidden any imperfections. Emphasis was placed on tuff architectural ornament, in full three-dimensional relief, and it is the best-preserved iconographic guide to the meaning of Mesoamerican architecture. Surviving façades retain a sheer vertical profile, rather than the usual mansard roof. These clean lines are echoed in the façades of Central Yucatán and the Puuc region, and may in fact originate at Copán.

106 By the mid-eighth century, Copán's Main Acropolis and Great Plaza had achieved their full growth, although nearby compounds of wealthy lineages continued to expand. The Copán River, to rear, later ate away structures until the U.S. Army Corps of Engineers constructed a new course for it in the 1930s.

The Copán Valley provides superb possibilities for the dramatic siting of architecture. The ancient city planners realized this and located their buildings to take advantage of specific views of the valley and surrounding mountains, especially the saddle through the mountains to the north. The ballcourt, for example, seems to reproduce the valley itself in its layout and orientation.

107 Structure 22, Copán, reconstruction of the inner doorway. One first steps through the fragmentary remains of a great monster mouth to gain access to this remarkable carved doorway. The king who built this structure, 18 Rabbit, was eventually captured and sacrificed by neighboring Quiriguá lords.

Eighth-century pyramids and structures dedicated to the rites of kingship crowd the acropolis, the final layer in what was at least a 600-year accretion. Kings were pronounced from Structure 22, where the private, elevated rear chamber framed by a bicephalic dragon is reached through a great open monster mouth, a symbolic cave entry to a sacred mountain. Young maize god sculptures once graced the exterior cornices, and the symbolic mountain may have been where the king brought forth the first corn from the Underworld. *106*

An international team of archaeologists has worked to reveal Copán's mysteries, both at its center and along its margins. Just beside Structure 22, Bill and Barbara Fash have recently reconstructed neighboring Structure 22a, apparently a *popol na*, or council house, where the king's *107* *108*

108 Apparently to unite the powerful and wealthy lineages, Copán lords built a *popol na*, or council house, where they might gather to advise and guide the king in his adjacent palace. Now known as Structure 22a, it features a fish on the front façade, probably a reference to the Fish family, whose compound lies south of the Main Acropolis.

109 One of the most beautifully sited of all Maya buildings, the ballcourt at Copán guides the eye from the Main Plaza to the steep hills beyond.

advisers would have conferred. Local lineages, including the Fish family, promote themselves from its façade, their names juxtaposed with woven mat, or *pop*, signs. Just south of the acropolis, other archaeologists have now found evidence of the Fish family compound. What might have been thought to be merely idle self-promotions seem, in fact, to have archaeological foundation. And during the eighth century, constituent lineages built luxurious quarters for themselves a few miles from the core that began to compete with the city center. The House of the Scribes in the Sepulturas group reveals the sophistication and wealth of the aristocracy at the end of the eighth century.

One of the last Copán kings, Yax Pac, as he is usually called, rebuilt many acropolis buildings, including Structure 11, his royal palace, and Structure 18, which may have held his tomb, although it was looted in antiquity. Structure 16 is the largest building on the acropolis, housing 83 within it the ancestral structures dubbed Rosalila and Margarita, the earliest funerary pyramids known at Copán, and its nine levels seem to refer to ancestry and the royal lineage in general, rather than to a single dynast.

Below the 25-m drop-off from the acropolis lies the Copán ballcourt, *109* the largest and most beautiful of all Classic courts. Like many smaller ones elsewhere, it unites two different areas of the central city. Unusual superstructures surmount the parallel buildings on its eastern and western sides. Each of these buildings has a plan cut by a central corridor running east-west, with mirrored configurations to north and south, as if ballcourts themselves. In its final phase, giant sculptural macaws lined the alleys.

Just to the south of the ballcourt stands the great Hieroglyphic *110* Stairway, a large pyramid whose steps are inscribed with 2,200 glyphs that relate the history of the Late Classic dynasty. Five three-dimensional rulers of Copán sit on projections from the staircase, and some are set directly over two-dimensional captive figures. In no other Maya building are sculpture, writing, and architecture more sensitively united. The carved scroll balustrade is an unusual element in Maya architecture, resembling the balustrade of the Pyramid of the Niches at El Tajín. *68*

110 Carved with 2200 glyphs, the text of the great Hieroglyphic Stairway at Copán is among the longest known. A supplicant would climb back in time as he or she ascended the stairs, reaching a shrine dedicated to the founder of Copán at the top. Eighth century AD.

111 The main structure, Chicanná, watercolor by Nigel Hughes. Worked in individual blocks that were then covered with a thin coat of stucco, the façade represents a great monster mouth through which one must pass to enter the chamber. AD 700–900.

The traditions that may have originated at Copán also thrived in Central Yucatán and the Puuc region. At Chicanná, as at most Chenes and Río Bec centers, the principal structures have great monster-mouth façades – presumably here again associated with ceremonies of kingship. Perhaps the proliferation of structures in Central Yucatán with monster-mouth façades reflects the widespread celebration of elite rituals. The mouth of the Chicanná structure is similar to the largely destroyed exterior of Structure 22, Copán, where the interior bicephalic monster framed a removed, interior chamber for private rites. Where blocks of ornament fell off in 1994, painting on stucco underneath was revealed.

Chenes structures are generally low-lying, galleried buildings. At Río Bec, great false temples frame such galleries – described as 'false,' in the accepted view, because there is no access to temple summits. In fact they may be funerary pyramids, directly combined with palaces, and conflations of the patterns established at Palenque or Tikal. Xpuhil, in south-

111
107

114

140

112, 113 The Pyramid of the Magician (*above*) and the Nunnery Quadrangle (*below*) at Uxmal.

114 What seem to be palaces and temples at Xpuhil, disposed like those of Piedras Negras (ill. 102), are in fact a single building, Structure 1. False openings beckon atop equally illusory stairs, in a Late Classic architectural style widely known as 'Rio Bec,' after a nearby site.

ern Campeche, for example, features stucco ornament that looks like stairs, but they cannot be walked on, nor their upper chambers entered.

Late Classic Puuc architecture first captured the imagination of modern Europeans and Americans through the writings and illustrations of Stephens and Catherwood, who spent months in the Puuc region. They visited Uxmal, Kabah, Sayil, and Labná to make drawings and to study the ruins there. There is still no finer introduction to the region and its ancient remains than their report of 1843. What attracted them and what still attracts the traveler today are the elegant quadrangles, fine veneer masonry, and beautiful mosaic façades that reflect shifting patterns of light in the hot clear sun of the Puuc hills.

Most of what is visible at Uxmal today seems to belong to the ninth century, ending with a final hieroglyphic date of 10.3.18.8.12 (AD 907).

Temple façades more typical of Petén and Usumacinta styles remain concealed by later reworkings: the west façade opens as a great monster mouth, in the fashion of Río Bec or Chenes buildings, and its axial staircase is precipitous. Opening towards the east is a structure of pure Puuc design, with a more gradual incline to its summit. From the Nunnery court, one can see only this final Puuc building; it looks like a second story on the eastern side of the quadrangle.

The juxtaposition of quadrangles with pyramids such as the Nunnery and the Pyramid of the Magician recalls the Palace and Temple of the *112* Inscriptions at Palenque, although the physical expression of Puuc architecture is new. The Palenque Palace, however, evolves from the inside out, while the Nunnery would seem to have been designed as a quadrangle. Indeed the Nunnery exemplifies the pioneering techniques of Puuc architecture: specialized 'boot' stones in vaults, providing increased stability and making possible some of the greatest vaulted spaces of ancient Mesoamerica; flying façades, the light, airy roofcombs set directly over the front weight-bearing wall, like the false storefronts of the American Old West; and veneer masonry, well-cut stones fitted together without mortar, hiding a rubble core.

Many elements from the Nunnery structures are repeated and elabo- *113* rated in the House of the Governor, the finest of all Puuc buildings. It, *115* too, was probably first conceived as part of a quadrangle, but no other structure was built. The plan of the House itself suggests three semi-detached structures, linked by sharp, corbeled doorways, innovatively used to open cross-corbel vaults within. The greater breadth of the central doorway and the uneven spacing of the flanking doorways (all of

115 The House of the Governor, Uxmal. Built to commemorate the tenth-century reign of the last important ruler of Uxmal, Lord Chac, this is one of the most elegant and beautifully proportioned structures of ancient Mesoamerica.

post-and-lintel construction), as first attempted in the east and west Nunnery buildings, alleviate the monotony that would result from even breadth and spacing, and the two pointed, recessed corbels vanish from view at sharp angles. The slight outward lean, or negative batter, of the structure gives it the appearance of lifting off its platform. The upper part of the vertical façade is, like most Puuc buildings, covered with a rich stone mosaic. Such mosaic designs may have been emblematic of certain rituals or certain families, and could be related to textile design. The decoration on the House of the Governor includes many elements: Chac, or rain god, masks; serpents; step frets; netted motifs; Maya thatched houses; and human busts. In the complexity of this ornament, the Uxmal artist seems to have drawn specifically on the east and west buildings of the Nunnery. The ruler of the era, Lord Chac, presides over the structure, the courtyard, and the range of hills before him from his three-dimensional representation over the central doorway. With its twenty-four rooms, the House of the Governor must have been the greatest administrative structure of its time, overseen by the ruler himself.

Perhaps the most remarkable feature of nearby Kabah is its monumental, freestanding arch, the only one of its kind. A *sacbe* 7½ miles long connects Kabah to Uxmal, and the arch marks the end of the elevated roadway. Unlike European city arches, which either denoted the opening in a wall or commemorated triumph, the arch at Kabah appears simply to proclaim the entrance to the city.

116 The Great Arch, Kabah, is set just at the edge of the city. The gateway grants access to the *sacbe* or causeway linking Kabah to Uxmal less than 8 miles away.

117 The Palace Tablet, Palenque. In commemoration of his accession in the eighth century, Lord Kan-Xul was portrayed in the act of receiving the symbols of office from his late parents. Pacal is shown at left, and he holds out a headdress of thin jade squares.

SCULPTURE

At the beginning of Late Classic times, strong regional styles emerged in monumental Maya sculpture. In the west, particularly at Palenque and Yaxchilán, two or three individuals were represented on a single relief, and the limestone slabs were set as wall panels or lintels, protected from the elements. Conservatism, on the other hand, generally prevailed at Tikal and the Central Petén, where stela imagery continued to conform to canons established in the Early Classic; but some innovative forms were introduced, such as carved wooden lintels. In the south, an impulse to three-dimensionality transformed the sculpture of Copán, while at Quiriguá, monuments of huge proportion were erected.

The Palenque artists selected a very fine-grained limestone for the interior wall panels that record dynastic history. The Palace Tablet commemorates the accession of the second son of Pacal, who became king of Palenque in 9.13.10.6.8, or AD 702. On the panel, the young king sits between his dead parents, who offer him attributes of kingship: a jade-plated headdress and a shield. The figures are all simply costumed, and one senses that their individual identity, not simply their ritual paraphernalia, ensures their right to dominion. New, seemingly less formal pos- 117 tures characterize Late Classic Palenque sculpture, and the courtly scenes depicted no doubt reflect something of the actual life that went on within the Palace chambers where most such sculptures were found.

100 Technically, the sarcophagus lid of twenty years earlier compares closely to the Palace Tablet, but the imagery of death is couched within the supernatural. The reclining king Pacal, known to have been some eighty years of age at his death, is shown as an idealized youth, and in the guise of two gods, God K (in the alphabetic system established at the beginning of this century), indicated by the tube puncturing his forehead, and the Maize God, whose beaded skirt he wears. As the Maize God, Pacal embodies the annual death and renewal of this Mesoamerican staff of life. God K is also characterized by a serpent foot, and Pacal twists his right foot to show the sole, perhaps to mimic the serpent.

A jade mosaic portrait mask was assembled directly onto the dead king's face, without any sort of wooden armature, and two stucco portrait heads were found in the tomb, presumably of Pacal and his wife. Many other fine stuccos have been recovered from Palenque. They reveal an interest in recording human physiognomy unparalleled in ancient America.

96 These fine, sensitive portraits of the ruling family find a foil in the rather gross depictions of subject persons in the East Court. The captives make gestures of submission to the individuals who would have stood above them on the terrace. On these slabs, hands, feet, and faces are crudely worked. Even the stone chosen reflects its subject: the buttery limestone of the accession panels is replaced by porous limestone less suitable for fine carving. Each figure is worked on an independent slab, and the compressed space for each person suggests oppression. The slabs may also have been re-used and re-cut to conform to a new configuration.

Often integrated with the architecture of Yaxchilán in the form of lintels or steps, the finest sculptures at this site display a regional style in which relief was executed on two distinct and removed planes. The resulting figures look as if they have been stamped out with a cookie cutter, and the glyphs around them often suggest the local architecture.

118, 119 On Stela 11, the figures stand inside a corbeled vault; on Lintel 25, Lady Xoc kneels in the rear chamber of a structure. Rituals associated with royalty were often recorded on Yaxchilán monuments: capture, sacrifice, autosacrifice, and visions of ancestors – all of which may derive from royal manuscripts. Many women are depicted too; the richly garbed Lady Xoc on Lintel 25 receives the vision of a warrior who appears in the mouth

146

118 Lintel 25, Yaxchilán. Lady Xoc, wife of Shield Jaguar kneels to receive a vision: a warrior, bearing a shield in hand and wearing a Tlaloc mask in 'X-Ray,' emerges from a serpent mouth. The rich drapery of the woman's garment is piled at her knees. The bloodletting tools that brought on this vision lie in a basket at her feet.

of a great serpent. Traces of red, green, and yellow polychrome remain on this and other Yaxchilán lintels, confirming what is supposed of most Maya sculptures – that they were once brilliantly painted.

On Stela 11, in the guise of Chac, the great king Bird Jaguar stands over three bound captives, prepared to carry out sacrifice. Bird Jaguar's cutaway mask recalls the Oxtotitlan painting of Olmec times, but the conceit particularly characterizes Late Classic Maya warriors. The dead parents of the ruler sit above, separated from the scene by a skyband, indicating their posthumous place in the heavens. Whether presiding over a scene or flanking it, as at Palenque, dead parents were frequently recorded, as if to confer legitimacy on a descendant. *119*

The obverse of Stela 11 shows the accession of Bird Jaguar, an event supported by the military success on the other side. Stela 11 and Lintel 25 were probably carved by a small atelier of sculptors whose work

119 (*above*) Stela 11, Yaxchilán. (*Left*) on the rear, Bird Jaguar, in an 'X-Ray' mask, wields an axe over three captives. (*Right*) the obverse shows Bird Jaguar (right) with his father. Mid-eighth century AD.

120 (*right*) Stela 14, Piedras Negras. Rulers of this site were portrayed within niches at the moment of their accession. This young eighth-century lord bore the glyphic title 'Turtleshell.' His mother stands in front of him.

121 (*far right*) Stela 12, Piedras Negras. The last dated monument (AD 795) of Piedras Negras shows a ruler presiding over a group of naked captives. At lower right, the sculptor has carved an old, humble man with great realism – perhaps a portrait.

148

spanned two generations of rule. Subsequent sculptors emulated their craft, but none equaled it.

The Yaxchilán artists also pioneered the introduction of new, active postures into normally staid stone sculpture. Lintel 8, for example, *27* shows Bird Jaguar and another lord grasping the hair of some captives, who bear their names emblazoned on their thighs. Such dynamic compositions ultimately culminate in the paintings of Bonampak. As Tatiana Proskouriakoff pointed out over twenty years ago, Tlaloc motifs *135* adorn the victors here, and throughout Late Classic art the Tlaloc

149

costume appears in scenes of warfare and sacrifice, as can also be seen on Lintel 25.

A higher relief distinguishes the sculpture of Piedras Negras. Here special attention was given to human faces, which were worked in three dimensions, especially on the handsome niche stelae. These monuments commemorated the accession to office of the various Piedras Negras rulers. On Stela 14, the young lord's tangible three-dimensionality plays against his mother's flat two-dimensional representation. Footprints mark the cloth draping the scaffold or ladder set in front of the niche, and swag curtains are pulled back at the top of the niche, as if the scene has just been revealed.

At the destruction of the site, enemies of the Piedras Negras dynasty smashed Throne 1 on the steps of the West Acropolis palace, where it remained for archaeologists to retrieve in the 1930s. Made at the end of the eighth century, the carving replaced an earlier throne figured on Lintel 3, another late carving, but whose subject treats détente with Yaxchilán a half century earlier. Along with Stela 12, these late eighth-century sculptures are among the most dazzling of Late Classic efforts and their workmanship runs counter to an indentification of artistic decline coupled with societal collapse.

Twelve individuals are grouped on four levels, probably steps, in a pyramidal composition on Stela 12. Eight captives are tied together in the lower register, and many show signs of torture. Two captains deliver the well-dressed, uppermost captive seated on draped cloth to the lord above. The text records a war event, and we see its aftermath here, victorious Piedras Negras displaying its trophies. Interestingly, the victims may be from Pomoná, a site known for its fine, Palenque-like carvings; indeed the workmanship of this monument resembles that style, not the more three-dimensional style with frontal faces of Piedras Negras. Artistic tribute may have been an aspect of elite warfare, and captives at other sites – Toniná, for example – were worked in the manner of their place of origin.

Static, single-figure compositions prevailed in the Central Petén throughout the Late Classic, conforming in some instances to canons established earlier. At Tikal, the texts on stone monuments were also laconic, unlike most monuments of the western region. Stela 16 presents a formal, frontal view of Ruler A, the king later buried in Temple I. Less public sculptures, such as the carved sapodilla-wood lintels of Temples I, II, and IV, display more complicated imagery and texts. The two lintels of Temple IV show Ruler B within a supernatural world. One depicts 122 him being borne on a litter and enthroned under an overarching feathered serpent. On the other, he sits enthroned over a flight of steps marked with symbols of rope and the main sign of the glyph emblematic of the site of Naranjo. A giant, anthropomorphic Jaguar God of the Underworld forms an architectural frame over the ruler.

At Naranjo, many monuments depict female dynasts, and the woman on Stela 24 stands over a humiliated captive. The cramped space of the lower register heightens the abject state of the prisoner. In two-dimensional carvings, frontal faces were generally reserved for captives.

An impulse to frontality may be seen in Early Classic Quiriguá Stela 26, although the contemporary Copán stelae resemble the works of the Petén. In the Late Classic, sculpture at these two southeastern sites moved from mere frontality to a near three-dimensionality. At Copán, larger-than-life portraits of standing rulers were carved nearly in the round. As at Tikal, many stelae were erected on the Main Plaza. By the reign of Yax Pac, the open space was heavily populated by royal ancestors. During his reign, however, there was also a return to two-dimensional works, perhaps re-introduced by his mother, a woman from Palenque. Carved steps, benches, and altars record numerous seated two-dimensional figures in profile. Altar Q, long misread as a gathering of astronomers, 124 actually shows the sixteen rulers of the city, all seated on their names, at the end of the eighth century. The ruler, at right, receives authority to rule from the first, at left, whose goggle mask indicates his antiquity.

During the reign of Cauac Sky, nearby Quiriguá grew wealthy, and according to the inscriptions this monarch captured his fellow ruler at Copán, 18 Rabbit. Cauac Sky was celebrated with a series of stelae, among them Stelae E and F, the tallest stone carvings of the ancient Maya. 125 Cauac Sky's face is worked in high relief, but the rest of his features are shown in two dimensions. Like their counterparts in tuff at Copán, these great prismatic shafts of sandstone were laid out in the clear expanse of the open plaza.

Later rulers at Quiriguá developed one of the most innovative types of Maya sculpture, the zoomorph. Huge river boulders were carved on all exposed surfaces as great composite jaguar, toad, crocodile, or bird forms. On Zoomorph P, a ruler emerges from a gaping front maw as if set within 126 supernatural architecture of the sort created in Structure 22, Copán. 107 Elaborate full-figure personifications of hieroglyphs were often inscribed on these great boulders as well, turning script into narrative sculpture.

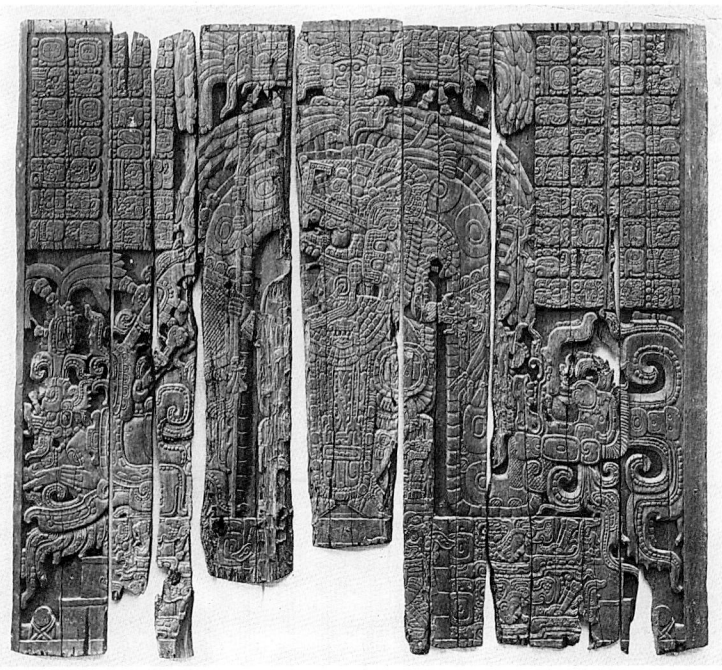

122 (*above*) Lintel 3, Temple IV, Tikal. Ruler B is borne high on a litter in this depiction – tied beams can be seen at lower right and left. The sapodilla wood of which the lintel is made is about 1200 years old.

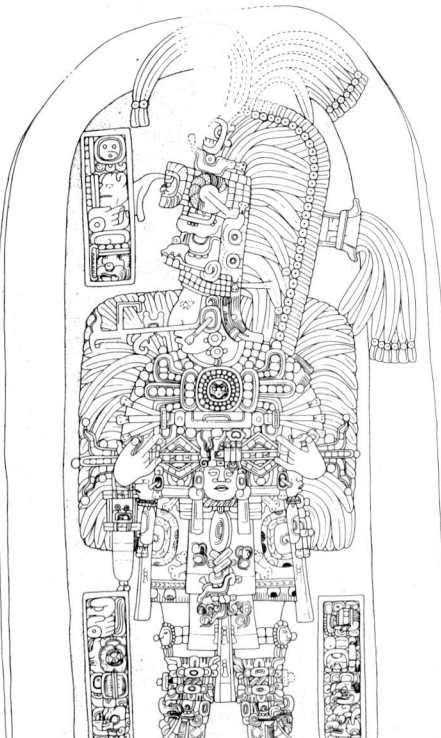

123 (*far left, below*) Stela 16, Tikal. On this stone monument erected to celebrate the *katun*, or twenty-year period, Ruler A holds a ceremonial bar and wears a great feather backframe.

124 (*below left*) On the front of Copán Altar Q, the first king (wearing goggles at left), Yax Kuk Mo', faces Yax Pac, the sixteenth, while the fourteen interposing monarchs line the monument. The nineteenth-century traveler, John Lloyd Stephens, had proposed that these figures are shown sitting on their names, an interpretation finally confirmed in recent years.

125 (*right*) Stela F, Quiriguá. The tallest Maya monuments were erected at Quiriguá, during the reign of Cauac Sky – depicted here – who bested the Copán king in an early eighth-century battle. Most such stelae were double portraits, carved both front and back.

126 (*below right*) Zoomorph P, Quiriguá. One of the latest known rulers of Quiriguá sits within the open maw of a great monster on this carved river boulder.

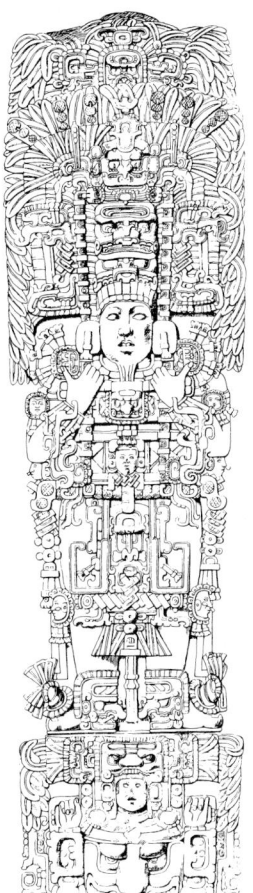
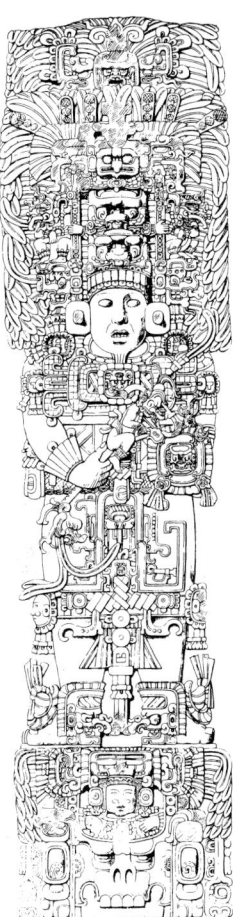

127 (*left*) A jade mosaic vessel, Burial 116, Tikal. Placed as an offering in Ruler A's tomb in the early eighth century, this Late Classic vessel recalls the form of Early Classic lidded tripods (ill. 90).

128 (*right*) Collected by Thomas Gann at Teotihuacan at the turn of the century, this fine Maya jade plaque shows an enthroned ruler attended by a court dwarf.

MINOR SCULPTURE

Most fine Maya objects of small scale have been recovered from royal burials, and many carry information relating to the life or afterlife of a given individual. The jade mosaic jar from Ruler A's tomb at Tikal, for example, is probably a portrait of the dead king. Jade-plated vessels of this sort are known only from Tikal, and the type is conservative, retaining Early Classic characteristics, such as the knob in the form of a human head. An extraordinary jade mosaic portrait mask was built onto Pacal's face in his crypt, unlike others assembled on wooden armatures, along with pounds of jade jewelry covering his body. At Altun Ha, a ruler was interred with a 9.7-pound (4.42-kg), three-dimensional carved jade head, an unusual representation of the Principal Bird Deity. Its shape sug-

127

129 Many finely carved bones – some of them human – were recovered from a single deposit in Ruler A's tomb at Tikal. On this one, paddlers guide a canoe and its occupants through underworld waters.

gests a miniature zoomorph. Fine jade plaques showing rulers accompanied by dwarves have been recovered from Nebaj, in the Guatemalan highlands, perhaps a place of manufacture, but they have also been found *128* far from the Maya region.

A number of incised bones (some human) were deposited as a single cache in Ruler A's funerary chamber, the scenes on some of them illustrating what we can presume to be the posthumous journey. On one pair *129* of bones the artist delicately incised and then filled with cinnabar a drawing showing the Maize God, the deified ideal of both rulership and renewal, in a canoe, being paddled to the underworld in the company of howling animals. In a gesture of woe, the king raises his hand to his brow.

Flint and obsidian were worked by Maya craftsmen into many shapes, and these are generally termed 'eccentrics.' Some of the eccentric flints, such as the many examples that reveal the profile of God K, might have been scepters carried by a lord. Others were perhaps designed as funerary offerings. An extraordinary example in the Dallas Museum of Art shows an earth monster with human figures on its back, and it may illus- *130* trate a concept of the afterlife.

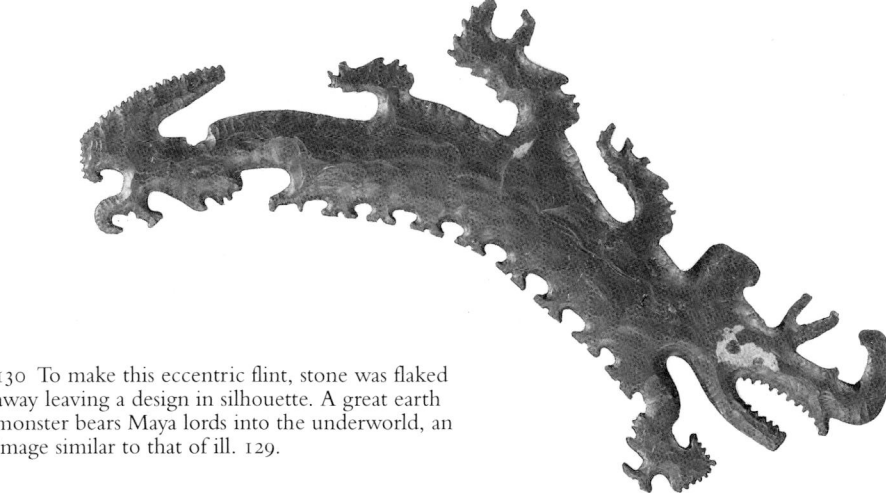

130 To make this eccentric flint, stone was flaked away leaving a design in silhouette. A great earth monster bears Maya lords into the underworld, an image similar to that of ill. 129.

131 Carved shell, Jaina Island. Along the Campeche coast, where the material abounded, conch was cut and carved into fine objects. Here a Maya lord seems to ride a fish monster. The piece may once have been inlaid with precious greenstone.

132 (*right*) Beautiful young woman and old man, Jaina Island. The moldmade bodies may testify to the popularity and timelessness of the scene, but this example received extraordinary hand-modeled details, including faces and headdresses, and tenacious pigments, including Maya blue. This example is also a whistle.

FIGURINES

For many years, figurines and shell carvings of high quality have been found on Jaina Island, just off the Campeche coast. The island may have functioned as a necropolis, and people of the Late Classic interred huge *131* numbers of offerings there. Conch was a common material, sometimes ornamented with inlay. Figurines must have been manufactured nearby: hundreds and hundreds are known from the island itself. Most were made in molds, but the finest were modeled by hand, at least in part, and small human fingerprints are often visible (suggesting to some that women made these objects). Tenacious pigments were used on the finished figures, especially blue, white, and yellow. Many Jaina figurines also function as whistles, ocarinas, or rattles.

Some supernatural beings depicted among the figurines, such as the Jaguar God of the Underworld, can be seen on painted ceramics too, but *132* perplexing religious scenes such as a young woman embracing an old

156

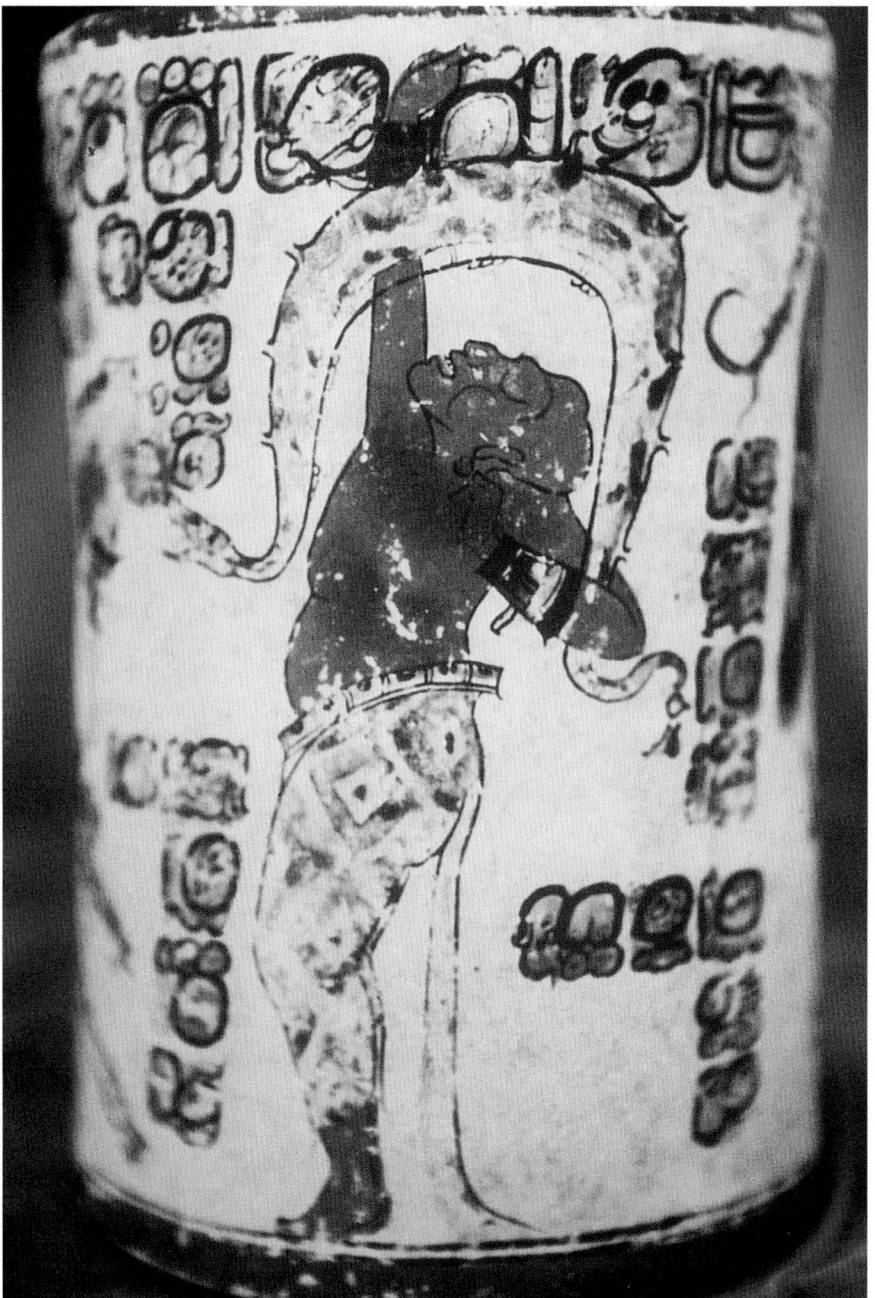

133 Maya lords transformed into their *uayob*, or shamanic companion selves, dance in ecstasy on this beautifully painted pot from Altar de Sacrificios. Dressed in snakeskin trousers, the bald dancer seen here throws back his head, hurls a boa constrictor in the air, and pierces the glyphic border with his raised hand.

man are known only from the ceramic repertoire of this small island. Even more lifelike ceramic sculptures have been found recently at Río Azul and Palenque. Few figurine cults in the world have produced such animated, compelling human miniatures as this Late Classic Maya tradition.

CERAMICS

Many of the scenes painted on Late Classic Maya narrative polychrome pottery elaborate a supernatural world, one the Maya themselves entered through states of altered consciousness. Some scenes occur without regard for geography or chronology, while other nevertheless standard narrations were made only in a single style. Some mythic scenes probably prescribed behavior for success in conquering the underworld, a theme later recounted in the Postconquest manuscript, the *Popol Vuh*. Painted in a fine black or brown line over a cream slip, frequently with a red rim band, such pots may have derived from lost Maya books, which has led Michael Coe to christen the tradition the 'codex' style. The color scheme itself, red and black, was the much later metaphor used by the Aztecs to mean writing itself. Several schools and master painters of this style have been identified, but a common theme celebrates the sacrifice of a baby jaguar by a dancing death god and Chac, sometimes with a dog and firefly looking on.

134

133 On a vase from Altar de Sacrificios, a site at the confluence of the Pasión and Usumacinta Rivers, a red rim and highlights have been added to a codex-style painting. Although often interpreted as a record of actual funerary rites, the scene instead depicts supernatural selves of shamanic transformation, two of whom dance in ecstasy. Adjacent texts name these figures as *uayob*, or shamanic other selves. One wears snake-patterned trousers, and as he hurls a boa constrictor into the air, he throws back his head, closes his eyes, and presses his hand right through the glyphic border. Maya vase painting of the Late Classic is self-conscious and theatrical, sophisticated in a way never matched elsewhere in the prehispanic New World.

Other regional vase painting styles can also be identified. In the region of Naranjo, a monochrome red-on-cream style predominated. The western Petén may be the source of the 'pink-glyph' style, in which rose tones were used and figures depicted in cutaway, X-ray fashion. Carved gray slateware was characteristic of northern Yucatán. In highland

134 The image on this codex-style pot has been photographically rolled out. A death god, right, pairs his dance steps with Chac, left, with the baby jaguar ready for sacrifice in between. The artist has used a fine brown wash behind Chac to suggest water.

Guatemala, potters generally included red backgrounds and painted the rim bands with chevron motifs. In Honduras, vases were carved from marble, perhaps by non-Mayas of the Ulua Valley, and these are occasionally found at Classic sites. At the end of Classic times, a new kind of pottery appeared in many parts of the Maya lowlands, and the iconography of these modeled and carved fine-orange vessels differs from the earlier painted ones, perhaps to be associated with new people or new trading patterns.

PAINTING

Fragments of polychrome paintings were uncovered periodically throughout the western Maya region in the late nineteenth and early twentieth centuries, particularly in the vicinity of Yaxchilán. Then, in 1946, Giles Healey stumbled upon a miraculously well-preserved sequence of Late Classic Maya wall paintings at the site now known as Bonampak, not far from the Lacanhá River, a tributary of the Usumacinta. The preservation of the paintings was a fluke: shortly after their completion in the late eighth century, water seeped through the poorly made limestone vault, building a layer of calcifications that encased the fragile paint.

135 Painted in the last decade of the eighth century, the wall paintings of Bonampak provide unusual views of noble life at the end of the Classic period. Seated on a throne, royal women pass ropes through their tongues. A servant, right, hands a sharp spine to the prominent woman in front; a child, probably a boy, in another woman's lap, may draw blood from his finger.

In Structure 1, the vaults, walls, benches, and door jambs of the three rooms had all been painted in bright colors on damp stucco. Hundreds of Mayas are depicted in a unified work celebrating the festivities and bloodshed of the last major dynastic accession at Bonampak. On three walls of Room 1, nobles in white mantles attend the presentation of a child; some ten months later – following the chronology of the painted glyphs – musicians and performers contribute to a great celebration in the child's honor. When another year has elapsed, a battle is waged and Bonampak emerges victorious. The battle covers three walls of Room 2. On the north wall, in a scene that encompasses the open doorway, sacrificial victims are displayed on the steps. The naked, humiliated captives are among the most handsome figures in Maya art, and even their tortured, bleeding hands were rendered lovingly by the artist. Above a skyband border appear cartouches marked with star signs. These seem to be the constellations of the morning sky on the date recorded, 2 August AD 792, when Venus rose as morning star and demanded a propitious sacrifice. History, for the Maya, seems to have been shaped by astrology and augury. In Room 3, the remaining captives are dispatched on a pyramid, *135* while royal women, clutching the little heir, sit on the throne and perform penance by running ropes and spines through their tongues. Linked together by rope, they liken themselves to the bound captives of Piedras Negras Stela 12 (ill. 121).

THE END OF THE CLASSIC MAYA

The momentum of Classic Maya civilization began to slacken and falter in the late eighth and ninth centuries. Stone monuments ceased to be erected from as early as AD 760 in certain areas, and gradually whole cities were abandoned. At some sites there is evidence of violence: at Piedras Negras, for example, monuments were dragged out of buildings and smashed. At Palenque and Copán, the ritual paraphernalia of the Classic Veracruz ballgame were left by late visitors. Tikal seems to have suffered a slower depopulation. Fine orange ceramics appeared at many sites. By about AD 900, perhaps slightly later in the north, Classic Maya civilization had collapsed.

For the ancient Maya, blood and blood sacrifice were the mortar of dynastic life, and sacrifice accompanied the rituals of office. At the end of Classic times, however, there is evidence that the pattern of capture and sacrifice gave way to warfare and dominion. The latest Yaxchilán monuments enumerate battle after battle; the final monument at Piedras Negras is Stela 12, where the booty of battle is laid at the ruler's feet. The *121* Bonampak murals were never completed, and we can deduce that the little heir perished before reaching majority in a battle like that painted in Room 2. Archaeologists have sought the explanation for the Classic Maya collapse in buried material remains (did their food supply change? What happened to the soils?), but the art and inscriptions relate the Maya's own last record of life around AD 800, and that record is of warfare. Warfare was the process, if not the cause, of the Classic Maya collapse that the Maya themselves chose to record.

CHAPTER EIGHT

Mesoamerica after the fall of Classic cities

The Classic Maya collapse was a gradual affair, affecting Maya cities at a far from uniform rate. Some well known centers, such as Palenque, abandoned the time-honored practice of raising stone monuments well before neighbors such as Toniná did so, while a large city such as Tikal continued with limited ceremonial activities for a considerable time. The burning and destruction of Classic Teotihuacan, on the other hand, marked a dramatic cessation in both the maintenance and the centralized, public use of the Way of the Dead and the major temples there, even if some residential quarters remained occupied. Meanwhile, in Oaxaca, when Classic Monte Albán was abandoned other centers of population grew up to take its place.

During this period of widespread disruption of Classic cities, their characteristic features did not disappear suddenly, nor was all knowledge of the past lost. At the time of the Conquest, for example, the Maya still wrote in a phonetic, hieroglyphic script probably perfected in Classic times, and had a literate Maya of the 1500s seen a Classic monument, he could have read and understood it.

Nevertheless, the turmoil of the late first millennium AD led many Mesoamerican peoples to uproot themselves and form new alliances or move to new territories. 'Foreign' influences can be observed in many places during the Terminal Classic (generally considered to be the ninth century). Mayas appeared in Central Mexico and Mexicans among the Maya. It was a time of seemingly unprecedented inter-regional contact, best seen today in the rise and fall of two cities, Tula and Chichen Itzá, one in Central Mexico and the other in Yucatán, both built in a cross-pollinated Maya-Mexican style during the Early Postclassic. During the Late Postclassic the Aztecs ruthlessly exploited the weaknesses of their neighbors in order to gain dominion over the whole of Central Mexico, and their civilization will be considered in Chapter Nine. The Maya of the Late Postclassic, however, show neither the innovation nor the craftsmanship of their Aztec contemporaries. Their art drew upon earlier models, and will be discussed at the close of this chapter, in conjunction with Chichen Itzá, the strongest influence on the later Maya.

One important marker used by archaeologists to chronicle change is pottery, and among elite wares there was a shift in styles and clays about AD 800 at several Classic Maya sites. Designs were now modeled and carved, rather than painted – color was no longer an element. Some designs appear to have been stamped out, or mass-produced. Even the clay used to make the vessels ceased to be local, and most scholars believe it to be of Gulf Coast origin, suggesting a foreign presence. Likewise, what we find in the art and architecture of the Maya city of Seibal argues for a Central Mexican or Gulf Coast infusion there about this time.

SEIBAL

The later buildings of Seibal exhibit a new architectural style. A great round platform was erected at the site, a rare feature in Mesoamerican, and particularly Maya, architecture. Round structures in use at the time of the Conquest were generally associated with the Central Mexican deity, Quetzalcóatl, and – as we shall see – his cult was beginning to take root during the Early Postclassic. Moreover, a new large radial pyramid at Seibal would seem to recall the unusual forms of Late Formative Uaxactún E-VII-sub or the Late Classic radial pyramids of Tikal's Twin Pyramid Complexes.

80, 105

A stela was set at the base of each staircase of the Seibal radial structure, each commemorating the date 10.1.0.0.0 (AD 849), as if that were a momentous year. One names lords of four separate polities, Tikal, Calakmul, San José de Motul, and Seibal itself, demonstrating the vitality of lineages in sustaining ritual practices. Most striking of all is the distinctive physiognomy depicted on Seibal monuments. Stela I, AD 869, for example, shows a new kind of portraiture. The ruler's face is not idealized, and the strong, slightly downturned lip suggests a harsh man. Many Seibal portraits show neither forehead deformation nor the extended bridge of the nose typical of most ancient Maya. Yet the greater emphasis on facial relief offers simply a new wrinkle on a pattern common at Piedras Negras and Quiriguá. Are the men represented foreigners? Or have the Maya simply absorbed and articulated foreign fashions once again?

136

On yet later monuments, both inscriptions and costume change. On Stela 3, for example, a date is recorded in a non-Maya system, and one of the glyphs used is a *cipactli*, or crocodile head, the first day name of the 260-day calendar in most Central Mexican systems. On this same monu-

136 Stela 1, Seibal. During the ninth century, new rulers – perhaps the Itzá – came to power at Seibal. Although they adopted the dress of the Classic Maya, they often confused and reinterpreted Classic symbols. Nevertheless, both the format and the message of Stela 1 convey rulership in a way that conforms to a millennium of Maya public presentation.

ment, individuals are shown with long, flowing hair and trimmed bangs, rarely revealed by Classic Maya in full dress. On other monuments, traditional Maya imagery appears in odd configurations, as if not understood clearly by the elite at Seibal. The exact ethnic identity of this ninth-century power may be a mystery, but the strong Central Mexican influence certainly suggests that the rulers of Seibal were Mexicanized Mayas, possibly the Olmeca-Xicalanca of the Gulf Coast renowned as traders at the time of the Conquest.

164

It is perhaps too tidy a solution to attribute contemporary developments further north to the same people who dominated Seibal, but powerful cosmopolitan, particularly Maya, influences undoubtedly made themselves felt at Cacaxtla and Xochicalco in Central Mexico at this time.

In 1975, a local schoolteacher led Mexican archaeologists to well-preserved, beautifully executed paintings in Maya style at Cacaxtla, Tlaxcala, a hilltop acropolis. One set of paintings had even been packed with fine sand by the ancient inhabitants to help preserve the stucco paint. In Structure A, the doorway is flanked by two stela-like portraits, one showing a standing Maya in bird costume; the other, a Maya in a full jaguar suit. The man in the bird costume and black body paint may be *140* the Terminal Classic prototype of the later Aztec Eagle Knight, but the *170* naturalistic proportions, skilled painting, and attention to both costume details and the human face reveal the Maya origins of the artist, while the shape of forehead and nose indicate the Maya ethnicity of the subject. Other influences are evident as well: borders show Teotihuacan motifs, and the glyphic style is not yet identified.

A second, nearly complete set of paintings framing a staircase features warriors with Central Mexican profiles in jaguar suits and adorned with the iconography of human sacrifice. They attack, defeat, dismember, and even disembowel warriors with Maya profiles who wear bird suits and lavish textiles, and at least two of the Maya figures may be women wearing upper body garments. The naturalistic representation of spurting blood and spilling entrails derives from a Maya canon of representation, but the subject matter suggests that Maya forays into Central Mexico may have resulted in grinding tribute payments and outright defeat. In the Red Temple, other fragments of paintings have been found that may record an economic reality: God L, the Maya patron of commerce, is depicted with his overstuffed trading pack along a staircase that records both particular victories and emaciated human captives at its foot, juxtaposing luxury with degradation. The rich blue pigments and the quality of line of the paintings correspond to those of Bonampak (Chapter *135* Seven), and they may have been painted around the same time, *c.* AD 800.

Some 80 miles to the southwest of Cacaxtla lies Xochicalco, a contemporary hilltop acropolis high above the Valley of Cuernavaca. Cosmopolitan influences abound here as well, and are particularly evident on the Pyramid of the Feathered Serpent. Seated figures of Maya *137*

137 At Xochicalco, Adela Breton observed undulating feathered serpents and seated lords. Xochicalco was a cosmopolitan city at the end of the Classic era, commanding fealty and trade from the smaller polities whose place names grace the exterior.

proportion, in Maya pose and dress, are carved among the undulations of great feathered serpents, or literally, Quetzalcóatl, while shell sections define an aquatic environment. The sculptors executed glyphic notations using an idiosyncratic system that features numerous unidentified place-names, possibly indicating political consolidation or a sort of council house, what to the Maya would be a *popol na*, like the one constructed at Copán (ill. 108). They also gave the images a double outline, a technique *cf. 70* characteristic of Classic Veracruz art, particularly at El Tajín.

A large, graceful ballcourt similar to that of Copán was situated at the heart of the site, adjacent to what were probably palace chambers. Other connections with the Classic Maya are seen on the three stelae excavated at Xochicalco. One shows the goggle-eyed and fanged face of Tlaloc, but the two others depict a strikingly three-dimensional human face, set within a helmet, framed by a more two-dimensional calendar sign above and skyband below. These stelae show resemblances to the 'niche' stelae *120* of Piedras Negras, where enthroned, three-dimensional rulers are portrayed within two-dimensional skyband borders, in scenes commemorating rulership. The works of art at both Cacaxtla and Xochicalco suggest that elites throughout Mesoamerica may have retreated to isolated sites like these, where they left a new, hybridized material culture.

MITLA

The abandonment of Classic cities in Central Mexico and the Maya area was paralleled in Oaxaca by the end of Monte Albán's long reign as the main city of the region, although the mountain continued to serve as a place of ritual activity and pilgrimage even after permanent occupation ceased. Instead, other Zapotec centers grew in the surrounding valleys, particularly to the south. Large, elegant palace complexes were constructed at both Yagul and Mitla, for instance.

The palaces at Mitla have long been admired for their elegant proportion and ornament. Courtyards with both interlocking and open corners are arranged along a general north-south axis. In Colonial times the townspeople built a church into the northernmost quadrangle and established a chapel on the summit of a large mound southwest of the palaces, thus transforming the ancient ruins into modern holy places.

138 Hall of the Columns, Mitla. This graceful building grants entry to private quadrangles within. Columns inside this building once supported a perishable roof.

The Group of the Columns, Quadrangles D–E, is the largest of the palace compounds and the most refined in proportion. Quadrangle E consists of four galleried buildings arranged around the sides of a plaza with open corners, while its northern building, the Hall of the Columns, provides the only access to D, a smaller, fully-enclosed quadrangle, maze-like in its plan. The Hall of the Columns is the most beautiful of Mitla structures. Like the House of the Governor at Uxmal (its contemporary), the building has a subtle outward lean, which visually alleviates the weight of its overhanging moldings, similar to those at Monte Albán.

The façades of Mitla buildings shimmer in the clear sunlight of Oaxaca. Geometric mosaics in a variety of designs and composed of individual veneer stones are set in rectangles across the exterior walls. In the private chambers of Quadrangle D the interiors are also cast with intricate patterns, quite conceivably replicating in stone fabrics which had once hung within palace rooms. The designs may refer to various family lineages, perhaps derived from woven textile patterns specific to group or place.

THE HUASTECS

At the very beginning of the Early Postclassic a regional style flourished in north Veracruz, among the Huastecs. This Mesoamerican group is

139 A so-called 'apotheosis' sculpture, Huastec culture (Early Postclassic). The strong three-dimensional quality of Huastec stone sculpture may be related to works at El Tajín and Classic Veracruz ceramic sculptures (ill. 74). The death deity on the back of this monument (*right*) is carried like a burden by the human on the front (*left*).

140 Stucco painting of a man in a bird suit, Structure A, Cacaxtla, AD 700–900. Like a Mesoamerican Daedalus, this handsome young warrior in black body paint wears a full bird suit, from headdress to wings to feet.

related by language to the Maya, but generations of separate evolution led to a distinct artistic expression. Particular emphasis in the Huasteca (as the region is known) was given to the cult of Quetzalcóatl, and as we shall see this was also true at Tula and Chichen Itzá. Circular buildings dedicated to Quetzalcóatl are found at small sites throughout the region.

Characteristic of Huastec sculptures are prismatic yet slab-like three-dimensional works. These have been called 'apotheosis' sculptures   *139* because of their dual imagery. A life-sized human figure is worked on the front of the monument, while a smaller image appears on the back – sometimes an infant, borne as if in a backpack, or in the case of the *139* example shown here, a skeletal death image. The oversized hands and the rich, incised pattern that covers the stone can be compared with later Aztec workmanship, particularly as seen in ill. 165. In fact, the carpeted body may represent the custom of body paint; the pleated adornments represent folded *amate* (fig) paper. The Aztecs conquered the Huastecs in the mid-fifteenth century and may have used Huastec art as a model for their own imperial style. It is also possible that these Huastec sculptures have a prototype in the Maya sculptures of Copán. There, a ruler and his predecessor are often recorded in three-dimensional relief on the front *125* and back of a stone shaft. The adult males of Huastec sculpture may be rulers, paired with their infant successors or dead predecessors.

THE TOLTECS

The rise of the Toltecs at Tula, in the state of Hidalgo, and at Chichen Itzá is generally attributed to the tenth century, although both sites were occupied long before. Ironically enough it was the later Aztecs who ensured the Toltecs a prominent place in history. No other people played such an important role in Aztec and Maya chronicles at the time of the Conquest. These historical annals – some of which were transcribed into the roman alphabet – provide information for events going back as far as the tenth century, even if for the period AD 1000 to 1300 the record is not at all complete. For earlier historical records in Mesoamerica, one must turn to Maya inscriptions (scarce as these are from AD 800 to 1000) and use them to compare contemporary archaeological data from other places.

The sixteenth-century documents weave a story of cyclical occurrences, where myth and history are one, and – unfortunately for us – geographical locations are often vague. We learn, for instance, of great events at the ancient city of Tula, but Tula, or *Tollan* (literally, 'place of reeds,' but generally understood to mean an urban settlement) is the name ascribed to many important centers from early Postclassic times on. To the Aztecs, both Teotihuacan and Tula, Hidalgo, were the Tula of the past, but their own city, Tenochtitlan, was also a Tula, as was Cholula, perhaps Chichen Itzá, and even Copán, as well. The sixteenth century reveals a particular view of the Toltecs:

The Tolteca were wise. Their works were all good, all perfect, all wonderful, all marvelous; their houses beautiful, tiled in mosaics, smoothed, stuccoed, very marvelous. . . . The Tolteca were very wise; they were thinkers, for they originated the year count, the day count; they established the way in which the night, the day, would work; which day sign was good, favorable. . . . (Sahagún, Book 10)

The later commentaries seem to have telescoped all past glories into the Toltec era, but they retained the term 'Toltec' to refer to their contemporary skilled craftsmen. As we shall see, the skill of the builders of Tula, Hidalgo, was not exceptional, and in fact, much of the workmanship there can be considered shoddy.

The historical annals reveal three important characters in the drama of the Toltec rise and fall. A great leader named Topíltzin Quetzalcóatl had achieved the rulership of Tula, Hidalgo, by AD 986. He led his people away from human sacrifice, the story goes, until the arrival in Tula of the deceiver Tezcatlipoca, known by a variety of names. Tezcatlipoca took on many disguises, charming and enchanting people, and in private consultation with Topíltzin pressed him to drink such quantities of an intoxicating beverage that the king humiliated himself in front of his people. After several confrontations and subversions, Topíltzin Quetzalcóatl, with a few supporters, fled Tula in shame. He went east to a place known as Tlapallan, or the 'red earth,' and vowed to wreak vengeance on Tula. In 1519, Hernando Cortés would be considered the avenging Quetzalcóatl, an identification on which he capitalized.

Postconquest Maya sources relate the arrival in the Maya region of a great culture hero named Kukulcan in AD 986. Kukulcan is a translation of Quetzalcóatl, or Feathered Serpent, into Yucatec Maya. He held sway at Chichen Itzá in Yucatán, it is said, until his death. The Feathered Serpent cult at Teotihuacan had promoted sacred warfare, so despite protestations about a peaceful Quetzalcóatl, such a cult at Tula and Chichen undoubtedly supported widespread warfare. Archaeology demonstrates that a series of structures were indeed begun at Chichen Itzá about this time that bear close links with those of Tula, thus apparently confirming the relationship.

Meanwhile, at Tula, Hidalgo, the Toltecs developed military and mercantile prowess, maintaining commerce and perhaps some social control far to the north and south. In the mid-twelfth century, however, the last king of Tula, Huémac, was forced to flee before growing factionalism and

141 Pyramid B, Tula. The French explorer Désiré Charnay first posited a direct connection between Tula and Chichen Itzá, and he recognized the similarity between this pyramid and the Temple of the Warriors at Chichen (ill. 150). Early Postclassic.

encroaching barbarians, repeating the pattern established by Topíltzin. Huémac settled in Chapultepec, on the western banks of Lake Texcoco in the Valley of Mexico, sources tell us. Tula was ravaged. Toltec power waned, but no later dynasty in Mesoamerica, whether Mixtec, Aztec, or Maya, would fail to invoke their glorious past.

TULA

Tula, Hidalgo, lies farther north than any other ancient Mesoamerican city. Located on the Tula River, the site is arid and windy, and although the stark surviving art and architecture suggests a military outpost, it was once a thriving urban center.

Tula was not only ravaged at its abandonment, but it was also looted systematically by the Aztecs. It has taken years of patient archaeological work to reveal the nature of the ancient city. What is now clear is that dense urban housing, laid out along a rough grid, surrounded the ceremonial core. Pyramid C is the largest of the central structures, but it was trenched for treasure and stripped of its sculpture in prehispanic times. Pyramid B is just slightly smaller, and stands today as the best-preserved major building at Tula. Its contiguous colonnades, which we can imagine to have had a perishable roof, may once have served as a royal residence. This relationship of massive pyramid to large, interior space formed by piers and courtyards recalls the arrangement at Teotihuacan, where the late Quetzalpapálotl Palace adjoins the Pyramid of the Moon, but on a reduced, even spartan scale.

141

The colonnade protects the single staircase of Pyramid B, restricting access to the summit of the pyramid. Against the four distinct levels of the structure, tenons once supported a façade of carved stone, which in turn was brightly polychromed – but only a small portion of the façade survives. Where still *in situ*, friezes of prowling jaguars, coyotes, and seated eagles with hearts in their beaks are punctuated by frontal single images of feathered, jaguar-like creatures from whose mouths emerge the

142 Atlantean columns, Pyramid B, Tula. These giant Toltec sculptures are warriors ready for battle; an *atlatl* is held at the side, and the butterfly pectoral and drum headdress are costume elements of those in combat.

faces of supernaturals with large eyes and bifurcated tongues, sometimes thought to represent the Morning Star, or Quetzalcóatl, but who in fact represents the War Serpent, whose headdress figured at Teotihuacan.

142   Great atlantean columns depicting Toltec warriors and feathered columns surmount the pyramid. The atlanteans functioned like caryatids and held up the roof; the feathered columns framed the doorway. Square pillars with warriors in low relief supported a rear chamber. Within the chamber, the atlantean Toltec warriors must have been an intimidating group. Their huge, blank faces convey the anonymity of the Toltec war machine, and the *atlatls* – or Central Mexican spearthrowers – borne in their hands threaten the viewer. Scant traces now remain of the bright polychrome that once colored these sculptures: the warriors' legs, for example, were painted in red-and-white candy stripes, usually indicative of sacrificial victims in Aztec art. Each atlantean consists of four drums held together by dowels, and both their uniformity and method of construction suggest mass production.

An innovation at Tula is the *coatepantli*, or freestanding serpent wall, which forms an L on the north side of the pyramid. With a border of geometric meanders, a single broad entablature supports a repeating relief of great rattlesnakes belching skeletal humans. Cut-out shell motifs of the sort associated in later art with Quetzalcóatl run across the top of the *coatepantli*.

Elevated benches within the palace adjoining Pyramid B may have served as thrones for the elite. Three-dimensional *chacmool* sculptures stood in front of these thrones. The discovery in the nineteenth century of similar *chacmool* figures in both Central Mexico and Yucatán helped spark the notion of Toltec hegemony, but, as we shall see below, the *chac-*

143   *mool* may be a Maya invention. The illustration here shows a fallen warrior, knife still held in place by an armband, and he holds out a flat paten, probably a receptacle for offerings brought to a ruler or deity on the throne behind. As is typical of most Toltec sculptures, the rough basalt retains its blockiness, despite the effort to create a three-dimensional effect.

Although carved stelae are not unknown in Central Mexico, they are not common, and the full-figure, frontal portraits roughly worked on Stelae 1 and 2 at Tula strongly suggest a Maya influence. Like earlier warrior stelae at Piedras Negras, the Tula stelae show the face worked in deep relief and the costume in shallow carving. In the illustration here

145   the figure is probably a ruler in warrior garb. The headdress of these

174

143 A *chacmool* from the Palace, Tula. These reclining sculptures of fallen warriors were set in front of thrones. The receptacle on the chest is for sacrificial offerings. Early Postclassic.

warriors comprises three 'bowties' surmounted by Tlaloc year-sign insignia and feathers. Among the Classic Maya and at Cacaxtla, Central Mexican motifs are worn both by warriors and by those engaged in sacrifice. These Tula stelae may reflect a strong Maya contact at the end of the Classic, and they may date to the early ninth century, when the tradition was still alive in the southern Maya lowlands. At Xochicalco, contemporary stelae called upon Maya forms and motifs in celebrating rulership; at Tula, the precedent is the Maya warrior.

During the Toltec era a distinctive type of pottery known as plumbate *144* ware was widely distributed throughout Mesoamerica. Traditionally thought of as a chronological and geographical marker of the Toltec Early Postclassic horizon, plumbate is nevertheless now generally considered to be of southwest Guatemalan origin, whence it dispersed to the rest of Mesoamerica. The name plumbate suggests a true, lead glaze of the sort used in the Old World, but in fact the glossy, metallic appearance derives from the high iron content of the clay and the reduced oxygen at the completion of firing. Indeed, plumbate perhaps deliberately imitates the

144 Plumbate wares mark the Toltec era of the ninth and tenth centuries, from Yucatán to Tula, although manufacture seems to have taken place in Chiapas. These ceramics carried new iconography across Mesoamerica, including the Maya god Pauahtun, featured on this vessel.

145 (right) Although crudely carved, this Early Postclassic stela from Tula is nevertheless dressed like a Maya warrior. The Tlaloc-and-year sign headdress is similar to that worn by the warrior in ill. 118.

sheen of metal, in much the same way as do wares made by the Chimú in the northern Andes. Even though metal objects have not been recovered from Tula itself, the Toltec era ushers in metalworking in Mesoamerica as a whole.

144   The plumbate potters often made human or effigy jars. Some of the human faces suggest portraits, while others seem to be those of deities. One unusual portrait is worked with mother-of-pearl over the terracotta, and the bearded face recalls the Toltec king, Topíltzin Quetzalcóatl, reputedly fair and bearded.

176

Tula was sacked in the late twelfth century. Its ravagers hurled the atlantean columns from the summit, interred them, and then dug a huge trench through Pyramid B, presumably looting any treasure there. The Aztecs later established a nearby hill as the locus of an important cosmic myth, so perhaps it was their ancestors, nomadic barbarians, who were among the despoilers of Tula. Whatever the truth of this, the Aztecs actively drew on the conventions and iconography of Tula when they designed their own capital.

Tula was in many ways an experiment: a seeming union of the Maya and Central Mexico, with a center farther to the north than any other in Mesoamerican history. In the end the experiment failed.

CHICHEN ITZÁ

The Toltec florescence at Chichen Itzá is far more exuberant and expansive than at Tula. Similar architectural features and motifs appear at both sites, among them serpent columns, *chacmools*, and Toltec warrior pillars, but the innovation and skill at Chichen suggests Maya stimulus and craftsmanship. To understand the transformation of Toltec Chichen, however, we must turn first to its earlier history as reflected in its architecture.

Chichen was undoubtedly occupied during the Classic, but despite many excavations and much speculation no precise chronology has so far been established for the site. What is most clear is that many buildings relate closely to the Late Classic Puuc developments at Uxmal, during the era when Teotihuacan had fallen into decline, perhaps unleashing new migrations across Mesoamerica. This early phase was then probably followed by a period of contact with a Mexicanized Maya group, the Itzá. Subsequently, Chichen began an era of construction when Toltec influences were pronounced. The relationship between the Itzá and the Toltecs remains obscure.

An examination of the site plan itself hints at the different phases of construction. The south half of the mapped portion, perhaps focussed on the use of water from the Xtoloc Cenote, follows the more chaotic and dispersed plan characteristic of Classic centers, with a rambling emphasis on a north–south axis. The north half of the site, on the other hand, has ordered colonnaded structures, mostly built during the Toltec era and perhaps all within a very short timespan, which spread from east to west, defining their own axis. A causeway or *sacbe* runs north to south, offering some unity to the plan. The *sacbe* terminates at the Sacred Cenote, a

146

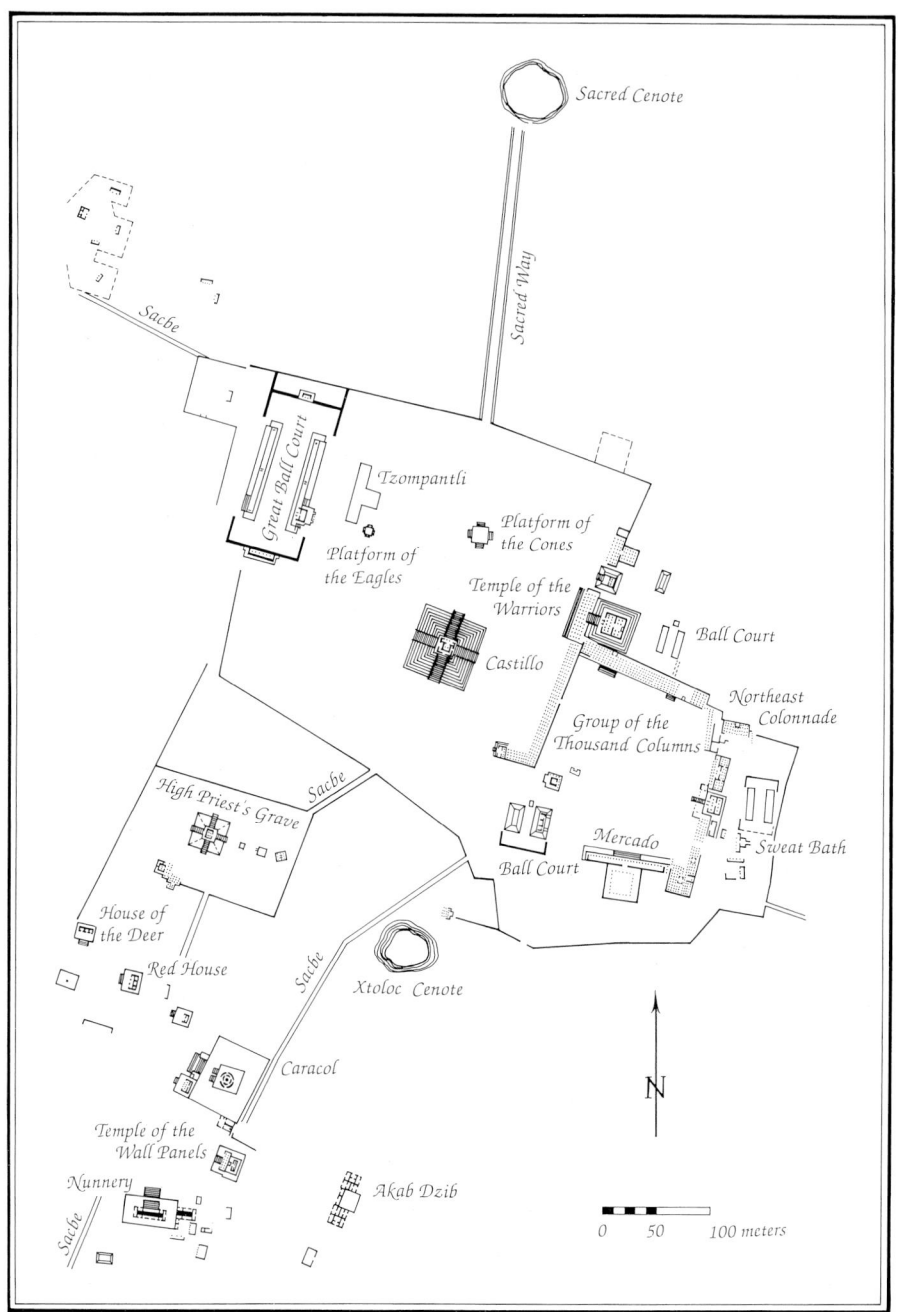

146 Plan of Chichen Itzá.

great natural sinkhole, and probably the source of the name of the site, literally, 'the mouth of the well of the Itzá.'

In 'Old' Chichen, buildings such as the Temple of the Three Lintels (a low-lying range-type structure with Chac masks at the corners) recall the galleries of the Puuc. The Red House and the House of the Deer are small temples set on raised platforms; their private rear chambers and orientation to one another suggest the plan and arrangement of the Cross Group temples at Palenque. Stonework, however, is limited to heavy blocks, and the finely cut façade masonry of the Puuc is missing. Nor are the specialized boot-shaped stones used for vaulting, and the arched doorway – so important visually at Uxmal – present at Chichen. In fact the visual refinements of negative batter and uneven spacing of doorways are entirely lacking in Chichen architecture, which in general cannot match the lyrical quality of Uxmal.

The first building that shows a dramatic shift away from more traditional Maya architectural practices is the Caracol, so-called for its plan, the core of which may deliberately resemble the section of a conch shell. Concentric vaults lead to an upper chamber via a spiral staircase. Stonework and vaulting remain of high quality. The great Mayanist Sir Eric Thompson decried its architectural style, claiming that it resembled 'a two-decker wedding cake on the square carton in which it came.' But one can equally well argue that the circles described within a trapezoid within a rectangle express an interest in geometry similar to that of Vitruvius in the Old World. As recent studies have shown, the unusual plan and placement of openings allow observation of the movements of Venus, whose synodic cycle of 236 days (Morning Star), 90 days (superior conjunction), 250 days (Evening Star), and 8 days (inferior conjunction) was of great importance to all Mesoamerican peoples. For the later Aztecs, round buildings were always dedicated to Quetzalcóatl (astronomically to be identified as Venus), who was seen with a conch shell in his manifestation as Ehécatl, the wind god.

Quetzalcóatl may have been known in earlier times – perhaps even then associated with feathered serpents, which can be seen on many monuments – but it is clear that this god grew greatly in significance during the Early Postclassic, very possibly coincident with the life of the historical individual of the same name (Topíltzin Quetzalcóatl, or Kukulcan to the Maya, literally 'Feathered Serpent'). But, as we have seen in earlier constructions at Teotihuacan, feathered serpents bear an integral relation to the cult of warfare. Just what this meant at Chichen Itzá

147
148

147 (*above*) The Caracol, Chichen Itzá. Tiny windows in the uppermost story were oriented for astronomical observations.

148 A cutaway drawing of the Caracol.

remains unclear, but the era was one when some of the tenets of Classic religion changed, with some new prominence for different deities. What provoked the changes in sacred imagery remains unclear, but ideological shifts often accompany geographic movement and chronological development.

The first Christian bishop of Yucatán, Diego de Landa, visited Chichen in the mid-sixteenth century, and made the earliest surviving European sketch of a Maya building. He drew a plan of what he called the Pyramid of Kukulcan, or Quetzalcóatl, which is now generally known as the Castillo. His plan shows a building of several levels with staircases flowing down all four sides of the building: even more remarkable is his written description of the 91 steps on a side of the structure,

149

149 The Castillo, Chichen Itzá. Like the funerary pyramids of Palenque or Tikal (ills. 99 and 104), the Castillo rises in nine distinct levels. The vertical profile and upper molding of the superstructure are characteristic of Toltec-era buildings at Chichen. This photograph was taken on the autumnal equinox, when seven serpent segments are illuminated along the main stairs.

150 Temple of the Warriors, Chichen Itzá. This structure shares the proportions and the use of a colonnade with Pyramid B of Tula, but the Chichen Itzá building is larger and far more beautiful. The colonnade in front of the structure supported a perishable roof. Early Postclassic.

with the north staircase heading off to the Sacred Cenote. Landa also noted the two 'dance platforms' in the plaza between the Castillo and the *sacbe* to the Cenote.

Landa's description includes many interesting observations for the modern viewer, not only in what he said but also in what he did not say. He noted the practice of making live human sacrifices into the sacred well (the theory of virgin sacrifice does *not* depend on Landa: for that we must turn to Tomás Lopez, who visited the site in 1552) and speculated that 'if this country possessed gold, it would be this well that would have the greater part of it.' Once Brasseur de Bourbourg rediscovered Landa's manuscript in 1864, feverish imagination focussed on the Cenote, with dreams of great treasure: divers at the turn of the century would eventually haul gold disks with Maya imagery from the well (ill. 1).

But given the state of both ruin and overgrowth that we might expect at Chichen Itzá by the sixteenth century (evidenced by Landa's own failure to see much of anything else at Chichen: he mentions only four buildings altogether and does not include, for example, the Caracol, which surely he would have been interested in and would have mentioned had he seen it), Landa's ability to see this one particular cleared portion of the site, from the Castillo to the Cenote, suggests that this quadrant had remained in perpetual use. Landa's attention was also drawn to the particular number of steps on each side of the pyramid and to the massive serpent heads on the northern face, perhaps indicating that the observation of astronomical phenomena at this building had continued unabated from the time of its construction.

Like the Caracol, the Castillo was oriented to acknowledge movements of the heavens, and on the equinoxes the nine levels of the pyramid cast a shadow that reveals a segmented serpent along the northern balustrade. The flight of stairs on that side has 92 steps, if one counts the serpent heads at the base; each of the other three staircases has 91, for a total of 365. Thus, both in numerology and orientation, the building recognizes the solar year. As we see the Castillo today, it is a radial pyramid of the sort first observed at Uaxactún in Protoclassic times and whose primary role would seem to have been to commemorate the completion of time.

Today, twice annually tens of thousands of visitors swarm onto the plaza in a modern ritual of equinox observation at the Castillo. The phenomenon was not rediscovered through careful archaeological observation and measurement, but rather seems to have grown up organically at

149

Chichen, probably by means of local Yucatec Maya, who had kept the plaza cleared in Landa's day and who had sustained memory continuously through the Colonial era.

In 1937, Mexican archaeologists exploring the Castillo found within it a complete pyramid-temple, also of nine levels, but with a single stairway to the north. Preserved in the temple chambers were a *chacmool* and jaguar throne, which remain *in situ* today. Given the pattern known at Tikal and Palenque, where earlier pyramids of nine levels held tombs of great kings, it seems likely that this one may also house a royal burial. Although the identity of that individual may never be known, the fact that this structure has always been associated with Kukulcan suggests that the great Toltec king himself may lie within the mass of the pyramid. The High Priest's Grave, a similar building that yielded a tomb in the nineteenth century, was recently restored to its ancient grandeur.

A typical feature of the final phase of construction at Chichen during the Early Postclassic is the large number of buildings distinguished by colonnades and serpent columns. The greatest of these is the Temple of the Warriors. Connecting colonnades extend to define a large, semi-enclosed court, the south side of which is flanked by the so-called Mercado and a small ballcourt. As with the Castillo, the outer building was discovered to enclose a smaller but similar structure, now known as the Temple of the Chacmool. ¹⁵⁰

One gains entry to the Temple of the Warriors itself through the maze of square pillars which would once have supported a perishable roof. Each pillar is carved on four sides. Some reliefs feature standing warriors with Toltec 'pillbox' headdress and weaponry; others show skirted figures, probably women, bearing offerings. Similar reliefs are worked on pillars of the rear chamber of Pyramid B at Tula, but the imagery there is limited to warriors. Anyone entering the Temple of the Warriors must have felt both the guidance of the offering bearers and the threat of the warriors.

The doorway at the summit of the temple is flanked by great feathered-serpent columns, whose plumed rattles once supported the door lintel. In the first chamber, a *chacmool* was set to receive offerings; in the rear chamber a great platform raised up by miniature atlanteans once served as the ruler's throne. A building such as the Temple of the Warriors may have been a seat of government, its function largely bureaucratic. The platform supports suggest the literal pillars of government, the warriors and offering bearers the means of its sustenance. The abundance

151 The *chacmool* excavated from the Platform of the Eagles, Chichen Itzá, in 1875 by Augustus LePlongeon, who unsuccessfully tried to take the stone sculpture to Philadelphia for the 1876 Centennial celebration.

of administrative buildings at Chichen Itzá is perhaps accounted for within a short construction era if we imagine that every regional governor – possibly an individual similar to the *bacab*, or governor, of the Conquest period – built a new establishment.

141 The Temple of the Warriors undoubtedly bears a striking resemblance to Mound B at Tula, but it also provides contrasts, and the scale and quality are Maya. Chambers within the Temple of the Warriors, for example, supported corbeled vaulting; stonework was elaborate and finely crafted – and the Temple is only one of several such buildings at Chichen. At Tula, the stonework seems mean and sparse by comparison, and Mound B stands alone as an impressive edifice. It is almost as if Toltec ideals were first given architectural expression at Chichen, and were then returned to Tula around the year 1000 in a provincial form. With the recent restoration of the adjacent and similar Temple of the Little Tables, the extent and repetition of the warrior template has become more obvious.

184

152 Part of the Great Ballcourt relief, Chichen Itzá. Members of the victorious team have begun to sacrifice their opponents. At the time of the Conquest, the Maya claimed that Mexicans – often specifically the Toltecs – had introduced human sacrifice to their land.

The most unusual structure at Chichen is the Great Ballcourt, the largest of all ballcourts in ancient Mesoamerica. Its playing area extends over a length of 146 m and a width of 36 m, defining a surface almost identical in size to a modern American football field, and several times the size of the average ballcourt. Unlike most Classic courts, the Great Ballcourt has vertical sides, a feature it shares with the Uxmal design. Rings, carved with entwined rattlesnakes, set into these side walls – presumably hoops through which the solid rubber ball passed or against which it was hit – are placed 8 m above the playing surface, almost out of range.

153

153 Almost too large to be played in by mere mortals, the Great Ballcourt of Chichen Itzá is the largest in Mesoamerica. Entwined serpents are carved on the rings set high in the side walls; carved reliefs adorn the sloping talus.

Carved reliefs centered under the rings reveal grisly scenes, perhaps documents of the events on the court. On the east side, two opposing teams of seven members each face one another. In the middle of the scene, the first player of the left team has decapitated the first player of the right, who, headless, kneels in front of a large ball marked by a great laughing skull. Six serpents of blood and a tree issue from the severed neck. The apparent victors on the left are more uniformly dressed than those on the right, who wear a variety of headdresses. All these ballplayers sport equipment of the sort generally associated with Classic Veracruz: *palmas*, yokes, and handstones; and the padding on arms and knees was designed to take the bruising blows of the heavy ball. Beaded scrolls with embedded *kan* crosses of the kind usually intended to represent precious liquid, particularly blood, form the background.

cf. 71–73

Three large platforms without superstructures guide supplicants toward the Sacred Cenote to the north. One of these platforms, the so-called *tzompantli*, or skull rack, is carved with rows of human skulls. A precedent for depicting human skulls on platforms exists at Uxmal, but the scale and number here indicate an increasing preoccupation with death at the end of Chichen's development, to which this platform and the two associated with it are generally attributed. Alternating jaguars and eagles devour human hearts on the Platform of the Eagles. These motifs also appear at Tula, and at both sites they linked the rituals of the ballgame to those of human sacrifice.

Three-dimensional sculpture regained prominence at Chichen during the Early Postclassic. Particular attention was given to thrones, *chacmools*, and mini-atlanteans, but even the design of plumbate pottery reflects the new concern for images in the round.

Thrones and *chacmools* are generally found together – for instance in the inner Castillo structure, Temple of the Chacmool, Mercado, and Temple of the Warriors – and they seem to replace the stela and altar of Classic times. In this we see the office itself commemorated rather than its occupant, whereas in Classic times the individual – and even the personality – who held such an office was the focus of the record. Thrones include large platforms supported by mini-atlanteans and built-in benches, but the most splendid one is the red jaguar found in the rear chamber of the inner Castillo structure. Bright red cinnabar covers the jaguar body and jade disks form feline spots in a color scheme characteristic of Classic thrones. On the seat of the red jaguar throne was a mosaic disk, or *tezcacuitlapilli*, a Toltec ornament worn at the back of the waist,

154 A wall painting from the Temple of the Warriors, Chichen Itzá. Copy and reconstruction by Ann Axtell Morris. Such scenes would seem to show a foreign conquest of Chichen in the Early Postclassic era, but there are no lakes near the site that resemble the one depicted.

assembled of precious shell and the rare turquoise traded from distant New Mexico or Arizona.

In front of the majority of thrones stand *chacmools*, the most famous of which was excavated from the Platform of the Eagles in 1875 by Augustus *151* LePlongeon, who gave them the name by which they are known today. The variety and number of Chichen *chacmools* exceeds that of Tula. Perhaps the inspiration for them came from the recumbent captives often carved beneath the feet of figures on Classic Maya stelae, an image which the Toltecs transformed into the three-dimensional idiom of their day. In recent years it has become apparent that Maya materials, forms, and iconography, often with roots in the Classic period, made a more profound impact on Central Mexico than has been previously acknowledged.

Stucco paintings have miraculously survived throughout Chichen Itzá. Scenes of Mayas and Toltecs once covered the interior of the Temple of the Warriors. In the illustration shown here, warriors with candy-striped *154* body paint are defeated by darker figures usually identified as Toltecs, who lead away their bound, naked captives. The houses depicted appear to be Maya, though the stone architecture resembles Central Mexican models. One temple stands within a body of water: is it Lake Petén Itzá, where the Mexicanized Itzá Maya may have lived before coming to Chichen? The naturalistic human renderings of earlier paintings, as at Cacaxtla or Bonampak, give way here to some shorter proportions, but non-naturalistic conventions reveal an intricate and lively landscape. Stylistically, the paintings have more in common with early Teotihuacan painting than with the tradition of Maya murals.

Pilgrimages to the Sacred Cenote continued to be made long after the Conquest, and objects dredged from the silt at the turn of this century spanned a millennium. The discovery of human skeletons confirmed the long-held suspicion that human sacrifice had taken place at the well. Among the finds rescued from the Cenote mire were offerings of copal, jade, and finely crafted repoussé gold disks. With their lively scenes of Mayas confronting Toltecs, the gold disks are not only important documents but also among the earliest Mesoamerican works where art is created from metal. The drawing of the human form and the layout of the scene, with basal panel reserved for an earth monster, reflects a development from the Maya tradition. On most of the disks warriors in Toltec dress dominate defeated Mayas.

Toltec, or Toltec-Maya, preeminence in the Early Postclassic may recall patterns of highland political dominance established earlier in Mesoamerica, and it certainly presages the tremendous success of the Aztecs. Such political success, however, does not guarantee priority in the aesthetic arena. Archaeologists may indeed prove one day that Tula truly reigned over the Maya, but the beauty, craft, and abundance of Maya works of the era will not be undermined.

THE DECLINE OF POSTCLASSIC MAYA ART AND ARCHITECTURE

Late Postclassic Maya art and architecture is mostly unimpressive, whether judged against Maya precedents or the splendors of Postclassic Central Mexico. Following the decline and abandonment of Chichen Itzá, Yucatán was loosely governed in the fourteenth and fifteenth centuries by a confederacy based at Mayapán and founded by Hunac Ceel, who had led a treacherous rebellion against Chichen. Mayapán in turn eventually fell prey to treachery and was abandoned in the mid-fifteenth century. Although remembered as a great city at the time of the Conquest, Mayapán was poorly built and highly derivative of Chichen Itzá in terms of its art and architecture.

What did set Mayapán apart, however, was its plan, which was unusual for a Mesoamerican city. It was apparently designed as a walled city, with a population that dwelt mainly within its bounds. Set at its heart is the Castillo, a small and ill-executed structure built along the lines of the Chichen Itzá Castillo. The Mayapán builders constructed the Castillo in badly cut stone held together only by mud and stucco. Mayapán lords also hauled old Chac masks from a site in the Puuc and reused them, perhaps to invoke ancient authority.

At least ten stone stelae have been discovered at Mayapán. The local limestone from which they are cut is of poor quality, but the stelae nevertheless show interesting imagery. Stela 1, for example, depicts a pair of *155* figures inside a thatched shrine, underneath a long but eroded glyphic text. Chac sits on a throne and gestures at a smaller figure, who may be a stone or clay image, placed on a box, possibly once a *tun* glyph. This stela, and the others like it, may in fact bear scenes connected with the *acantun*, a part of the New Year's ceremonies shown in the Dresden Codex and discussed by Bishop Landa.

155 Despite the absence of stelae at Chichen Itzá, the lords of Mayapán revived the practice of erecting such monuments, although with a change from the historical iconography of the Classic period. Texts do not survive, but glyph blocks construct a shrine, topped by thatch, in which the god Chac receives adoration.

156 The site of Tulum, overlooking the Caribbean.

Large ceramic figures of the Late Postclassic have come to light throughout northern Yucatán. Most prevalent among these are images of Chac, who was thought to exist both as a single deity and as a group of four. Typically, these figures hold human hearts in the hand: they must have looked gruesome anointed with blood, as Spanish chroniclers tell us they were. The Postclassic potters used a coarse clay, with various substances, or tempers, added to lower the firing temperature. Most of the figures were once brightly polychromed, some with a stucco paint that obscured imperfections. Only the most tenacious pigments, particularly blue, survive.

Christopher Columbus's son Ferdinand accompanied his father on the Fourth Voyage to the New World, and he described the great seagoing canoes of Maya traders that they saw among the Bay Islands off Honduras. Some canoes were piled high with fine cotton mantles, a standard unit of exchange at the time of the Conquest, along with other embroidered garments. Other canoes carried foodstuffs – grains, roots, and fermented corn beverage – and copper bells and hatchets, as well as cacao beans, another unit of exchange. What is clear is that the Caribbean coast sustained considerable commerce, and that commerce in turn provided the basis for the growth of Caribbean Yucatán centers. Tulum and Tancah were probably the largest of these. On his voyage to Yucatán in 1518, Juan de Grijalva sighted what may have been Tulum, and reported that the city was bustling with activity. The small shrines on the island of Cozumel and at other places along the coast may have been no more than way-stations for travelers – a function they later served for famous Caribbean pirates who worked the same coast.

Tulum is beautifully situated overlooking the Caribbean. The sea ₁₅₆ forms the fourth side of a rectangle with the three walls that surround the main ceremonial structures. Unlike Mayapán, the populace lived outside the walls. The temples of Tulum are small, even diminutive, with some doors too small for easy entry. Most buildings were shabbily constructed and heavily stuccoed. The negative batter, used to subtle effect at Uxmal, was here carried to such an extreme that some buildings look as if ready to pitch over. The cornices of Structure 16 reveal great faces, and the sharp outward slant of the structure makes the eyes bulge and the chin recede.

Elaborate paintings cover the walls – both interior and exterior – of many Tulum buildings. The palette of these works is limited to red, blue, and yellow, all outlined in black. Stiff conventional gestures as well as the proportional system suggest influences from Late Postclassic Mixtec painting. Some of the imagery also hints at contact with Central Mexico: the example here shows a deity covered with turquoise mosaic; his eyes ₁₅₇

157 Many interior wall paintings such as this one (reconstruction) have been preserved at Tulum. The figure here has the facepaint of Tezcatlipoca, an Aztec deity. Exterior stucco was also painted, but little more than traces of those brilliant pigments survive today. Late Postclassic.

are banded with what appears to be black obsidian. This masking is
177 typical of the Central Mexican deity, Tezcatlipoca. The most famous
turquoise mosaic masks to have survived the Conquest were those given
to Hernando Cortés by Motecuhzoma, but Grijalva's record shows that
he also collected some in Yucatán, and perhaps such costume elements
provided the means by which religious iconography was shared.
Although the Aztecs were not well informed about their Maya neighbors
in Yucatán, the Maya nevertheless knew a great deal about this Central
Mexican power by the eve of the Conquest. Foreign elements and even
a foreign stylistic impact, however, should not be taken as evidence that
Tulum was occupied by foreigners: the glyphs that accompany the paintings of Tulum are purely Maya, indicating that they were written for a
literate Maya audience. Outside influences do nevertheless show the
complicated iconographic interaction at the time of the Conquest. At
Santa Rita, in what is now northern Belize, Thomas Gann had copies
made of Late Postclassic paintings that were destroyed shortly after he
found them in 1896. Their style also bears a resemblance to Mixtec painting, but the unusual iconography is largely Maya, as is the writing.

Probably contemporary with the paintings of Tulum are the four surviving Maya manuscripts. Of these, the finest, most complete, and oldest
158 is the Dresden Codex, preserved today in the Dresden Sachsische
Landesbibliothek. Cortés was given several Mesoamerican manuscripts in
1519. He sent these to his king, Charles V in Vienna, where the Dresden
Codex was discovered in the eighteenth century, so it may have come as
part of the Cortés collection. The survival of the Dresden is fortuitous,
since the first bishop of Yucatán, Diego de Landa, gathered up and
burned every 'idolatrous' manuscript that he could find. Technically a
screenfold rather than a bound codex, the Dresden was painted primarily in black and red, but with bright polychrome on some pages, on a
stucco surface over native fig-bark paper. This red–and–black color
scheme may have been an ancient one for Mesoamerican writing. The
Aztecs used the metaphor *tlilli tlapalli*, 'the black, the red' to refer to
writing, although their own books did not conform to such a color
scheme. Pages are divided into registers, and the glyphs and figural
illustrations create a unified text. Most of the book is filled with auguries
and predictions most useful in an agricultural context. The rituals of the
New Year's ceremonies are described. Calculations deep into the past and
future are also related, as are the movements of the Venus gods and Chac,
the rain god. The Venus calculations also provide confirmation of the

192

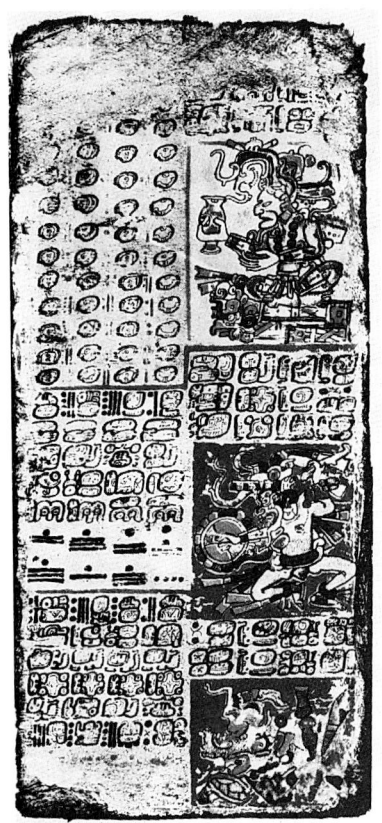

158 Pages 46 and 47 of the Dresden Codex. Perhaps dating to as early as the thirteenth century, this folding-screen book written on bark paper includes elements – such as calculations on the Venus pages shown here – that may have been copied from an older, perhaps Classic-period, manuscript. Here the Venus gods are shown as malevolent forces who cast spears.

standard correlation constant used to derive equivalents for Maya and Christian calendars.

Only a few pages survive of the Paris Codex, and the Madrid manuscript – the third of the remaining Maya texts – is less interesting artistically: it appears to have been made with great haste. Its style is very close to the paintings at Tancah. In 1973 a few pages of a fourth text, an ancient Maya Venus table, came to light, known as the Grolier Codex after the club in New York where it was first exhibited, but it is now kept in the National Museum in Mexico City.

At the time of the Conquest various highland Guatemala Maya ethnic groups – Cakchiquel, Quiché, Pokomán, and Tzutuhil – warred over territory and, perhaps more importantly, access to resources. Hilltop acropolises provided strongholds during this era, at Iximché, Utatlán, Mixco Viejo, and Cahyup, among other places. Following the Conquest of Central Mexico, the victorious Spaniards swept down into Guatemala. From Iximché the Cakchiquels took the foreigners' side against their old enemies, the Quiché. By 1527, all groups of Maya had been subjugated, and the Spanish were able to establish a new capital at Ciudad Real, the first in a series of modern capitals that would be wracked by severe earthquakes. Iximché, like the other fortified cities, was abandoned. Its plan reveals the nature of political organization there. Iximché was laid out to accommodate, architecturally, two important Cakchiquel lineages. Buildings were largely executed in duplicate: two ballcourts, two palaces, and so forth. The steep profiles of the structures, with emphasis on the tablero, recall the profiles of Classic Monte Albán.

159

Sculptural efforts continued in what is now Guatemala after the Conquest. Cortés left his sick horse with the Itzá lords in Tayasal, in the Petén, and after his departure, the horse died. Many years later, when Spaniards passed that way again, they found a stone or wooden image of the horse, enshrined in a temple! Stone cult objects have been made in Guatemala even more recently: on a hill near Chichicastenango, a stone image is still venerated by local Quiché Maya.

Both in highland Guatemala and in Yucatán the Maya quickly adopted the Latin alphabet, and various systems of romanization of Maya languages have developed. In some cases, ancient books were transcribed. The *Popol Vuh*, for example, the single most important sixteenth-century

159 Pyramidal platforms, Iximché. Cakchiquel lords reigned from Iximché at the time of Pedro Alvarado's brutal sweep into Guatemala. They helped the Spanish defeat the Quiché.

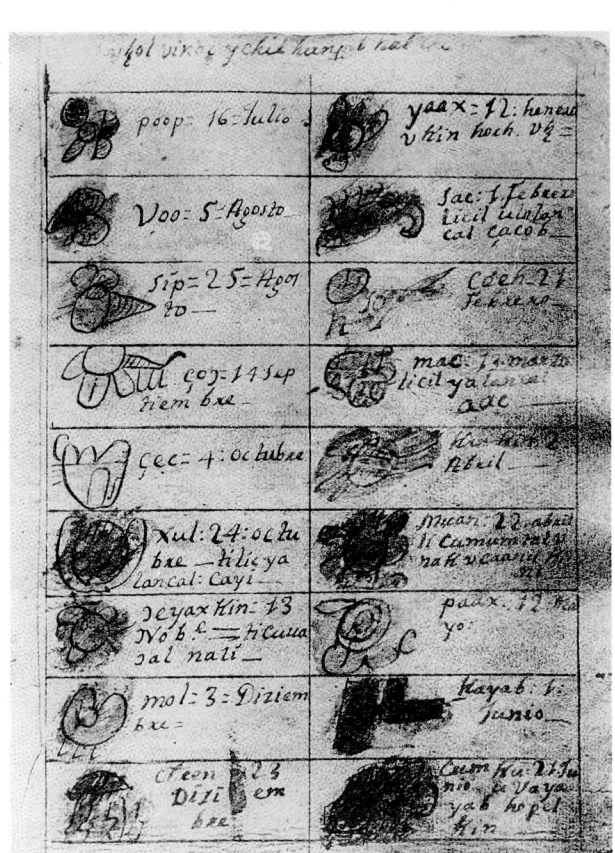

160 Page 23 from the book of Chilam Balam of Chumayel. By the time this manuscript was written during the Colonial period, the glyphs – here showing the Maya months – were little more than vestigial ornaments. The text is in Maya, written in the Roman alphabet.

document in terms of Maya religious narrative, was written down by a noble Quiché. Others, such as the many books of Chilam Balam, emphasizing cyclical historical events and prophecies, were written by noblemen in Yucatán. In the margins of the Chumayel manuscript of Chilam Balam, the eighteenth-century scribe added glyphic cartouches, perhaps from the source he was copying. The glyphs he drew had lost most of their meaning: the meaning was now carried by the alphabetic script. Here we see one step in the end of an ancient tradition and its transformation into the form that would help sustain memory in the modern world. Interestingly enough, in both Guatemala and Yucatán, through seminars led originally by Linda Schele and Nikolai Grube, many Maya have seized on the opportunity to write in glyphs once again. The ancient writing may yet live on.   160

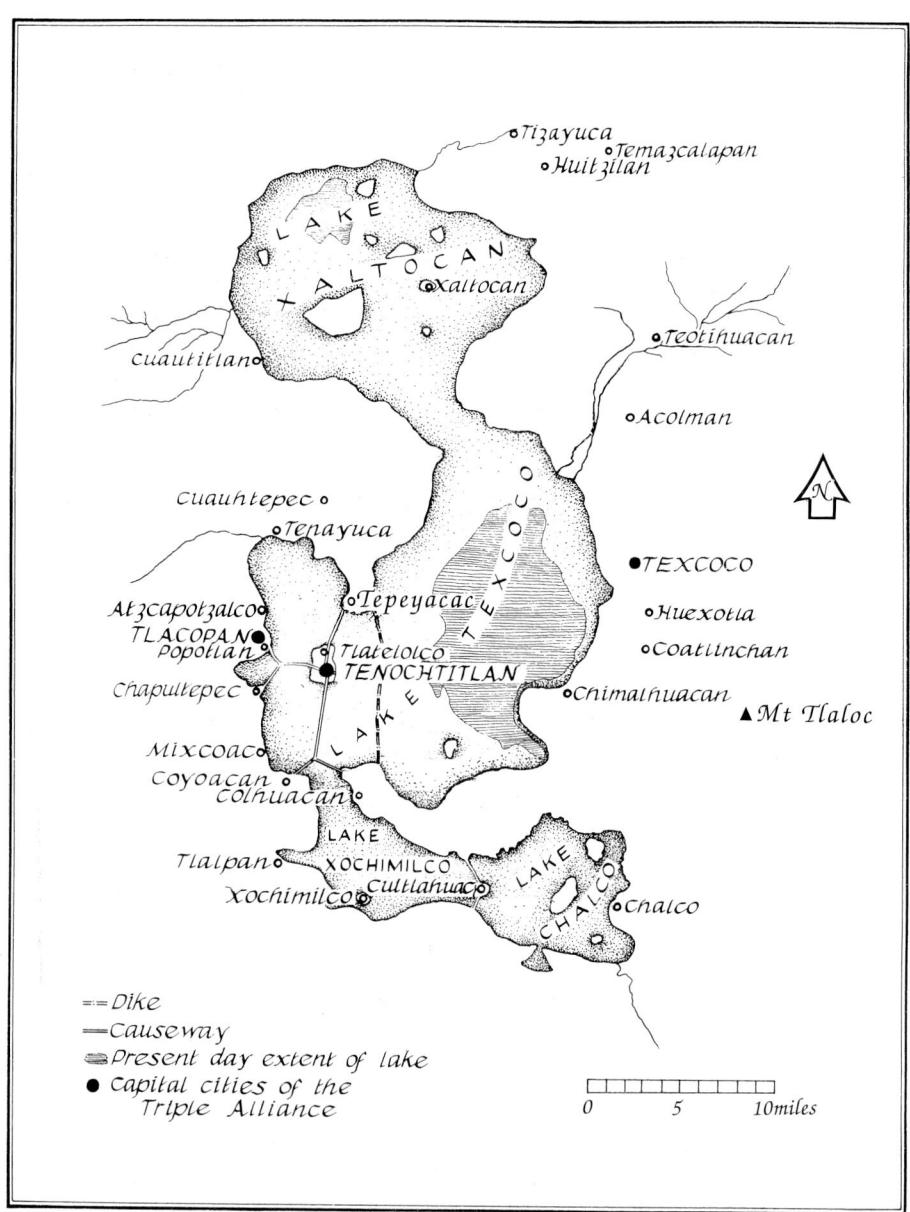

The Valley of Mexico in Aztec times.

CHAPTER NINE

The Aztecs

By 1515, rumors were circulating in Tenochtitlan, the Aztec capital, of strange occurrences. Descriptions came back to Motecuhzoma II from the coast that great floating temples or mountains had been seen on the sea. Evil omens were studied. In 1509, a bright comet had alarmed Motecuhzoma, and during the last ten years of his reign he surrounded himself with soothsayers. According to some sources, a sense of gloom prevailed in Central Mexico, particularly in the mind of the ruler. Was Quetzalcóatl, the deified king of the Toltecs, about to make a return, to wreak his vengeance? Was the fifth sun about to collapse in violent cataclysm, provoking the end of this cycle of life? The melancholic poetry of the king of neighboring Texcoco suggested the transience of life.

> Just as a painting
> We will be dimmed,
> Just as a flower
> We shall become desiccated . . .
> Ponder on this,
> Eagle and Jaguar Knights,
> Though you were carved in jade,
> Though you were made of gold,
> You also will go there
> To the land of the fleshless.
> We must all vanish,
> None may remain.

> (After N. Davies, *The Aztecs*,
> after Leon-Portilla, *Trece Poetas*, p. 50)

The Aztecs were the last of the great native Mesoamerican civilizations. Theirs was still a young culture at the time of the Spanish Conquest, and, despite the difficulties that Motecuhzoma II had in suppressing insurrection, they would probably have endured for a century or so had Hernando Cortés and his men not arrived when they did. For the Spanish, Tenochtitlan was the fulfillment of a fantasy, the sort of place they had heard of in the late medieval romances of Amadís de Gaula. Years later, when Bernal Díaz del Castillo, a soldier with Cortés, wrote a chronicle of the Conquest, he could still recall his excited first impressions of the Aztec capital:

> When we saw so many cities and villages built both on the water and on dry land, and this straight, level causeway, we couldn't resist our admiration. It was like the enchantments in the book of Amadís, because of the high towers, *cues* [pyramids] and other buildings, all of masonry, which rose from the water. Some of our soldiers asked if what we saw was not a dream.

> (*The Discovery and Conquest of Mexico*, trans.
> A. P. Maudslay, New York 1956)

AZTEC HISTORY

According to early chronicles Tenochtitlan was founded in 1345. Before that the Aztecs scraped out a mean living on the old volcanic beds south of Lake Texcoco, near the present site of the National University. (The term Aztec, referring to the dominant people of Central Mexico, became current only in the nineteenth century, but it is convenient and will be used here. They knew themselves as the Mexica.) The Aztecs served as mercenary soldiers for more successful groups. In the early fourteenth century, before they moved to Tenochtitlan, they asked their neighbors and overlords in Culhuacan for a royal bride, in order to establish a ruling lineage. The city offered the ruler's daughter. Having accepted, the Aztecs invited the Culhuacan ruler to visit. When he attended the shrine of what was reputed to be a new deity, he found instead an Aztec priest wearing the flayed skin of his daughter. In response to this obscene offense the Aztecs were driven from their settlement. Some fled into Lake Texcoco and made their way to an island, where they founded Tenochtitlan, which is now Mexico City.

Such acts characterized the early history of the Aztecs, who claimed to be nomadic barbarians, from the mythical place Aztlán, supposedly in northwest Mexico. It is in fact possible that these Náhuatl speakers were already in Central Mexico before they embarked on their search for the new home described to them by Huitzilopochtli, their cult god, a war and hunting deity. By the time of the fall of Tula, in any case, the Aztecs had Central Mexican connections, and were perhaps accomplices in the

Toltec downfall. The birth, or possibly rebirth, of Huitzilopochtli took place on a hill near Tula, according to Aztec legend. The god promised to lead them to an island in a lake, where an eagle would sit in a cactus. Tenochtitlan was that home.

During the fourteenth century the Aztecs were vassals to more powerful cities around the lake, such as Azcapotzalco to the west. With the accession of Itzcóatl in 1426, however, the situation changed dramatically. Under his leadership, and with the aid of his second-in-command, a military adviser who bore the title of Cihuacóatl, or 'Woman Snake,' the Aztecs crushed their former masters and began to consolidate the lake cities under their direction. Their military might made them greatly feared. They formed the Triple Alliance of Texcoco, Tenochtitlan, and Tlacopan, with control east and west of the lake. Under Motecuhzoma I (1440–1468), the empire grew considerably, particularly to the south. Major waterworks and causeways were built, and *chinampa* agriculture (often called 'floating gardens' but in fact a type of raised-field farming) expanded. Mid-fifteenth century crop failures and other disasters, however (a snowstorm sank *chinampas* and caused thatched roofs to collapse) afflicted Motecuhzoma's reign. Then a successful New Fire ceremony was held in 1455 to commemorate the end of the 52-year cycle (see Chapter Three), and almost miraculously, we are told, the natural disasters ceased. To prevent food shortages from occurring in the future Motecuhzoma began a new campaign of conquest to the east, particularly in the Huastec region, where agricultural bounty was more certain. Under his administration the Aztecs also began what was known as 'flowery war,' or perpetual warfare for the purpose of gaining and offering sacrificial victims, often in gladiatorial combat. The main target of such warfare was Tlaxcala, a state to the east of the Aztecs and by now largely surrounded by them.

Axayácatl and Tízoc, the rulers to succeed Motecuhzoma I, were less successful on the battlefield. Much energy was expended simply in controlling the dominion already established, and forays to the west brought the Aztecs into unsuccessful combat with the Tarascans, who had the benefit of metal weapons. Perhaps because he was jealous of its commercial success, Axayácatl brought the northern part of Tenochtitlan's island, Tlatelolco – known for its wealthy merchants – firmly under Aztec control. The last ruler of the fifteenth century, Ahuítzotl (1486–1501), was a great soldier who stepped up the pace of both conquest and sacrifice. Parts of Guatemala, Oaxaca, and even El Salvador were incorporated into the Aztec realm. These last three rulers of the fifteenth century were brothers, grandsons of Motecuhzoma I.

Motecuhzoma II, a son of Axayácatl and destined to be the last independent ruler of the Aztecs, was installed as *tlatoani*, literally 'speaker,' in 1502. (The Spaniards equated the title with emperor, but the word suggests 'he who speaks for the people.') By this time, the population of the island had grown to about 200,000. Known more for his religious preoccupations than his military skills, Motecuhzoma presided over troubled times in Aztec history, even before the landing of the Spanish. There were ominous portents, and Motecuhzoma could not be reassured. Perhaps a larger problem was the nature of the Aztec 'empire' itself. The Aztecs kept no standing armies. Following an initial subjugation, they depended on local rulers, sometimes puppets, to carry out their administration, particularly in the fulfillment of tribute and the worship of the Aztec cult god, Huitzilopochtli. By the late fifteenth century, the Aztecs were overextended. More and more, distant provinces rebelled and Aztec might had to be wielded to restore control. The 'flowery war' with Tlaxcala became more than a military exercise, and other parts of the realm grew restless. In the end the very fierceness of Aztec retaliation was their undoing, for their enemies eagerly joined forces with the Spanish. Without the Tlaxcala warriors, the Spanish Conquest of Mexico would have been delayed many years.

Even at their first sighting of the Mesoamerican mainland, Spanish explorers knew they had discovered cultures far more sophisticated than any they had encountered in all the twenty-five prior years of their dominion in the Caribbean. At first they reconnoitered the coast of Yucatán, but their progress was impeded by hostile Maya. The Spanish found them living in small cities, with ceremonial centers where 'idols' were kept in temples. The 'idols' offended and disgusted the Conquistadores, who therefore had no scruples about stripping these cult images of the gold and copper that adorned them. The metal wealth of the Postclassic Maya was negligible, however, and under the leadership of Cortés in 1519 attention was turned directly to the Valley of Mexico, to the people that informants of the time called 'Culhua' or 'Culhua-Mexica.' What drew Cortés to Tenochtitlan was not only the lure of gold; Cortés also perceived a great unknown kingdom, from which, if he could conquer it (with only 500 men and less than twenty horses in his original army), he would gain great power and prestige.

In the summer of 1519 Cortés founded Veracruz (the 'true cross') on

163 In the mid-sixteenth century, this plan of the center of the ancient Aztec capital was drawn up for Father Sahagún in a manuscript known today as the Primeros Memoriales. The Twin Pyramid of Huitzilopochtli and Tlaloc is at the top of the drawing. Beneath Quetzalcóatl, in white, are the skullrack and ballcourt. Only three doorways granted access to the precinct.

tage of the natural topography of the Valley of Mexico. The twin pyramid was framed by the volcanoes Ixtaccíhuatl and Popocatépetl to the east, recalling the positioning of the Pyramid of the Moon with Cerro Gordo *47* at Teotihuacan. The ceremonial precinct was also laid out to acknowledge the movement of heavenly bodies. During the wetter season, appropriate for agriculture, the sun rose every day behind the blue Temple of Tlaloc, the ancient rain and earth god; in the drier months, the sun emerged from the red Temple of Huitzilopochtli, whose associations with warfare, hunting, and fire were appropriate for this season. On the mornings of the two annual equinoxes, however, the sun rose between these two temples and faced the Temple of Quetzalcóatl instead. Quetzalcóatl, of course, was expected to return from the east to wreak vengeance; this temple was thus positioned to keep the vigil.

In the union between Tlaloc and Huitzilopochtli on the Templo Mayor, the old established deity of the Toltecs and perhaps Teotihuacan

164 At Malinalco, west of Tenochtitlan, a mountainside was carved in Aztec times to set temples into the living rock. The thatched roof is a modern restoration.

gave legitimacy to the new cult of the Aztecs. The two seasons of the tropical world, wet and dry, were also thus united. The Temple suggests too the expression *atltlachinolli*, literally 'water-conflagration,' used by the Aztecs to mean warfare, especially sacred war. In the very pairing of Tlaloc and Huitzilopochtli they made this metaphor the center of Aztec religion.

The Aztecs therefore echoed and recreated within the ceremonial precinct the natural topographic features surrounding Tenochtitlan. At other sites around the Valley of Mexico, however, they carved the mountains themselves, transforming natural forms into manmade ones. At Texcotzingo, a hill east of Lake Texcoco, baths and shrines were worked directly into the cliffside, making it a pleasure garden. Shrines were constructed at the summits of many other mountains in the Valley of Mexico too. At Tepeyacac, Tonantzin, an earth and mother goddess, received offerings at what would become the site of the Virgin of Guadalupe, Mexico's patron saint. To the east, the Tlaloque, or rain gods, dwelt atop Mount Tlaloc: to the Aztecs, it was the gods' raucous parties and the hurling of pots of water that led to thunderous rainstorms. At Malinalco,

164

206

a ceremonial center was built into a mountainside. The most important building there is a round structure carved out of the living rock. To enter the inner chamber one steps through an open pair of monster jaws and onto a giant tongue. A circular bench with jaguars and eagles carved as seats curves round the interior, and a deep hole of narrow diameter at the center of the floor enters the heart of the mountain. The jaguar and eagle pelts suggest that this was a chamber for the military orders of Jaguar and Eagle Knights, who may have conducted penitential rites here, perhaps offering their own blood directly into the earth.

SCULPTURE

The Aztec word that comes closest to the European concept of a god is *teotl*, which even sounded to Spanish ears like a corruption of *dios*. But the Aztec concept of *teotl* is different from the European concept of god, and although Huitzilopochtli may have been a solar deity, he was not Apollo. Rather, *teotl* called up a series of natural forces, like the Polynesian *mana*. The Aztecs captured the representation of gods in stone and wooden images, but the sacred force dwelled in sacred bundles kept separately inside shrines and temples. Huitzilopochtli's power lived in the bundle carried by the Aztecs on their long migration and then kept at the Templo Mayor, although the Spanish saw the sculptural representation as the force of idolatry.

The theme of blood sacrifice is important to much Aztec sculpture. The Spaniards were appalled by the accumulation of human blood they found on these 'idols.' One Spanish soldier, Andrés de Tapia, described the experience of seeing a large and terrifying sculpture encrusted with jewels, gold, and human blood. That sculpture may have been the great Coatlícue, or 'she of the serpent skirt,' a depiction so fearsome that it was systematically re-interred at various times after its accidental discovery in 1790 in excavations near the Cathedral, within the old ceremonial precinct. It is probably the greatest of known Aztec sculptures.

The Coatlícue is both a two-dimensional work, intricately patterned, and a great three-dimensional portrait. Like many Aztec sculptures, it is also carved on its underside with an earth monster – indeed some early students therefore erroneously imagined that it was meant to be suspended in the air. The bulky figure is shaped like a mountain, and she leans forward, pressing upon viewers and enveloping them in shadow. Particularly in profile, she also resembles the great twin pyramid. The

165

head is severed and replaced by two snakes, symbolic of flowing blood. Another snake descends from her groin, suggesting both menses and penis. Her hands and feet have been transformed into claws, and she wears a necklace of severed hands and extruded hearts. It is a nightmare cast within female form. It is also a powerful, imaginative sculpture, representative of the superb work created in Tenochtitlan in the fifty years preceding the Conquest, in what has been termed the 'metropolitan' style by George Kubler.

The Coatlícue may once have resided in the Huitzilopochtli chamber of the twin pyramid, for Coatlícue figured as Huitzilopochtli's mother in Aztec cosmic myth. According to legend, Coatlícue kept a temple shrine on a hill near Tula called Coatepec, or 'hill of snakes.' After tucking a ball of down feathers in her bosom, she became pregnant with Huitzilopochtli. Repelled by her condition, her children, especially her daughter Coyolxauhqui, plotted her death. When Coatlícue's enemies attacked her and sliced off her head, Huitzilopochtli rose from her severed trunk fully grown and armed. He banished the attackers and mutilated his evil sister, severing her extremities, so that she collapsed at the base of the shrine.

The myth was permanently commemorated at the twin pyramid. Serpents lined the base, as if to suggest the placename of Coatepec.

165 (*opposite*) Rediscovered in the late eighteenth century, this sculpture of the goddess Coatlícue was so fearsome that it was reburied for some years. Two serpents form her head, and she wears a necklace of hands and hearts.

166 A huge stone relief of Coyolxauhqui as a dismembered goddess, from the base of the twin pyramid, Tenochtitlan. Discovered by workmen excavating the cellar of a bookstore in 1978, this sculpture sparked renewed interest in the remains of the Aztec sacred center, subsequently the focus of extensive excavation.

Within the Huitzilopochtli shrine was a sculpture of that deity, probably made of wood and now lost, and perhaps the great Coatlícue, preserved in headless form. The recent excavations in the Templo Mayor have *166* revealed a great round stone of Coyolxauhqui at the foot of the pyramid, mutilated and humiliated, a permanent record of conquest and probably the place of much subsequent sacrifice. Coyolxauhqui was also understood to be the moon and Huitzilopochtli the sun, so the myth repeats the dominance of the greater heavenly body over the lesser, even the three-dimensional over the two-dimensional. In their positioning, we *162* should also recall the Codex Mendoza frontispiece and its setting of defeated figures at the bottom of the page.

Such extraordinary Aztec sculptures reveal the energy given over to the new, imperial style. As parvenus in Mesoamerica, however, the Aztecs had many established sources upon which to draw. Enclaves of foreign artists, particularly from Oaxaca, lived in Tenochtitlan, bringing their own styles and techniques to the metropolis. The Aztecs returned to Tula, Hidalgo, to sack the site, and brought back Toltec sculptures – perhaps *chacmools* and warrior figures – to their own capital. They also derived inspiration from the rich three-dimensional tradition of the Huastec region of the Gulf Coast, particularly after conquering much of the area in the mid-fifteenth century. And, almost like archaeologists, the Aztecs were continually uncovering elements of the past. The recent excavations in the Main Temple precinct revealed caches of objects, particularly of antiquities even in Aztec times. Olmec, Teotihuacano, and West Mexican stone pieces have been found as offerings. Whether through tribute, looting, or the collection of heirlooms, the Aztecs were the recipients of many works of art that they studied, cherished, buried again, or incorporated into their own visual imagery.

167 The Stone of Tízoc is essentially a historical monument, worked in the conventionalized, stiff-figured manner characteristic of manuscript painting, particularly in Oaxaca, where historical screenfold writings had long been made. Like a Roman emperor depicted as Hercules, the minor Aztec ruler Tízoc is shown in the garb of Tezcatlipoca, a principal Central Mexican Postclassic deity known by his smoking mirror and serpent foot (like God K of the Maya), and in this role he takes a captive. This image appears fifteen times on the Stone, confirming the prowess of Tízoc (in fact he was a failure as a military strategist), but set within a cosmic scheme: a solar disk defines the upper surface of the stone; gnawing schematized earth monsters with reptilian skin lie under the protagonists'

feet. From such a depiction, we can probably assume that the *tlatoani* was perceived to be divine by this time. Motecuhzoma II, we know, was thought of as a god during his lifetime.

No single image of ancient Mesoamerica is better known than the great Calendar Stone: it is reproduced on ashtrays, keychains, liquor labels, and is popular both in and outside Mexico. Like the Stone of Tízoc and the Coatlícue, the stone was saved from the axe by some farsighted priest late in the eighteenth century when it was found near the Cathedral. Despite its name, the Calendar Stone does not function as any sort of useful calendar but works rather as a record of calendrical cata-

168

167 (*above*) The Stone of Tízoc commemorates the brief reign of this minor fifteenth-century ruler. Victorious warriors hold captives by the hair, as do the victors in ills. 27 and 180. A solar disk is carved on the upper surface.

168 The great Calendar Stone features a solar diadem with an earth monster within at its center. Although not a functioning calendar by any means, the twenty day signs appear on the disk.

clysm. It represents an expanded cosmic scheme related to the one recorded on the Stone of Tízoc. The basic representation is of a solar diadem, borne by encircling fire serpents and framing the twenty day names. At the center is the outline of the day sign, Ollin, or Movement, within which are described four dates. These commemorate the Four Suns, or previous eras, known by the day names on which destruction took place. On Four Wind, for example (upper left), the world and its inhabitants were destroyed by great winds. According to the Aztecs, the current world would end in cataclysm on Four Movement, the larger date inscribed. At the very center of the stone is a frontal face bordered by clawed extremities that grasp human hearts. Cecilia Klein has identified this as the Night Sun, but it may instead be the face of the female earth monster, usually found on the hidden underside of other monuments. The image thus created is of the sun fallen on earth, the cataclysm complete, the Aztec world ended. On the Stone of Tízoc, the sun and earth were kept apart by rulership and captive sacrifice. The Calendar Stone is exhibited and reproduced as a wall panel today, but it was probably set on the ground, with blood offerings anointed on the earth monster to keep the apocalypse at bay.

Many small cult images are known, and it is likely that they were placed in shrines throughout Late Postclassic Central Mexico. Most common among these are female maize deities, generally standing figures with headdresses like temple roofcombs. Many such figures are flat and blocky, without the skilled execution of imperial works but also lacking the more horrifying Aztec imagery. The Late Postclassic potters also produced a great many female water deities, on the whole shown kneeling, with their hair tied like drapery pulls at the sides of the head. In provincial works, emphasis thus fell on more beneficient images of fertility.

Another common fertility figure, this time male, was Xipe Totec, 'our lord the flayed one.' Xipe Totec was a god of planting, and his ritual imitated the observed natural life of the maize kernel. A human skin was flayed, and a young man wore it until it rotted off (one dreads to think of the stench), allowing the new, clean youth to emerge, like a sprout from the husk of the old seed. Xipe's cult was at first celebrated most along the Gulf Coast, especially among the Huastecs, but with their conquest the cult spread in Central Mexico. Many ceramic and stone images of Xipe are known, and the flayed skin is often shown with almost loving detail. Unlike the female maize deities, the Xipe figures were also executed in rich three-dimensional forms. Three-dimensional sculpture had a sus-

169

169 The impersonator of Xipe Totec, 'our lord the flayed one,' wears the skin of a flayed human. By the end of a twenty-day ritual in honor of Xipe, the skin would have rotted. Like the shoot of a new plant, the human emerged. An imitation of a plant life cycle, Xipe Totec was a god of springtime. Note the extra set of hands that dangle limply.

tained life along the Gulf Coast, from Olmec times to the Spanish Conquest, and the sensual, rounded shapes of Xipe sculptures probably derive from this tradition.

The Gulf Coast also gave rise to a tradition of large, hollow ceramic sculptures. The recent excavations in the ceremonial precinct produced the finest such specimen ever to be found in the Valley of Mexico. Made *170* in four separate pieces, the sculpture represents a life-sized eagle warrior, poised just as if to take flight. Bits of stucco show that he was probably once covered with feathers. One of a pair who flanked a doorway, the warrior is reminiscent of the eagle jamb figure painted at Cacaxtla some *140* centuries before. The beauty and natural proportions of this figure reach out across the centuries, transcending cultural boundaries. It is difficult to believe that the same culture that made the Coatlícue would also create this Eagle Knight. What we find, nevertheless, is a pluralism of aesthetic ideals rarely matched in history, and perhaps best compared with our own era. Naturalism was enshrined at the same time as abstraction; beauty and terror both inspired awe. We know relatively little from the Aztecs of the conceptual ideals of their sculpture, but we do have a description of what a beautiful young male sacrificial victim should be:

170 Life-sized, this idealized young eagle warrior is posed as if to take flight. Gulf Coast sculptors, skilled in firing such large terracotta works, were probably the makers.

171 This large, 45-cm-long, red carnelite grasshopper, or *chapulín* in Náhuatl, probably refers to Chapultepec, or 'hill of the grasshopper,' just west of Lake Texcoco.

[He was] like something smoothed, like a tomato, or like a pebble, as if hewn of wood. [He did] not [have] curly hair, [but] straight, long hair; [he had] no scabs, pustules, or boils . . . not with a gross face, nor a downcast one; not flat-nosed nor with wide nostrils, nor with an arched . . . nose nor a bulbous nose, nor bent nor twisted nor crooked – but his nose should be well-placed, straight . . . [he should be] not emaciated, nor fat, nor big-bellied, nor of prominent, hatchet-shaped navel, nor of wrinkled stomach . . . nor of flabby buttocks or thighs . . .

(Florentine Codex, Book 4, Sixth Chapter, trans. Dibble and Anderson)

In the face of the Eagle Knight, we see that perfection.

Naturalism inspired many Aztec works of small scale, among them fine images of squash, cacti, shells, and snakes. The bright red carnelite grasshopper shown here may have functioned as some kind of emblem for the *171* place Chapultepec, the source of fresh spring water for Tenochtitlan, for its name means 'hill of the grasshopper.'

Other Aztec sculptures also served as temple or palace furnishings. *Chacmools* had probably long been used as receptacles for human hearts, and a number of Aztec ones have been found. The earliest known Aztec *chacmool* was recently discovered *in situ* on the Tlaloc side of the twin pyramid, in an early context. It may even have been brought from Tula, with other looted treasures. It is the only *chacmool* to survive with bright polychrome, but most Aztec sculptures were probably painted. In fact, given modern taste, we might be unpleasantly surprised if we were to see them in their original condition. Another very sensuously carved *chac-* *172* *mool* excavated in 1943 outside the ceremonial precinct could have been moved away from the temple compound at the time of the Conquest.

215

172 The recumbent figure of this rain god *chacmool* wears a Tlaloc mask and a pendant with an archaistic motif, as if to refer to antiquity in general. The underside of the monument is worked with aquatic motifs.

The recumbent figure wears a Tlaloc mask and bears a *cuauhxicalli*, a vessel for sacrificed human hearts, on his chest. Tlaloc insignia are inscribed on the vessel's upper surface. The underside of the whole sculpture is worked with a Tlaloc among other aquatic motifs, as if the monument were floating in a liminal state. Like the dead and dying figures at Cacaxtla, this *chacmool* wears a jade plaque from an earlier culture (it would appear to be a Classic Zapotec or Maya piece), as if to associate the antique form of the sculpture with an antique culture. The *chacmool* seems very likely therefore to have come from the Tlaloc side of the twin pyramid, which bore other symbols of antiquity as well.

173   The Temple Stone was found near the palace of Motecuhzoma II in 1831, and probably functioned as his throne, although it has been called the 'Monument of Sacred War.' It records the date in 1507 of the last New Fire ceremony, normally celebrated at the completion of a 52-year cycle. On the sides, seated deities draw blood from their loins, and this blood drawn in penance supports the legitimate ruler. Above, Motecuhzoma would be seated on an earth monster, with the solar disk at his back. In

216

173 The Temple Stone. Also known as the 'Monument of Sacred War,' this miniature temple was probably a throne in Motecuhzoma II's palace. When the lord was seated, he would appear to carry the sun on his back.

this way, he bore the sun; he also prevented it from collapsing onto the earth. The *tlatoani* was thus the conduit of order, the figure whose very person keeps the upperworld and underworld in their appropriate positions.

MINOR ARTS

Many musical instruments were worked with designs that indicate their importance in Aztec ritual life. A number of *teponaztlis*, the higher-toned, longitudinal drums, and *huéhuetls*, the deeper, upright drums, have survived from prehispanic times. A fine *huéhuetl*, reputedly from 174 Malinalco, may have been associated with the orders of Jaguar and Eagle Knights there and might even have been used to accompany rites in the Malinalco chambers. The drum carries the date of the destruction of the 164 Fifth Sun, Four Movement. Jaguars and eagles dance ecstatically around the instrument, and all emit speech scrolls of the twined *atltlachinolli*, 'water-conflagration,' or warfare symbols. They also carry banners to

175 (*below*) A large gold pectoral from Tomb 7, Monte Albán, Late Postclassic. Below the skeletal deity's head are signs in the Mixtec calendrical system. Both filigree and lost-wax techniques were mastered by these Oaxacan craftsmen.

174 A *huéhuetl*, or large upright drum, reportedly from Malinalco (ill. 164). Deerhide would have been stretched across the top of the cylinder, and the drum was played with the hand. The *teponaztli*, a longitudinal drum, was played with drumsticks.

indicate that they are sacrificial victims, as if perhaps to pronounce their willingness to be sacrificed to the Fifth Sun, and such sacrificial events were probably accompanied by music.

Other fine Aztec works were made of feathers or covered with feather mosaic, turquoise mosaic, and gold. Little of the goldwork survives, thanks to the destructive lust of the Conquistadores. Virtually the only pieces for us to study and admire are of Mixtec manufacture, discovered in Oaxaca during this century. In Tenochtitlan, the Mixtecs were recognized as the greatest metalworkers of the era, and an enclave lived there to practice their craft. Oaxaca, the region of the Zapotecs and Mixtecs,

176 Perhaps sent to Charles V by Cortés, this exotic Aztec feather headdress has been preserved in Vienna since the Conquest. Some scholars have speculated that Motecuhzoma II himself might have worn it.

was spared much of the violent destruction of the Conquest, and in the immediate aftermath the area was not identified as a great source of raw metals. Cortés received much of Oaxaca as a grant from Charles V, but luckily did not know the location of all Mixtec gold treasure. In 1932 Alfonso Caso excavated a royal tomb on Monte Albán that had been re-used by the Mixtecs in Late Postclassic times. He discovered a superb cache there of over a hundred gold objects, along with fine artifacts of silver, pearl, jade, rock crystal, obsidian, and bone. At last the skills that earned Dürer's accolades became evident to the twentieth century. The most spectacular object is the large pectoral of a skeletal deity, worked in *175* a lost-wax method.

The malleability, color, and inert nature of gold have always made it an appealing raw material, although the Aztecs valued jade more highly. They referred to gold as *teocuícatl*, or 'excrement of the gods.' Given the destruction of the Conquest, we will probably never know the nature of Aztec goldwork to any greater extent.

High-quality Aztec feather painting (a mosaic technique, really, of finely cut exotic bird feathers) has also not survived, although detailed feather paintings are known with Postconquest, Christian imagery. Aztec headdresses and shields on the other hand have endured. At an 1890 conference in Paris, Zelia Nuttall first suggested that the fine featherwork 176 preserved in Vienna might be Motecuhzoma's headdress. To prove its wearability, she made and wore a reconstruction. With its extraordinary green quetzal and blue cotinga feathers, gold, and beads, the original headdress certainly may have been a royal garment, but there is no evidence that it was the property of Motecuhzoma II in particular. Illustrations in the chapter on featherworking in the Florentine Codex, the sixteenth-century encyclopedia (see below), show the making of a similar headdress.

Motecuhzoma II sent Cortés a chest containing turquoise mosaic masks and feather costumes of various deities in 1519. Guided by his interpreters to put on the Quetzalcóatl costume, Cortés strengthened the perception that he was that deity. Such costumes and masks may have

177 Probably part of a whole costume of the deity Tezcatlipoca, this mask is made of turquoise mosaic, obsidian, and gold pyrites over a human skull.

178 Ceramic cup from Cholula, with decoration of three jaguars. Bright polychrome slip was used by Cholula potters to draw intricate patterns and figural scenes. The pottery was in demand throughout the Valley of Mexico at the time of the Conquest.

179 (*right*) Hundreds of Tlaloc effigies were unearthed from the Tlaloc side of the Templo Mayor. This unusual ceramic effigy vessel was painted bright blue after firing.

been offered to the earlier explorer Grijalva as well. These curiosities were sent to Europe, but it is no longer certain which ones were in Motecuhzoma's gift. One of the masks in the British Museum is of the deity Tezcatlipoca, with black obsidian bands set against a bright blue *177* face. Pyrites form the eyes. Unlike many of the other masks, this mosaic is built over a human skull, and its wearer would have been unable to see.

Bernal Díaz described the sumptuous meals prepared for Motecuhzoma II. Tens of dishes would be served up for the king's pleasure, including turkey, boar, venison, rabbit, quail, duck, pigeon, and human flesh. Motecuhzoma would sit and eat behind a screen, alone. Díaz informs us that Motecuhzoma ate only from Cholula pottery (so *178* named although it was made at various places in the Valley of Puebla). With their rich polychrome slip design over fine, thin pottery, Cholula wares were far superior to the Aztec product. Many designs and color patterns can be related to the Borgia group of manuscripts (see below).

Some unusual ceramics have been recovered from the Templo Mayor excavations. Two fine vessels were found on the Huitzilopochtli side that were made in an archaizing fashion, imitating Toltec work, and the cremated bones they contained could be royal remains, perhaps even of *179* Motecuhzoma I. Remarkable bright blue pigment was preserved on a Tlaloc effigy vessel, found on the Tlaloc side of the temple. Like many fifteenth- and sixteenth-century Aztec Tlaloc images, the deity has the braided 'cruller' over his nose that characterizes the Classic Maya Jaguar God of the Underworld, and may link ancient concepts of war.

Shortly after his accession to power in 1426, Itzcóatl decided to have history rewritten. Manuscripts were collected and destroyed, making way for a new record of official Aztec history and religion. Nevertheless, it is obvious from the variety of historical and mythic information later written down in the Roman alphabet that a great diversity of religious and historical ideas continued long after Itzcóatl's edict. The supremacy of Huitzilopochtli as a cult god was fought throughout the region, and in fact Tezcatlipoca seems to have remained the supreme deity among those claiming Toltec descent.

Sadly the Spanish Conquest was more effective than Itzcóatl's purge, and, even though books were common among the Aztecs, no manuscript survives that can be attributed to Preconquest Tenochtitlan. Examples from other regions remained intact, however, and various schools of manuscript painting thrived for fifty years after the Conquest. Books served many purposes for the Aztecs: genealogies were kept, 260-day ritual calendars were consulted, and religious esoterica were guarded in screenfold manuscripts. For generations after the Conquest, Mixtec screenfolds were brought to Colonial courts to document testimony in land disputes. Painted in thin stucco on deer hide, these manuscripts were sometimes scraped and re-used; for sixteenth- and seventeenth-century purposes, 'idolatrous' lore might be purged in order to allow legal use of the genealogical records. The Codex Selden relates the genealogy of one prominent Mixtec family. Red guidelines indicate the boustrophedon, or back-and-forth, reading order of the manuscript, and we can observe the *180* highly conventionalized nature of representation. In the section illustrated here, the Postclassic heroine 6 Monkey is seen avenging the murder of her father and brothers. Footprints indicate travel or movement: at the center of the page, 6 Monkey (her name tied to her like a cartoon balloon) hides in a hill, as she has been counseled to do. She later leads a

180 Page 6, Codex Selden. Although additions were made after the Conquest to this Mixtec manuscript on deerskin, most of the pages were completed in prehispanic times. A young woman named 6 Monkey is the heroine of this portion of the genealogy. The story reads from bottom to top, following the footprints. In the second register from the top, as the footprints show, 6 Monkey goes into hiding – and only her lower body is visible.

181 Folio 1, Codex Féjerváry-Mayer. The cover page of this prehispanic manuscript presents concepts of the world order: the four cardinal points are associated with particular colors, birds, and trees with a maltese-cross frame of 260 dots, referring to the calendar round and its completion.

cf. 27, 167 successful military campaign, and is depicted holding her subjugated captive in the posture characteristic of male victors.

There are many surviving Mixtec genealogies, and although they are embedded within a context of mythic origins (some families derive from trees, others from stones), they are essentially historical. They are also not without interesting contradictions: the heroic 8 Deer of one narration is just another captive in a different history. The complexity of such interlocked families and narratives is what gives modern scholars a better view of ancient life and political organization.

Another collection of Postclassic manuscripts to survive is known as the Borgia Group, so named after the largest and most complex of these screenfolds, now in Rome. Of these, the Borgia, Cospi, and Vaticanus B manuscripts may share a common origin in Puebla or Tlaxcala. Most of

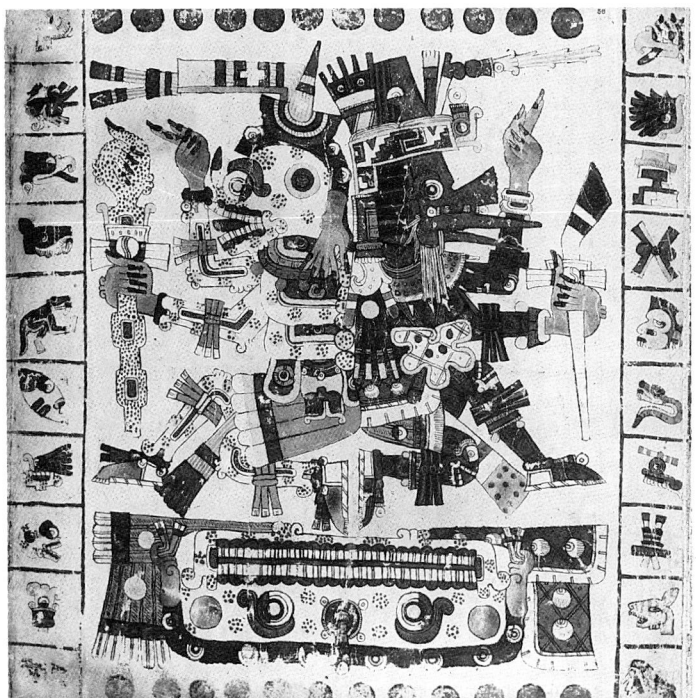

182 Page 56, Codex Borgia. Framing one end of a divination cycle are these paired deities, Mictlantecuhtli and Quetzalcóatl in the guise of Ehécatl, the wind god. They stand over an open-mouthed earth monster, and the twenty day names run along the sides of the page.

the Borgia manuscripts incorporate divining almanacs of the 260-day calendar with other religious material. No histories are known. Calendrical and cosmic concerns are expressed together on the front page of the Féjerváry-Mayer, and the page has the character of a medieval carpet *181* page. Two-hundred-and-sixty dots are laid out in the form of a maltese cross, recalling the Maya completion sign. Radiating in four directions *cf. 24* from the image of the sacrificed body of Xiutecuhtli, the young fire god, are four world trees surmounted by four directional birds. Such a picture conveys notions of world creation and world order within the frame of the calendar.

The Borgia manuscript is the single most complex surviving *182* Mesoamerican book. The Venus pages in the center of the manuscript contain the travels of Quetzalcóatl in the underworld. The divination

225

pages of the 260-day calendar have a border of paired deities. The opposition of Mictlantecuhtli, the chief death god, with Ehécatl, an aspect of Quetzalcóatl, emphasizes the principle of duality in Mesoamerican thought, for Quetzalcóatl was also perceived to be a creator god.

THE EARLY POSTCONQUEST ERA

After the Conquest, the production of indigenous art and architecture slowly ceased, except for personal residences and attire. Temples were dismantled and their stones used to build the churches, civic buildings, and houses of the conquerors. Disease, strife, and despair all took their toll, as did forced labor in mines. In the sixteenth-century history of New Spain, the only light for the native population was the arrival of mendicant preaching friars. Charles V charged three religious orders, the Franciscans, Dominicans, and Augustinians, with the conversion of the new land. They came in groups of twelve, emulating the Apostles, and among their number were educated, enlightened individuals, instilled with ideas of the Renaissance. Just as Europe was in the throes of the Reformation, the new souls for conversion presented the Catholic church with another and different sort of challenge. Millions were converted and they needed schools and churches. This gave rise to one of the most energetic building programs in the history of the world. Hundreds of monastic complexes were constructed with native labor under the direction of friars who rarely had any knowledge of architectural principles. The Franciscans arrived first and built establishments throughout the Valley of Mexico; Dominicans came next and entered Oaxaca. The Augustinians, who arrived last, led the conversion to the north.

The predominant type of church constructed was the open-air chapel, a medieval form revived to meet the needs of the Mesoamerican population, who were unused to large interior spaces. The architecture was Christian, but Precolumbian imagery nevertheless stood under and within in both obvious and subtle ways. In some cases, Mesoamerican ideas were used to convey the new teachings of Christianity. At the Augustinian establishment at Ixmiquilpan, the paintings that line the nave show Eagle and Jaguar Knights doing battle with centaurs, who are portrayed as villains. On one level, we can understand this to show a converted indigenous population in native armor fighting the pagan Chichimecs of the north. The Spaniards, however, were interpreted at

183 Battle of eagle knights and centaurs, Postconquest wall painting, Ixmiquilpan, Hidalgo. Under the guidance of Augustinian friars, native artists incorporated European and Precolumbian motifs in several sixteenth-century programs of decoration.

first by native Mesoamericans to be combinations of man–horse, like centaurs, and so we must also see an indigenous spirit in these paintings.

Much of the architectural sculpture associated with the monastic establishments was worked in very low relief, a technique typical of Aztec *cf. 165* ornament but one which also came about when woodcut images were transferred to three-dimensional forms. Many of the large atrium crosses, however, had obsidian embedded in them, recalling an Aztec practice of incorporating an obsidian heart into many sculptures.

The two Precolumbian art forms that succeeded above all others in the early Colonial era were manuscript making and feather painting. Native scribes recorded histories, divinatory almanacs, and religious tracts, generally under the guidance of Franciscan priests. The earliest manuscript of the early Colonial period, the Codex Borbonicus, was long thought to pre-date the Conquest, but it has now been shown that throughout this screenfold on native paper, spaces were left for romanized glosses. The first part of the manuscript is a divinatory guide of the

227

184 Folio 34, Codex Borbonicus. Calendar priests feed the flames during a New Fire ceremony. Aztec deities are drawn along the left-hand side of the page: at the right, a pregnant woman is shown sequestered within doors, as prescribed by the ceremony.

260 days, with auguries and patrons. The two center pages relate complex notions of calendar and time, and the last pages chart the 365-day cycle and the feasts of the months. The European influence is most obvious in *184* this last section. In the drawing of a New Fire ceremony, for instance, fire priests hold bound fagots, while the depiction of the knots shows a knowledge of perspective.

185 (*opposite*) Folio 47, Codex Mendoza. Organized by province, the center section of the Codex Mendoza is a copy of Motecuhzoma II's tribute roll. Here, luxurious goods from the far southern reaches of Aztec dominion in Guatemala – jaguar pelts and bird feathers – are illustrated as the required payment. Province names run down the left-hand side of the page.

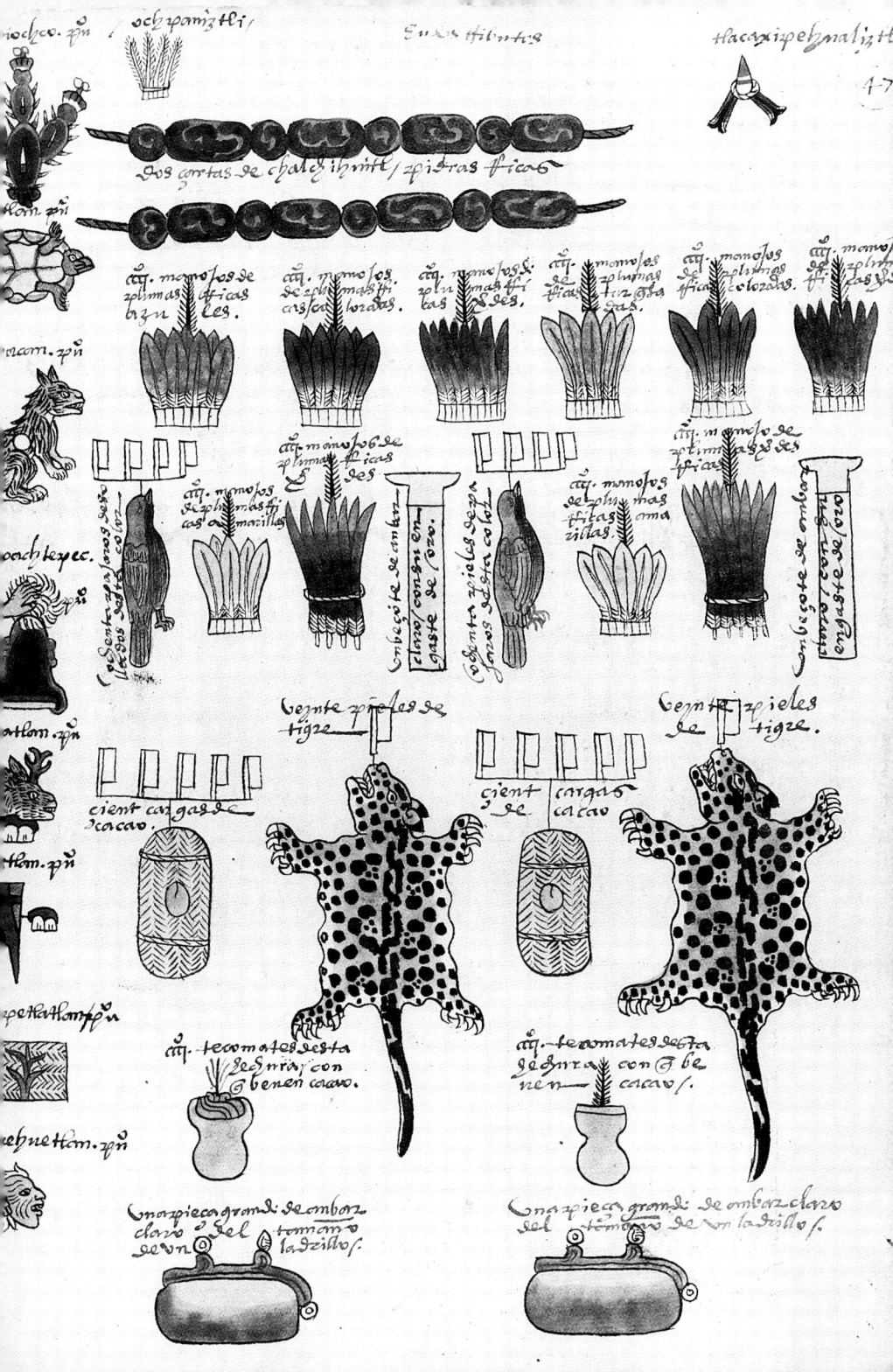

Dos sartas de chalchihuitl / piedras ficas

ccc. moxoxos de plumas ficas azules.

ccc. moxoxos de plumas ficas coloradas.

ccc. moxoxos de plumas ficas coloradas.

ccc. moxoxos de plumas ficas tregadas.

ccc. moxoxos de plumas coloradas ficas.

ccc. moxoxos de plumas ficas.

ccc. moxoxos de plumas ficas amarillas.

ccc. moxoxos de plumas ficas coloradas.

cabeçote se embra tores con engaste de oro.

ccc. moxoxos de plumas ficas coloradas.

ccc. moxoxos de plumas ficas amarillas.

ccc. moxoxos de plumas ficas verdes.

cabeçote se embra tores con engaste de oro.

veinte pieles de tigre.

veinte pieles de tigre.

cient cargas de cacao.

cient cargas de cacao.

ccc. tecomates desta hechura con que benen cacao.

ccc. tecomates desta hechura con que benen cacao.

una pieça grande de ombar claro del tomaño de un ladrillo.

una pieça grande de ombar claro del tomaño de un ladrillo.

European paper soon replaced native fig paper entirely; the screenfold gave way to the bound book. But indigenous painting traditions and conventions survived for some time, perhaps inspired by prehispanic books still available for consultation. The frontispiece of the Codex *162* Mendoza may have its roots in a carpet page such as page 1 of the *181, 185* Féjerváry-Mayer. The luxurious tribute list of the Mendoza must have been copied directly from a similar record kept by Motecuhzoma, but – as Donald Robertson has pointed out – transferred from screenfold to codex form.

Ostensibly, the aim of the friars was to understand indigenous religion in order to extirpate it, but in the *Florentine Codex, The General History of the Things of New Spain* (*c.* 1566–77; 1585) – a thirteen-book encyclopedia organized along the lines of a medieval compendium such as that of Bartholamaeus Anglicus – one senses that Father Bernardino de Sahagún's goals exceeded mere religious needs. His interest in the New World was truly catholic. His record, written in Náhuatl and illustrated by native artists, is the single most important document of Aztec life. Father Sahagún's manuscript went through several drafts, and illustrations *163* for an early version show stronger Precolumbian traditions, perhaps copied, and less concern for shading and landscape, both of which interest the illustrators of the later Florentine Codex. In one volume of the later work, information on metalwork and feather painting is lavishly illustrated, and a headdress like the one in Vienna today is shown. Background landscapes include European castles, surely drawn after some European book. The sole copy, known as the Florentine Codex, survived only because it was delivered into Italian, not xenophobic Spanish, hands.

This surviving manuscript tradition was the final stage of Mesoamerican art and architecture. By the end of the sixteenth century the intellectual friars had been supplanted by parish priests who took less interest in their native flocks. The ravaged indigenous population had shrunk by now from twenty million on the eve of the Conquest to a mere million. Perhaps not quite the cosmic cataclysm predicted by the Aztecs, it was nevertheless one of the worst catastrophes in history. There were even too many churches for the population by 1580. The great art and architecture of Mesoamerica vanished under modern buildings or encroaching wild growth, or in other instances was simply destroyed. Not until the end of the eighteenth century would modern man begin the serious investigation of Mesoamerican antiquities.

Select bibliography

Abbreviations

BAEB   Bureau of American Ethnology, Bulletin
CIW   Carnegie Institution of Washington
HMAI   Handbook of Middle American Indians
INAH   Instituto Nacional de Antropologia e Historia
MARI   Middle American Research Institute, Tulane University
PARI   Pre-Columbian Art Research Institute, San Francisco
PMM   Peabody Museum, Harvard University, Memoirs
PMP   Peabody Museum, Harvard University, Papers
RRAMW   Research Reports on Ancient Maya Writing

1 Introduction

For an alternative survey in English of Mesoamerican Precolumbian art and archaeology, one might turn to George Kubler, *Art and Architecture of Ancient America*, 3rd edition (Pelican), 1984 (it also includes the art and architecture of Central and South America). The 16 volumes and 5 supplements of the *Handbook of Middle American Indians*, ed. Robert Wauchope et al. (Univ. Texas), 1964–95, offer the most comprehensive consideration of all aspects of Mesoamerica. Mary Miller and Karl Taube's *Gods and Symbols of Ancient Mexico and the Maya* (Thames and Hudson), 1993, provides a comprehensive guide to the religious symbolism of Mesoamerican art. Valuable archaeological surveys that encompass the entire Mesoamerican region include Muriel Porter Weaver's *The Aztecs, Maya, and Their Predecessors*, 3rd edition (Academic Press), 1993; and Michael Coe's paired volumes, *Mexico*, 4th edition (Thames and Hudson), 1994, and *The Maya*, 5th edition (Thames and Hudson), 1993. Many older art historical surveys have sharp insights into particular works of art, even if some of the archaeological data is now out of date: Pál Kelemen, *Medieval American Art* (Macmillan), 1943, Elizabeth Easby and John Scott, *Before Cortés: Sculpture of Middle America* (Metropolitan Museum of Art), 1970; Miguel Covarrubias, *Indian Art of Mexico and Central America* (Knopf), 1957, José Pijoán, *Historia del arte precolombino* (*Summa Artis X*), Barcelona, 1952; Ignacio Marquina, *Arquitectura Prehispánica*, Mexico City, 1951; Doris Heyden and Paul Gendrop, *Pre-Columbian Architecture of Mesoamerica* (Abrams), 1975. Eduard Seler, *Gesammelte Abhandlungen*, Berlin, 1902–23. New journals, among them *RES*, *Mexikon*, *Latin American Antiquity*, and *Ancient Mesoamerica*, serve as up-to-the-minute sources.

The term 'Mesoamerica' has been in use since mid-century (Paul Kirchhoff, 'Mesoamerica,' *Acta Americana* 1, 1943: 92–107). Nigel Davies has recently re-examined and evaluated diffusionist thought in a highly readable book (*Voyagers to the New World*, (W. Morrow), 1979). Bernal Díaz wrote the most comprehensive and lucid eye-witness report of the Conquest (*The Discovery and Conquest of Mexico*, trans. A.P. Maudslay, New York, 1956). Of all early travelers who looked at ancient ruins, John Lloyd Stephens' accounts are the most interesting today (*Incidents of Travel in Central America, Chiapas, and Yucatán*, 2 vols. (Harper), 1841). Bernardino de Sahagún's *Florentine Codex, A General History of the Things of New Spain*, trans. A.J.O. Anderson and C. Dibble, in 13 books (School of American Research and University of Utah), 1950–1982, is an encyclopedia of prehispanic life in Central Mexico.

Gordon Willey and Jeremy Sabloff have written a history of archaeological exploration (*A History of American Archaeology*, 3rd edition (W.H. Freeman), 1993), but like R.E.W. Adams' 'Maya Archaeology 1958–1968, A Review,' *Latin American Research Review* 4:2, 1969, 3–45, there is limited consideration of ancient art. One of the most interesting historical views was written by an historian: Benjamin Keen, *The Aztec Image in Western Thought* (Rutgers), 1971.

2 The Olmecs

A single volume published in Spanish, *Los olmecas en mesoamerica*, ed. John Clark (Citibank), 1994, offers up-to-date archaeology and art history of the Olmec, including information on recent excavations at Teopantecuanitlan, El Manatí, and San Lorenzo. General books and collections of essays to consult on Olmec subjects include: *Regional Perspectives on the Olmecs*, eds. Robert Sharer and David Grove (Cambridge), 1989; Beatriz de la Fuente, *Los hombres de piedra*, 2nd edition (UNAM), 1984; Elizabeth Benson, ed., *The Olmec and their Neighbors* (Dumbarton Oaks), 1982; Ignacio Bernal, *The Olmec World* (Univ. California), 1969; Michael D. Coe *America's First Civilization: Discovering the Olmec* (American Heritage), 1968; and Susan Milbrath, 'A Study of Olmec Sculptural Chronology,' *Dumbarton Oaks Studies in Pre-Columbian Art and Archaeology* no. 23, 1979. Coe has written on San Lorenzo (with Richard Diehl): *In the Land of the Olmec*, 2 vols. (Univ. Texas), 1980; for La Venta, see P. Drucker, Robert Heizer, and R.J. Squier, *Excavations at La Venta, Tabasco, 1955*, BAEB 170. On early ceramic art: Michael D. Coe, *The Jaguar's Children: Preclassic Central Mexico* (Metropolitan Museum of Art), 1965; Carlo Gay, *Xochipala: The Beginnings of Olmec Art* (Art Museum, Princeton), 1972. Painting and petroglyphs are discussed by David C. Grove, 'The Olmec Paintings of Oxtotitlan Cave,' *Dumbarton Oaks Studies in Pre-Columbian Art and Archaeology* no. 6, 1970; and Grove, *Chalcatzingo: Excavations on the Olmec Frontier* (Thames and Hudson), 1984. P. David Joralemon has written on the iconography: 'A Study of Olmec Iconography,' *Dumbarton Oaks Studies in Pre-Columbian Art and Archaeology* no. 7, 1971; also, 'The Olmec Dragon: A Study in Pre-Columbian Iconography,' in H.B. Nicholson, *Origins of Religious Art and Iconography in Preclassic Mesoamerica* (UCLA), 1976, 27–72; see also Kent Reilly, 'The Shaman in Transformation Pose: A Study of the Theme of Rulership in Olmec Art,' *Record of the Art Museum, Princeton University*, 1990. The theory of 'recycled' monuments has been articulated by James Porter, 'Olmec Colossal Heads as Recarved Thrones,' *RES* 17/18, 1989: 22–29.

3 The Late Formative

The most stunning addition to the Late Formative corpus was published by F. Winfield Capitaine, 'La Estela 1 de La Mojarra, Veracruz, Mexico,' *RRAMW* 16, 1988. For the evolution of writing and its early forms, as well as important decipherments, see Michael D. Coe, 'Early Steps in the Evolution of Maya Writing,' in H.B. Nicholson, *Origins of Religious Art and Iconography in Preclassic Mesoamerica* (UCLA), 109–22; Matthew Stirling, 'An Initial Series from Tres Zapotes, Vera Cruz, Mexico,' *National Geographic Society, Contributed Technical Papers*, 1:1 1940; J. Eric S. Thompson, *Maya Hieroglyphic Writing*, 2nd edition (Univ. Oklahoma), 1960; Alfonso Caso, *Los calendarios prehispánicos* (UNAM), 1967; Heinrich Berlin, 'El glifo 'emblema' en las inscripciones mayas,' *Journal de la Société des Americanistes*, NS 47, 1958, 111–19; Tatiana Proskouriakoff, 'Historical Implications of a Pattern of Dates at Piedras Negras,' *American Antiquity* 25, 1960, 454–75; and 'The Lords of the Maya Realm,' *Expedition* 4:1, 1961, 14–21; Yuri Knorosov, *The Writing of the Maya Indians*, trans. and ed. Tatiana Proskouriakoff and Sophie Coe, *Harvard University Russian Translation Series 4*, 1967. Joyce Marcus's *Mesoamerican Writing Systems* (Princeton), 1993, provides summaries of some points of view and treats Mesoamerica comprehensively. *Research Reports on Ancient Maya Writing*, published since 1986, offer a steady diet on new hieroglyphic readings. David Stuart's 'Ten Phonetic Syllables,' *RRAMW* 14, 1987, is a model of carefully argued decipherment. Linda Schele's privately published *Copán Notes* and *Texas Notes* are a source for the latest readings of texts and iconography. Michael Coe's *Breaking the Maya Code* (Thames and Hudson), 1992, offers insights into the foibles and successes of decipherment.

The Late Formative in Oaxaca is discussed by John Scott, 'The Danzantes of Monte Alban,' 2 vols., *Dumbarton Oaks Studies in Pre-Columbian Art and Archaeology* no. 22, 1980, and Ignacio Bernal, 'The Ball Players of Dainzu,' *Archaeology*, 21, 1968. See also the book by Richard Blanton listed here under the Chapter 5 bibliography. Archaeoastronomical principles in ancient American art and architecture are discussed in Anthony F. Aveni, *Skywatchers of Ancient Mexico* (Univ. Texas), 1981. D.M. Earle and D.R. Snow, 'The Origin of the 260-day Calendar: the Gestation Hypothesis Reconsidered in Light of its Use among the Quiche-Maya,' in Fifth Palenque Round Table, 1985, pp. 241–44.

Various interpretations of West Mexican clay sculptures have been put forth by Furst and Von Winning (Peter Furst, 'West Mexican Tomb Sculpture as Evidence for Shamanism in Prehispanic Mesoamerica,' *Antropológica*, 15, 1965; Hasso von Winning and O. Hammer, *Anecdotal Sculpture of West Mexico*, Los Angeles, 1972). Mark Miller Graham has proposed that some shamanic 'horns' are really conch shells, 'In Place of a World that Never Was,' ms. in possession of the author, 1990. Catalogues by Michael Kan et al., *Sculpture of Ancient West Mexico*, 2nd edition (LA County Museum), 1985, and Jackie Gallagher, *Companions of the Dead* (LA County Natural History Museum), 1983, provide both clear interpretations and excellent illustrations. M. Foster and P. Weigand have carried out extensive excavations, *The*

Archaeology of West and Northwest Mesoamerica, Boulder, 1985.

The rise of the early Maya civilization is studied by John Graham, Robert Heizer, and Edwin Shook, 'Abaj Takalik 1976: Exploratory Investigations,' *Univ. Cal. Arch. Res. Facility* no. 36, 85–114; David Freidel, 'Civilization as a State of Mind: The Cultural Evolution of the Lowland Maya,' in G. Jones and R. Kautz, eds., *The Transition to Statehood in the New World*, Cambridge, 1981, pp. 188–227; Ray T. Matheny, 'El Mirador, Peten, Guatemala,' *Papers of the New World Archaeological Foundation* no. 45, 1980. A compelling picture of early Maya civilization and religious formation has been drawn by David Freidel, Linda Schele, and Joy Parker in *Maya Cosmos* (W. Morrow), 1993. See also, Garth Norman, 'Izapa Sculpture, Part 1, Album,' *Papers of the New World Archaeological Foundation* no. 30, 1973.

4 Teotihuacan

Three recent volumes provide comprehensive views and sharp insights into Teotihuacan art and archaeology: Janet Berlo, ed., *Art, Ideology, and the City of Teotihuacan* (Dumbarton Oaks), 1992; Kathleen Berrin and Esther Pasztory, eds., *Teotihuacan: Art from the City of the Gods* (The Fine Arts Museums of San Francisco, Thames and Hudson), 1993; and Kathleen Berrin, ed., *Feathered Serpents and Flowering Trees* (The Fine Arts Museums of San Francisco), 1988.

René Millon's archaeological 2-vol. report, *Urbanization at Teotihuacan, Mexico* (Univ. Texas), 1974, remains useful, as do some of the ideas floated by Laurette Séjourné in *Un palacio en la ciudad delos dioses* (INAH), 1959. Karl Taube's 'The Teotihuacan Spider Woman,' *Journal of Latin American Lore* 9:2, 1983, 107–189, initiated new thinking about the female cults at the site.

5 Classic Monte Albán, Veracruz and Cotzumalhuapa

On Monte Albán, see Richard E. Blanton, *Monte Albán: Settlement Patterns at the Ancient Zapotec Capital* (Academic Press), 1978; also John Paddock, ed., *Ancient Oaxaca* (Stanford), 1966; Caso and Bernal studied the urns of Oaxaca, *Urnas de Oaxaca*, INAH Memorias 2, 1952. See also Marcus, as above (Chapter 3). Also to be considered are studies of the Middle Classic: Esther Pasztory, ed., *Middle Classic Mesoamerica, AD 400–700* (Columbia), 1978.

On Veracruz sculpture, see M. Goldstein, ed., *Ceremonial Sculpture of Ancient Veracruz* (Brooklyn), 1988. Recent archaeology is treated in B. Stark, ed., *Settlement Archaeology of Cerro de las Mesas, Veracruz, Mexico* (Institute of Archaeology, UCLA), 1991.

For El Tajín, see J. Garcia Payón, *El Tajín, Guía Oficial* (INAH), 1957; Michael E. Kampen, *The Sculptures of El Tajín* (Univ. Florida), 1972; and S. Jeffrey K. Wilkerson, 'Man's Eighty Centuries in Veracruz,' *National Geographic Magazine* 158:2, August 1980, 203–31.

For the Mesoamerican ballgame, one might start with T. Leyenaar and Lee A. Parsons, *Ulama: the Ballgame of the Mayas and Aztecs*, 2000 BC–AD 2000, Leiden, 1988, and Mary Miller and S. Houston, 'The Classic Maya Ballgame and its Architectural Setting: A Study of Relations between Text and Image,' *RES* 14, 1987, 46–65.

For Cotzumalhuapa, see Barbara Braun, 'Sources of the Cotzumalhuapa Style,' *Baessler-Archiv* 51, 1978, 159–232, and Lee A. Parsons, *Bilbao, Guatemala: An Archaeological*

Study of the Pacific Coast Cotzumalhuapa Region, 2 vols. Milwaukee Public Museum, 1967–69.

6 and 7 The Early and Late Classic Maya

Several important books have dramatically changed the history of Maya art, archaeology, and Maya history itself. Chief among these are: Linda Schele and Mary Ellen Miller, *The Blood of Kings: Ritual and Dynasty in Maya Art* (Kimbell Art Museum), 1986, and (Thames and Hudson), 1992; Linda Schele and David Freidel, *A Forest of Kings: The Untold Story of the Ancient Maya* (W. Morrow), 1990; and David Freidel, Linda Schele, and Joy Parker, *Maya Cosmos: Three Thousand Years on the Shaman's Path* (W. Morrow), 1993. Robert Sharer's new version of Morley's *The Ancient Maya*, 5th edition (Stanford), 1994, is the most encyclopedic archaeological resource on the Maya to reflect this changed picture. In addition to Coe's *The Maya* (as in Ch. 1), Norman Hammond's *Ancient Maya Civilization* (Cambridge; Rutgers), 1982, is worth consulting, as are Elizabeth Benson, ed., *City-States of the Maya: Art and Architecture* (Rocky Mountain Institute for Pre-Columbian Studies), 1986; Gene Stuart and George Stuart, *Lost Kingdoms of the Maya* (National Geographic), 1993; *Die Welt der Maya*, Hildesheim, 1994. Although Sir Eric Thompson's works are all dated, *The Rise and Fall of the Maya Empire* (Univ. Oklahoma), 1956, and *Maya Hieroglyphic Writing* (Univ. Oklahoma), 1971, should be consulted.

Every reader can learn something from the four volumes of the first keen observer of Maya art and architecture, John Lloyd Stephens: *Incidents of Travel in Central America, Chiapas, and Yucatán* (Harper), 1841, and *Incidents of Travel in Yucatán*, 1843. Claude Baudez and Sydney Picasso, *Lost Cities of the Maya* (Thames and Hudson), 1992, offers a good, brief historiography.

Some examples of the extensive work in the Maya area carried out by the Carnegie Institution of Washington are: Oliver G. Ricketson and Edith B. Ricketson, *Uaxactún, Guatemala, Group E, 1926–1931*, CIW Pub. 477, 1937; A. V. Kidder, Jesse D. Jennings, and Edwin M. Shook, *Excavations of Kaminaljuyú, Guatemala*, CIW Pub. 561, 1946; A.L. Smith, *Uaxactún, Guatemala, Excavations of 1931–37*, CIW Pub. 588, 1950. Tatiana Proskouriakoff based her careful reconstructions on such archaeological reports (*An Album of Maya Architecture*, CIW Pub. 558, 1946). For technical observations on Maya architecture, see Lawrence Roys, 'The Engineering Knowledge of the Maya,' CIW *Contributions*, II (1934).

Both Early and Late Classic sculptures are discussed and illustrated in Sylvanus G. Morley, *Inscriptions of Petén*, 5 vols., CIW Pub. 437, 1937–38; Alfred Percival Maudslay, *Biologia Centrali-Americana: Archaeology*, 5 vols., London 1899–1902; *Corpus of Maya Hieroglyphic Inscriptions*, vols. 1–5, Peabody Museum, Harvard University, 1977–. See also Teobert Maler, *Researches in the Central Portion of the Usumatsintla Valley*, PMM 2, 1901–03. Proskouriakoff has written the single most comprehensive study of Maya sculpture to date, *Classic Maya Sculpture*, CIW Pub. 593, 1950.

On Tikal, see William R. Coe, *Tikal, a Handbook of the Ancient Maya Ruins* (University Museum, Philadelphia), 1967; 'Tikal: Ten Years of Study of a Maya Ruin in the Lowlands of Guatemala,' *Expedition* 5:2, 1963, 5–56. The most synthetic of the Tikal works is the unpublished dissertation of Clemency Coggins, 'Painting and Drawing Styles at Tikal: An Historical and Iconographic Reconstruction,' Ph.D. diss. Harvard, 1975. See also the excellent publication by Christopher Jones and Linton Satterthwaite, *The Monuments and Inscriptions of Tikal: The Carved Monuments* (University Museum, Philadelphia), 1982. For excavation reports, see William Coe, *Excavations in the Great Plaza, North Terrace and North Acropolis of Tikal*, 6 vols. (University Museum, Philadelphia), 1990.

On Palenque: Merle Greene Robertson, *The Sculpture of Palenque*, 4 vols, *The Temple of Inscriptions* (Princeton), 1983–92; Peter Mathews and Linda Schele, 'Lords of Palenque: The Glyphic Evidence,' *Primera Mesa Redonda de Palenque, Part 1*, ed. M.G. Robertson (R.L. Stevenson School), 1974, 63–76; Alberto Ruz Lhuilier, *El Templo de las Inscripciones, Palenque* (INAH), 1973.

For Copán and Quiriguá, see Elizabeth Boone and Gordon Willey eds., *The Southeast Classic Maya Zone* (Dumbarton Oaks), 1988, pp. 149–94; William Fash, *Scribes, Warriors, and Kings: The City of Copán and the Ancient Maya* (Thames and Hudson), 1991; D. Webster, ed., *The House of the Bacabs* (Dumbarton Oaks), 1989; E. Schortman and P. Urban, eds., *Quiriguá Reports II*, Papers 6–14 (University Museum, Philadelphia), 1983; Sylvanus G. Morley, *Inscriptions at Copán*, CIW Pub. 219, 1920; *Introducción a la Arqueología de Copán, Honduras*, 3 vols., Proyecto Arqueológico de Copán, Tegucigalpa, Honduras, 1983.

On Yucatán: Jeff Kowalski, *The House of the Governor* (Univ. Oklahoma), 1986; Harry Pollock, *The Puuc* (PMM), 1980; V. Miller, *The Frieze of the Palace of the Stuccoes, Acanceh, Yucatán, Mexico* (Dumbarton Oaks), 1991.

On Belize: David Pendergast, *Altun Ha, British Honduras (Belize): The Sun God's Tomb*, Royal Ontario Museum of Art and Archaeology, Occasional Paper 19, Toronto, 1969; A.F. Chase and D.Z. Chase, *Investigations at the Classic Maya City of Caracol, Belize: 1985–87* (PARI), 1987.

For Yaxchilán: C. Tate, *Yaxchilán: Design of a Maya Ceremonial Center* (Univ. Texas), 1992.

For Bonampak: Mary Ellen Miller, 'Maya Masterpiece Revealed at Bonampak,' *National Geographic Magazine*, February 1995, pp. 50–69; and *The Murals of Bonampak* (Princeton), 1986; Frans Blom and Gertrude Duby, *La selva lacandona*, 2 vols., Mexico City, 1955–57; A. Espinosa, M. Rosas, B. Sandoval, and Abelardo Venegas, *Bonampak* (Citicorp), 1988; M. Nájera Coronada, *Bonampak* (Edo de Chiapas), 1991.

On Piedras Negras: William Coe, *Piedras Negras Archaeology: Artifacts, Caches, and Burials* (University Museum, Philadelphia), 1959; A. Stone 'Disconnection, Foreign Insignia, and Political Expansion: Teotihuacan and the Warrior Stelae of Piedras Negras,' in *Mesoamerica After the Decline of Teotihuacan AD 700–900*, eds., Richard Diehl and Janet Berlo (Dumbarton Oaks), 1989, 153–72.

For religious iconography, see Karl Taube, *The Major Gods of Ancient Yucatán* (Dumbarton Oaks), 1992; Elizabeth Benson and Gillett Griffin, eds., *Maya Iconography* (Princeton), 1988; Merle Greene Robertson, *Mesa Redonda de Palenque* (Palenque Round Table) (R.L. Stevenson School, Univ. Texas, PARI), 1973–present.

On Maya jades, A.L. Smith and A.V. Kidder, *Excavations at Nebaj, Guatemala*, CIW Pub. 594, 1951; Tatiana Proskouriakoff, *Jades from the Cenote of Sacrifice, Chichen Itzá, Yucatán*, PMM 10: 1, 1974. For figurines, see Mary Ellen Miller, *Jaina Figurines* (Art Museum, Princeton), 1975; Roman Piña Chan, *Jaina, la casa en el agua* (INAH), 1968.

The chronology and terminology for Maya ceramics drives from the Uaxactún excavations (Robert E. Smith, *Ceramic Sequence at Uaxactún, Guatemala*, 2 vols., MARI Pub. 20, 1955). Recent studies have focussed on iconography: Michael D. Coe, *The Maya Scribe and His World*

(Grolier Club), 1973; *Lords of the Underworld* (Art Museum, Princeton), 1978; R.E.W. Adams, *The Ceramics of Altar de Sacrificios*, PMM 63:1, 1971. Justin Kerr has begun to publish the complete corpus, *The Maya Vase Book*, Volumes 1–4, 1989–. For the best single-volume art historical and archaeological analysis, see B. Reents-Budet, *Painting the Maya Universe* (Duke), 1994. For the Early Classic, see N. Hellmuth, *Mönster und Menschen*, Graz, 1987. *The Classic Maya Collapse*, ed. T. Patrick Culbert (Univ. New Mexico Press, 1973), considers the end of Classic Maya civilization from several points of view. A synthetic view of the end of high Maya civilization in the southern lowlands has appeared, *Lowland Maya Civilization in the 8th c. AD*, eds. Jeremy Sabloff and John Henderson (Dumbarton Oaks), 1992.

8 Mesoamerica after the fall of Classic cities

On Xochicalco: J. Litvak-King, 'Xochicalco en la caída del clásico,' INAH *Anales de Antropología*, VII, 1970, 131–44. *Mesoamerica After the Decline of Teotihuacan AD 700–900*, eds., Richard Diehl and Janet Berlo (Dumbarton Oaks), 1989, offers keen insights into Xochicalco, Cacaxtla, Tula, and iconographic shifts, as well as theoretical views.

A flurry of publications accompanied the discovery of the Cacaxtla paintings. Best of these is Donald McVicker, 'The Mayanized Mexicans,' *American Antiquity* 50:1, 1985, 82–101. See also Marta Foncerrada de Molina, 'La pintura mural de Cacaxtla, Tlaxcala,' *Anales del IIE, UNAM* 46, 1976, 5–20; Diana Lopez de Molina, 'Los murales prehispanicos de Cacaxtla,' *Boletín INAH*, 1977, 2–8. The presence of foreigners in the Maya area is discussed by Sir Eric Thompson, *Maya History and Religion* (Univ. Oklahoma), 1970, and John Graham, 'Aspects of non-Classic Presences in the Inscriptions and Sculptural Art of Seibal,' in Culbert, *Collapse*, pp. 207–19 (above, Chapter 7).

Articles in Kent V. Flannery and Joyce Marcus, eds., *The Cloud People: Divergent Evolution of the Zapotec and Mixtec Civilizations* (Academic Press), 1983, consider the Early Postclassic in Oaxaca. The volume is also valuable for earlier eras in Oaxaca.

On the Toltecs, see Richard Diehl, *Tula: the Toltec Capital of Ancient Mexico* (Thames and Hudson), 1983; Nigel Davies, *The Toltecs Until the Fall of Tula* (Univ. Oklahoma), 1977; also, *The Toltec Heritage from the Fall of Tula to the Rise of Tenochtitlan* (Univ. Oklahoma), 1980; Jorge Acosta, 'Resumen de las exploraciones arqueológicas en Tula, Hidalgo, durante los VI, VII y VIII temporadas 1946–1950,' INAH *Anales* 8, 1956, 37–116. Désiré Charnay first noted the resemblances between Tula and Chichen Itzá (*Ancient Cities of the New World*, New York, 1888).

Various reports summarize the many years of excavations by the Carnegie Institution of Washington at Chichen Itzá. The most important studies: Karl Ruppert, *Chichen Itzá*, CIW Pub. 595, 1952; A.M. Tozzer, *Chichen Itzá and its Cenote of Sacrifice*, PMM 12, 1957; Earl H. Morris, Jean Charlot, and Ann Axtell Morris, *The Temple of the Warriors at Chichen Itzá, Yucatán*, 2 vols., CIW Pub. 406, 1931. On Toltec art forms at Chichen Itzá, see George Kubler, 'Serpent and Atlantean Columns: Symbols of Maya-Toltec Polity,' *Journal of the Society of Architectural Historians*, 41, 1982; Mary Ellen Miller, 'A Re-examination of the Mesoamerican Chacmool,' *Art Bulletin*, 67:1, 1985, 7–17; Clemency Coggins and O. Shane, eds., *Cenote of Sacrifice: Maya Treasures from the Sacred Well at Chichen Itzá* (Univ. Texas), 1984. C. Lincoln's dissertation, 'Ethnicity and Social Organization at Chichen Itzá, Yucatán, Mexico' (Ph.D.

diss., Harvard), 1990, provides a fresh look at the assumptions that have shaped all Chichen work.

The final Carnegie project was carried out at Mayapán: H.E.D. Pollock, Tatiana Proskouriakoff, and Edwin Shook, *Mayapán*, CIW Pub. 619, 1962. For Tulum, see Samuel K. Lothrop, *Tulum: An Archaeological Study of the East Coast of Yucatán*, CIW, Pub. 335, 1924; also, particularly for the copies of the murals there, Arthur Miller, *On the Edge of the Sea: Mural Painting at Tancah-Tulum, Quintana Roo, Mexico* (Dumbarton Oaks), 1982. Thomas Gann visited Santa Rita and published the murals there: 'Mounds in Northern Honduras,' *BAE*, 19th Annual Report, 1900. A.L. Smith, *Archaeological Reconnaissance in Central Guatemala*, CIW Pub. 608, 1955, presents Postclassic architecture of the Guatemalan highlands.

F. Columbus wrote his father's biography, and reported the great canoes of the Maya (*The Life of the Admiral Christopher Columbus by his Son Ferdinand*, trans. and ed. Benjamin Keen, (Rutgers), 1959). Juan de Grijalva, as recorded in *The Discovery of New Spain in 1518*, trans. and ed. Henry R. Wagner (Cortés Society), 1942, collected exotic objects from the Maya.

On Maya pre- and post-Conquest books: Sir Eric Thompson, *The Dresden Codex* (American Philosophical Society), 1972; J.A. Villacorta and C.A. Villacorta, *Codices Maya*, Guatemala City, 1930; the Grolier Codex is illustrated in Coe, *The Maya Scribe* (see Ch. 7 above). The Popol Vuh has been translated many times. Cited here is Munro S. Edmonson, *The Book of Counsel: The Popol Vuh of the Quiché Maya of Guatemala*, MARI Pub. 35, 1971; A.M. Tozzer published a heavily annotated version of Bishop Landa's account of Yucatán (*Landa's Relación de las cosas de Yucatán*, PMP 18, 1941); also useful is the William Gates translation (*Yucatán Before and After the Conquest*, Baltimore, 1937, reprinted by Dover, 1978). See also Dennis Tedlock's translation, *The Popul Vuh* (Simon and Schuster), 1985. On religious practice at the time of the Conquest, Inga Clendinnen, *Ambivalent Conquests: Maya and Spaniard in Yucatán, 1517–1570* (Cambridge), 1987.

9 The Aztecs

Several recent books provide an excellent entrée to the study of the Aztecs: Esther Pasztory, *Aztec Art* (Abrams), 1983; Richard Townsend, *The Aztecs* (Thames and Hudson), 1992; Elizabeth Boone, *The Aztec World* (Smithsonian), 1994. Richard F. Townsend's, 'State and Cosmos in the Art of Tenochtitlan,' *Dumbarton Oaks Studies in Pre-Columbian Art and Archaeology* no. 20, 1979, is a fine examination of a few major sculptures. H.B. Nicholson and Eloise Quinones Keber, *Art of Aztec Mexico: Treasures of Tenochtitlan* (National Gallery, Washington), 1983, provides valuable commentary on the many Aztec objects exhibited at the National Gallery in 1983.

On specific monuments, see Cecilia F. Klein, 'The Identity of the Central Deity on the Aztec Calendar Stone,' *Art Bulletin* 58:1, 1976, 1–12; Justino Fernandez, *Coatlicue, estética del arte indígena antigua*, Mexico City, 1954.

On excavations at the Templo Mayor: J. Broda, D. Carrasco, and E. Matos Moctezuma, *The Great Temple of Tenochtitlan: Center and Periphery in the Aztec World* (Univ. California), 1987; Elizabeth Boone, ed., *The Aztec Templo Mayor* (Dumbarton Oaks), 1987.

The most readable history of the Aztecs is Nigel Davies' *The Aztecs* (Macmillan), 1973, and (Univ. Oklahoma), 1980; he follows fairly closely the information from Father Diego Duran's *Historia de las Indias de Nueva España*. For the

Conquest of Mexico, see Bernal Díaz del Castillo (see Ch. 1) and Hernando Cortés, *Letters from Mexico*, trans./ed. A.R. Pagden (Yale), 1986.

Inga Clendinnen's *Aztecs: An Interpretation* (Cambridge), 1991, provides an engaging social history; Serge Gruzinski, *The Conquest of Mexico* (Cambridge), 1992, offers the freshest take on the Mesoamerican mind since T. Todorov, *The Conquest of Mexico* (Harper), 1981, first raised the possibility of entering it.

Many aspects of Aztec life are documented in Bernardino de Sahagún, *Florentine Codex* (see Ch. 1); on Aztec ideology, see H.B. Nicholson, 'Religion in Pre-Hispanic Central Mexico,' *HMAI*, 10:1 395-446; also, Miguel Leon-Portilla, *Aztec Thought and Culture* (Univ. Oklahoma), 1963. For music, see Robert Stevenson, *Music in Aztec and Inca Territory* (Univ. California), 1968.

Mixtec goldwork is discussed by Alfonso Caso, *El Tesoro de Monte Albán* (INAH), 1969. All New World gold and silver are considered by Andre Emmerich: *Sweat of the Sun and Tears of the Moon: Gold and Silver in Pre-Columbian Art* (Univ. Washington), 1965.

The manuscripts mentioned in this chapter are all available in facsimile edition. *Codex Selden*, commentary by Alfonso Caso, glosses by M.E. Smith (Sociedad Mexicana de Antropologia), 1966; *Codex Féjerváry-Mayer* (Akademische Druck u. Verlagsanstalt), 1971; *Codex Borgia*, Commentary by Eduard Seler (Fondo de Cultura Económica), 1963; Elizabeth Boone, *The Codex Magliabechiano* (Univ. California), 1985; F. Berdan and P. Anawalt, eds., *The Codex Mendoza* (Univ. California), 1992; Serge Gruzinski, *Painting the Conquest* (UNESCO), 1992; *Codex Borbonicus*, Graz (Akademische Druck u. Verlagsanstalt), 1974. The Postconquest manuscripts are described by Donald Robertson, *Mexican Manuscript Painting of the Early Colonial Period: The Metropolitan Schools* (Yale), 1959.

Early Postconquest life and art are best examined in Robert Ricard, the *Spiritual Conquest of Mexico* (Univ. California), 1966; Constantino Reyes, *Arte Indocristiano* (INAH), 1981; Manuel Toussaint, *Colonial Art of Mexico*, rev. and trans. Elizabeth Wilder Weismann (Univ. Texas), 1967; George Kubler, *Sixteenth-Century Architecture of Mexico* (Yale), 1948; John McAndrew, *The Open-Air Churches of Sixteenth-Century Mexico: Atrios, Posas, Open Chapels, and Other Studies* (Harvard), 1965; Serge Gruzinski, *Conquering the Indian Mind: the Making of Colonial Indian Cultures in Spanish Mexico, 16th–18th Centuries*, 1992.

List of illustrations

Unless otherwise indicated, photographs are by the author and site plans by Martin Lubikowski. Measurements are given in centimeters (and inches).

Abbreviations

AMNH American Museum of Natural History, New York
INAH Anstituto Nacional de Antropologia e Historia
MNA Museo Nacional de Antropologia, Mexico
NGS National Geographic Society
UM University Museum, University of Pennsylvania.

bat assemblage, H 19 (7⅜), MNA. **32** Clay figure, Monte Albán, Zapotec, MNA. **33** Colima dog, H 20.9 (8¼), MNA. **34** Nayarit ballcourt, 45 × 26 (17¾ × 10¼), Yale University Art Gallery, Stephen Carlton Clark BA 1903 Fund. **35, 36** Nayarit couple, H 60 and 58.4 (23⅝ and 23), Yale University Art Gallery, Stephen Carlton Clark BA 1903 Fund. **37** Mezcala temple models, H 12 and 15 (4¾ and 5⅞), MNA. **38** Structure 5, Cerros, photo D. Freidel. **39** Stela 1, Nakbé, drawing Richard D. Hansen UCLA RAINPEG Project. **40** Stela 1, Izapa, 193 (76), photo courtesy Matthew W. Stirling and NGS. **41** Stela 5, Izapa, H 158 (62¼), photo Brigham Young University, Utah–New World Archaeological Foundation. **42** Stela 11, Kaminaljuyú, H 182.8 (72), photo M. D. Coe. **43** Silhouette sculpture, H 146.6 (57¾), photo courtesy Museum of the American Indian, Heye Foundation, New York.

4 Teotihuacan

44 Isometric view of Teotihuacan, after G. Kubler. **45** Airview of Teotihuacan, photo © R. Millon. **46** *Talud-tablero*, after Marquina. **47** Pyramid of the Moon, Teotihuacan. **48** Pyramid of the Sun, Teotihuacan, photo W. Bray. **49** Isometric view of Zacuala compound, after L. Séjourné. **50** Teotihuacan mask, 10 × 18 (4 × 7¼), MNA, photo Michael Zabé. **51** Teotihuacan figurines, H 9.5 (3¾), photo courtesy Museum of the American Indian, Heye Foundation, New York. **52** Necklace of teeth, shell, and human jawbone, 20 × 20 (8 × 8), INAH, photo Michael Zabé. **53** Temple of Quetzalcóatl, Teotihuacan, photo J. Soustelle. **54** Mass-produced urn from Late Teotihuacan, photo Irmgard Groth-Kimball. **55** Goddess with Claws, fresco on a wall fragment, probably from Techinantitla, Metepec, AD 650–750, 66 × 77 (26 × 30½), lent anonymously to the Fine Arts Museum of San Francisco, photo John Bigelow Taylor. **56** Wall painting from Tetitla, H 72.7 (28½), MNA, photo Michael Zabé. **57** Thin orange ceramic pot, 21 (8¼), MNA, photo Irmgard Groth-Kimball. **58** Tripod vessel with lid, H 20.9 (8¼), Dumbarton Oaks Research Library and Collection, Washington D.C. **59** Plan, Kaminaljuyú B-4, after Kidder, Jennings and Shook 1946. **60** Pyramid, Cholula, lithograph after L. Castoñeda, Paris 1843.

5 Classic Monte Albán, Veracruz and Cotzumalhuapa

61 Monte Albán, photo Colin McEwan. **62** Plan, Monte Albán after Blanton, and Kubler. **63** Stela 4, Monte Albán, H 186 (73¼). **64** Tomb 104 façade, Monte Albán, 91 (35⅞). **65** Tomb 104 painting, Monte Albán, from Covarrubias 1957. **66** Tomb 105 painting, Monte Albán, from Caso 1936–37. **67** Ceramic urn, H 43.1 (17), Yale University Art Gallery, New Haven, Stephen Carlton Clark BA 1903 Fund. **68** Pyramid of the Niches, El Tajín, after Nebel 1829. **69** South Ballcourt, El Tajín. **70** Ballcourt panel 4, El Tajín, H 156 (61⅜), photo M. D. Coe. **71** *Palma*, H 58 (22⅞), MNA. **72** Granite yoke, 12 × 37 × 40.5 (5 × 14½ × 16), Museum purchase, gift of the Friends of the Art Museum in honor of the Sixtieth Birthday of Gillett G. Griffin. Art Museum Princeton University. **73** *Hacha*, H 28 (11), MNA. **74** Hollow figure, Veracruz style. **75** Stela 8, Cerro de las Mesas, photo R. H. Stewart, NGS. **76** 'Smiling face' figure, H 35.6 (14), AMNH. **77** Wheeled Veracruz figure, H 19.3 (7¾), AMNH. **78** Cotzumalhuapa ballgame stela, H 282 (111), Staatliche Museen Preussischer Kulturbesitz, Berlin. **79** Pantaleon head.

6 The Early Classic Maya

80 E-VII-sub, Uaxactún, photo AMNH. **81** A-V, Uaxactún, drawing by G. Kubler. **82** North Acropolis, Tikal. **83** Rosalila structure, Copán. Christopher A. Klein/National Geographic Image Collection. **84** Stela 29, Tikal, H 205 (80¾), drawing by W. R. Coe. **85** Stela 31, Tikal, H 230 (90½), UM. **86** Po panel, H 44.5 (17½), photo Joe Tagliarini. **87** Leiden Plate, H 21.6 (8½), Rijksmuseum voor Volkenkunde, Leiden. **88** Rio Azul tomb painting, photo I. Graham. **89** Turtle flange bowl with water-bird lid, Tikal, Petén, H 15.5, D 19.5 (6, 7¾), Museo Nacional de Arqueologia y Etnologia, Guatemala City, photo © Justin Kerr. **90** Tripod vessel, Tikal, UM, photo W. R. Coe. **91** Quadrupod bird, H 26 (10¼), New Orleans Museum of Art. **92** Old god effigy, Tikal, H 36 (14⅛), UM. **93** GI cache vessel, Stendahl Collection, Los Angeles.

7 The Late Classic Maya

94 Plan, Palenque, after Stierlin 1964. **95** Palenque Palace. **96** East Court, Palenque Palace. **97, 98** Buildings at Palenque, after Stierlin (*left*) and Marquina (*right*). **99** Temple of the Inscriptions, Palenque. **100** Sarcophagus lid, Palenque. L 372 (146½), rubbing M. G. Robertson. **101** Structure 33, Yaxchilán, after Marquina. **102** West Acropolis, Piedras Negras, drawing by T. Proskouriakoff. From T. Proskouriakoff, *An Album of Maya Architecture* (reprinted Norman: University of Oklahoma Press, 1963); by permission. **103** Plan, Tikal, after Morley and Brainerd. **104** Temple 1, Tikal. **105** Twin Pyramid Complex, drawing by M. Lubikowski after W. R. Coe. **106** Main Acropolis and the Great Plaza, Copán, drawing by T. Proskouriakoff. Courtesy the Peabody Museum, Harvard University. **107** Structure 22, drawing A. P. Maudslay. **108** Structure 22a, Copán, photo E. Theodore. **109** Copán ballcourt, photo courtesy the Peabody Museum, Harvard University. **110** Hieroglyphic Stairway, Copán, drawing T. Proskouriakoff. **111** Main structure, Chicanná, watercolour by Nigel Hughes. **112** Pyramid of the Magician, Uxmal, photo J. Sabloff. **113** Nunnery Quadrangle, Uxmal, photo Irmgard Groth-Kimball. **114** Structure 1, Xpuhil, drawing by T. Proskouriakoff. Courtesy the Peabody Museum, Harvard University. **115** House of the Governor, Uxmal, photo G. Kubler. **116** Great Arch, Kabah. **117** Palace Tablet, Palenque, photo M. G. Robertson. **118** Lintel 25, Yaxchilán, H 127 (50), Copyright British Museum. **119** Stela 11, Yaxchilán, H 358 (140⅞), photo T. Maler, courtesy the Peabody Museum, Harvard University. **120** Stela 14, Piedras Negras, H 281.9 (111), UM. **121** Stela 12, Piedras Negras, H 313 (123), Museo Nacional de Arqueologia, Guatemala City, photo T. Maler, courtesy the Peabody Museum, Harvard University. **122** Lintel 3, Tikal, H 205.7 (81), Museum für Völkerkunde, Basel. **123** Stela 16, Tikal, H 352 (138½), drawing by W. R. Coe. **124** Altar Q, Copán, photo Yale gift, Joseph A. Baird. **125** Stela F, Quiriguá, H 731.5 (288), drawing A. P. Maudslay. **126** Zoomorph P, Quiriguá, H 220.9 (87), Copyright British Museum, photo A. P. Maudslay. **127** Jade mosaic vessel, Tikal, H 24.5 (9½), UM. **128** Gann jade, H 14 (5½), Copyright British Museum. **129** Bone, Burial 116, Tikal, after A. Trik. **130** Eccentric flint, H 24.8 (9¾), Dallas Museum of Art, The Eugene and

Margaret McDermott Fund in honor of Mrs Alex Spence. **131** Jaina carved shell, H 8 (3⅛), Dumbarton Oaks Research Library and Collection, Washington D.C. **132** Male/female Jaina pair, H 24.8 (9¾), Detroit Institute of Arts, Founders Society purchase, Katherine Margaret Kay Bequest Fund and New Endowment Fund. **133** Altar de Sacrificios vase, H 25.4 (10), Museo Nacional de Arqueologia y Etnologia, Guatemala City, photo T. Grider. **134** Codex-style pot, Metropolitan Museum of Art, New York, rollout photo © Justin Kerr 1975. **135** Room 3 Bonampak.

8 Mesoamerica after the fall of Classic cities

136 Stela 1, Seibal, H 237 (93¼). **137** Pyramid of the Feathered Serpent, Xochicalca, pen and ink drawing by Adela Breton, courtesy of City of Bristol Museum and Art Gallery. **138** Hall of the Columns, Mitla. **139** 'Apotheosis' sculpture, H 158 (62½). The Brooklyn Museum, Henry L. Batterman and Frank S. Benson Funds. **140** Cacaxtla painting. **141** Pyramid B, Tula, photo W. Bray. **142** Atlantean columns, Tula, photo Irmgard Groth-Kimball. **143** *Chacmool*, Tula, H 66 (25⅞), photo M. D. Coe. **144** Plumbate vessel, H 16 (6¼), Yale University Art Gallery, New Haven. Gift of Mr and Mrs Fred Olsen, photo Joseph Szaszfai Yale Audio Visual Center. **145** Tula stela, H 122 (48), MNA. **146** Plan, Chichen Itzá, after Morley and Brainerd. **147** Caracol, Chichen Itzá, photo W. Bray. **148** Section, Caracol, AMNH. **149** Castillo, Chichen Itzá. **150** Temple of the Warriors, Chichen Itzá. **151** *Chacmool*, Chichen Itzá, H 148.6 (58½), MNA. **152** Great Ballcourt relief, from Marquina. **153** Great Ballcourt, Chichen Itzá. **154** Wall painting, Temple of the Warriors, Ann Axtell Morris, Carnegie Institution of Washington. **155** Mayapan Stela 1, drawing T. Proskouriakoff, courtesy the Peabody

Museum, Harvard University. **156** Tulum, photo Irmgard Groth-Kimball. **157** Painting, Tulum, after copy by M. A. Fernandez 1939–40. **158** Dresden Codex, Sächsische Landesbibliothek, Dresden. **159** Pyramidal platforms, Iximché. **160** Book of Chilam Balam, Firestone Library, Princeton University.

9 The Aztecs

161 The Valley of Mexico, after Coe 1984, drawing by P. Gallagher. **162** Codex Mendoza, Bodleian Library, Oxford MS Arch. Selden A1. **163** Primeros Memoriales from Codex matritense. **164** Malinalco. **165** Coatlicue, H 257 (99), MNA. **166** Coyolxauhqui stone, H 340 (133⅞), photo Smithsonian Institution. **167** Stone of Tízoc, D 275 (104½), MNA, photo INAH. **168** Calendar Stone, D 360 (141¾), MNA. **169** Xipe Totec, H 40 (15¾), Museum für Völkerkunde, Basel. **170** Eagle warrior, H 190 (75), INAH, photo Salvador Guilliem. **171** Carnelite grasshopper, L 45.7 (18), MNA. **172** Rain god *chacmool*, H 73.6 (29), MNA. **173** Temple Stone, H 123 (48⅜), MNA. **174** *Huéhuetl*, H 115 (45¼), photo INAH. **175** Gold pectoral, H 12.2 (4⅞), MNA. **176** Feather headdress, H over 124 (48). Museum für Völkerkunde, Vienna. **177** Skull mask, Copyright British Museum. **178** Cholula pottery cup, H 12 (4¾), The Metropolitan Museum of Art, New York. All rights reserved. **179** Tlaloc effigy vessel, H 35 (13¾), Templo Mayor collection. **180** Codex Selden, Bodleian Library, Oxford MS Arch. Selden A2. **181** Codex Féjérváry-Mayer, Board of Trustees of the National Museums on Merseyside. **182** Codex Borgia, Vatican Library. **183** Wall painting, Ixmiquilpan. **184** Codex Borbonicus, Bibliothèque de l'Assemblée Nationale, Paris. **185** Codex Mendoza, Bodleian Library, Oxford MS Arch. Selden A1.

Index

Numerals in italics are illustration numbers

143, *112*; Seibal 163; Tula 173–74; Pyramid of Quetzalcóatl 180; Twin Pyramid Complex, Tenochtitlan 203–05, *166*; Pyramid of the Feathered Serpent 165

quetzal feathers 11, 220
Quetzalcóatl 40, 81, 86, 163, 165–66, 169, 174, 179, 180, 197, 201, 204, 205, 220, 225, 226, *163*, *182*; Topíltzin Quetzalcóatl 171, 176
Quetzalpapálotl palace 173
Quiriguá 103, 145; Early Classic ruler portrait 113; tallest Maya stelae 151, *125*; Zoomorph P 151, *126*

radiocarbon dating 17, 52, 58, 80
Remojadas 100
Río Azul *see* painting
Río Bec 140
Rivera, Diego 54
ritual interment 20, 25, 29
Robertson, Donald 230
Rodríguez, María del Carmen 31
Ruler A 62, 118, 131, 134, 150, 154, 155, *123*
Ruler B 151, *122*
Ruz, Alberto 127

San José de Motul 163
San Lorenzo Tenochtitlan 17, 19–24, 26, 28, 38, *4–7*
Santa Cruz Quiché *43*
Schele, Linda 16, 195
sculpture *see* individual sites
Seibal 163–64, *136*
Shield Jaguar 106
Stephens, John Lloyd 15, 45, 123, 142, *124*
Stone of Tízoc 210–12, *167*
Storm God 67, 71, *58*
Stormy Sky 112, 113, *85*
Stuart, David 16
Sullivan, Thelma 67
sun symbolism 60, 216, *167*, *168*, *173*

talud-tablero style 69, 73, 78, 94, 108, 120, 194, *46*

Tancan 193
Tapia, Andrés de 207
Techinantitla 78
Temple Stone 216, *173*
Templo Mayor *see* Aztecs
Tenochtitlan 9, 11, 14, 16, 19, 58, 197, 200, 201, 202, 203, 304, 209, 210, 218, 222; description by Bernal Díaz 198, 203, 218; *see also* Aztecs
Teopantecuanitlan 34, *17*
Teotihuacan 9, 10, 11, 65, 67–82, 83, 84, 86, 89, 116, 120, 162, 170, 173; architecture 68–72, *44*, *45*, *49* ; sculpture 72–75, 83, *51*, *54*, *55*, *57*; painting 75–80, 90, 91, 92, *56*; fall 80–82; influence 103, 112, 119
Tezcatlipoca 192, 221, 222, *157*, *177*
Thompson, Sir Eric 44, 179, 182
Tikal 26, 62, 114, 120, 162, 163, *129*: Late Formative 59; temples 64, 118, 131–34, *103*, *104*, *122*, *123*; artistic links with Monte Albán 90; rise in Early Classic 103; architecture 105, 106–09, 120, *82*; sculpture 109, 113; painting 115; eighth-century revival 131; Late Classic sculpture 154
Tlaloc 67, 73, 78, 112, 149, 166, 175, 205–06, 216, *144*, *172*, *179*
Tlapacoya 34
Tlatilco 'pretty ladies' 34
Tlaxcala 82, 165, 200, 201
Toltecs 10, 82, 170–72, 175, 210; *see also* Tula and Chichen Itzá
Toniná 150, 162
Totonacs 82, 92–93
Tres Zapotes 17, 38
Tula 9, 162, 169, 172–77, 198, 215, 141–45
Tulum 190–91, *156*; wall paintings 191–92, *157*
Twin Pyramid Complex *see* pyramids
tzompantli 186, 204

Uaxactún 86, 104, 105, 106, 112, 119, 120, 183, *81*; Late Formative 59, 65; Early Classic architecture, radial pyramid 104–05, *80*

Urcid, Javier 86
Usumacinta River 130
Uxmal, Pyramid of the Magician 143, *112*; Nunnery 143–44, *113*; House of the Governor 143–44, 168, *115*

Valley of Mexico 204, 205, 206, 226, *161*
Veracruz 11, 17, 21, 73, 83, 101, 102, 200–01; the Wrestler 22, *5*; Classic 92–101; Huastecs 92, 168–70, *139*, as Aztec sacrificial victims 204, cult of Zipe Totec 212; *see also* El Tajín

Weigand, Phil 56
were-jaguar 19, 37
West Mexico; autonomous development 54; shaft tombs 55; artifacts and architecture 54–59, *33–37*
world tree, Izapa 64
Wrestler, the 21, *5*

Xipe Totec 212, *169*
Xochicalco *see* Maya
Xochipala, Guerrero 32, 34, *18*
Xochipala figurines 32, *18*
Xpuhil 140, *114*
Xtoloc 177

Yaxha 120
Yaxchilán 103; historical inscriptions 47; stone monument 113; Late Classic architecture 130, *101*, and sculpture 146, 147–49, 150, *119*; battle scenes 114
Yax Kuk Mo' *124*
Yax Pac 138, 151, *124*
yoke 97, 100, 102, *72*
Yucatan 9, 135, 158, 162, 188, 190, 192, 195, 200

Zapotecs 38, 39, 45, 49, 51, 54, 86, 90, 218; writing system 48; at Teotihuacan 72; at Mitla 167; *see also* Monte Albán
zoomorph 151, *126*